OCEANUS

SEPTENTRIO

NOVA ZEMLA

NALIS

Mare Pitzorke

Samoieda

Oceanus

Deucalidonius

MARE

ATLANTI

Açores Insulæ al. Flandricæ

CUM

Canariæ Insulæ Salvagenæ

MEDITERRANEUM

TARTARIA

Cathaya

Ergimul Tanguth

NA CHI

BARBARIA

AFRICA

Numidia

Libia Interior

GUINEA

Mare Arabicum et Indicum

Gange

Golfo de Bengala

CHINE Philippinas

OCEANUS

ÆTHIOPICUS

MAR DI INDIA

MARE LANTCH. DOL

Beach

NOV GUI

Promontorium terræ Australis

MAGALLANICA

A JOURNEY BACK IN TIME THROUGH MAPS

Kevin J. Brown

WHITE STAR PUBLISHERS

A JOURNEY BACK IN TIME THROUGH MAPS

Contents

Introduction

This illustrated book provides a history of the world, through maps from some of the earliest known maps to 20th century propaganda maps. The history illustrated here is not merely geographical, but also a perceptual history of how we see the world, each other, and, ultimately, ourselves. The maps herein illustrate a variety of religious, social, and economic ways of seeing and relating to the world.

The first two maps, the Tabula Peutingeriana and the Hereford Mappa Mundi, represent both the beginning and the end of our voyage. The contrast between them exemplifies the ideals of mapmaking and the inherent conflicts that cartographers struggle with: science and religion, the physical and the spiritual, reality and fiction, factual and practical, neutrality and persuasiveness.

We begin our journey with the Tabula Peutingeriana, a map that, in form and function, is both modern and primitive. The Tabula Peutingeriana is not mathematically scaled, and so is often considered somewhat primitive compared to some later maps. Instead, it is a practical route map, showing mileage and distances between cities and waystations on the ancient Roman road system. As such, it might be best understood by modern standards as being akin to the very modern London Underground Map. Both maps focus on routes and waypoints and dismiss such notions as relative scale to make the map more accessible and readable. They are both practical maps offering clear instructions on how to get from point A to point B. This was as useful in ancient Rome as it is in modern London.

The underlying elements of the Roman Empire were conquest and commerce, both of which were facilitated by the Empire's vast and well-maintained road network. The collapse of the Roman Empire also led to the general failure of the Roman road system and with it the ease of travel and commerce that it had facilitated. As Europe slipped into the Dark Ages, extensive travel became less and less common and regional governments more fragmented. The European world turned inward, focusing more upon religious and spiritual values. This was the world of Richard of Haldingham and Lafford's Hereford Mappa Mundi. Where the Tabula Peutingeriana was a practical navigation tool for a physical empire, the Hereford Mappa Mundi offered a spiritual navigation through Biblical meta-geographies. It, in contrast to the Tabula Peutingeriana, was of little practical use and although it contained geographical elements, but, practically, these could not be used to navigate the physical world.

Each of these maps exemplifies a kind of cartographical ideal. The Tabula Peutingeriana was brilliantly designed, practical, and was a useful tool with which one could easily navigate a sprawling real world empire. The Hereford Mappa Mundi was a persuasive tool intended to provide spiritual guidance and direction, but was of little practical use. The history of cartography can be understood in terms of continuous movement between these ideologies and a slow toing and froing between one cartographic perspective and another. Therefore, while these are the earliest maps we will deal with, they are also the endpoints of our journey and understanding them will lead the way to understanding all of the other maps.

The next entry in our work is Waldseemüller's 1507 Universalis Cosmographia. The publication of this map coincided

The SOLAR SYSTEM

The SUN as seen through a Telescope appears of an uneavenness on any kind. But near five firmy mountains Centrado his limb appears free from mountains very Elevation. Strata of many Surface which disappear often much and in the limb it self, that they may be taken for real Mountains and Valleys

Sun

The Cause of an Eclipse of the Sun and of the Moon

COMETS or Blazing Stars are probably of equal Genera-tion and Duration with the Planets. They are dense Bodies generally much less than the Planets but with much deeper Atmo-spheres which when those Bodies come near the Sun produce a shining Tail opposite to the Sun

Saturn India time and more stupid thing of Solar Matter surrounding him

Four Satellites may move round Jupiter as under

The Comet of 1680 according to S.r Isaac Newton in its near-est Approach to the Sun was 2000 times hotter than red hot Iron, and had it been a Globe of Iron so heated quite thro would not have been Cold in 50000 years. The Velocity of this Comet near its Perihelion was 15000 Miles in a Minute, and the Length of its Tail 80 Million Miles.

Orbit of Jupiter

Orbit of Mars

Orbit of the Earth &c.
Orbit of Venus
Orbit of Mercury
Sun

Colour of Saturn Tail long a crooked Colour of Blood

November 16.th Incl. 37°

The Ring of Saturn is a Phenomenon which has no parallel in the Solar

The Ring of SATURN and his Ring seen thro a Telescope

Mercury as seen thro a Telescope

The Diameter of the Penumbra or Shadow of the Earth at the Moon is above 4,900 Miles The Diameter of the true Shadow of the Moon at the Earth is 180 Miles

Poles of the Earth, are two Points in the Surface of the Earth diametrically opposite to each other; One of which is called the North Pole and the other the South Pole. The Axis of the Earth is a streat Line drawn from Pole to Pole, and about which the Diurnal Motion is performed from West to East in 24 Hours, whereby the Sun and Stars appear to move from East to West in the same Time. The Equinoctial Line is a great Circle all of its Parts being 90 Degrees distant from either of the Poles. Meridians are great Circles passing round the Earth and thro the Poles. The Sensible Horizon is that which separates between the upper and lower part of the Sky or Firmament. The Rational Horizon is the Earth, and parallel thereto by a Semi Diameter of the upper and lower Tropic of Capricorn are two lesser Circles the Tropic of Cancer and the between North, and the other 23½ South of the Equi. The Arctic Circle and Antarctic Circles the one 23½ from... lesser Circles the one 23½ from...

WESTERN HEMISPHERE OR THE N

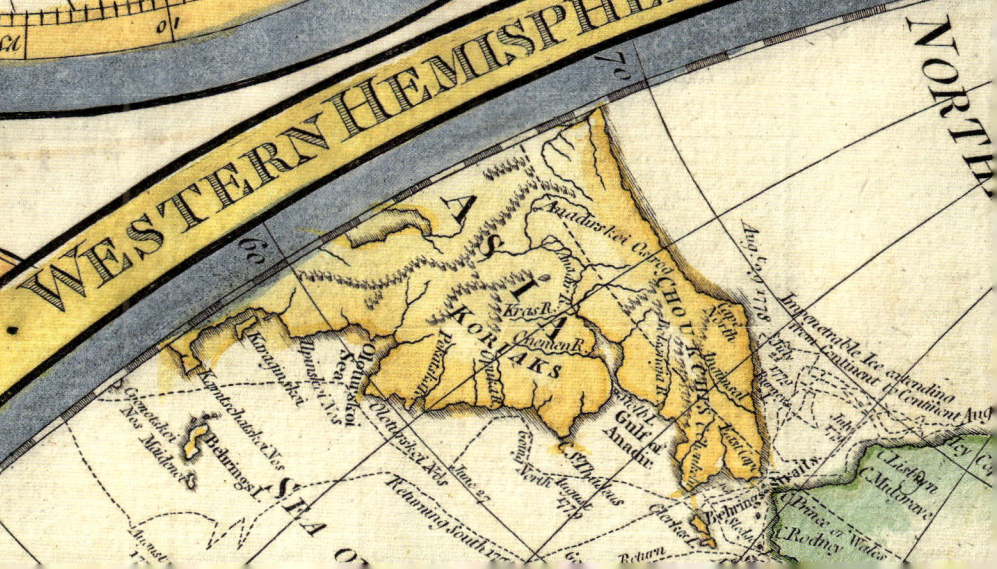

NORTH

ASIA

KORIAKS

SEA OF

with, and some might say exemplified, the birth of the Early Modern Era (1500-1800). The birth of the Early Modern Era was marked by the 1492 Discovery of America and the dawn of the Age of Discovery. It also roughly corresponded to the European Renaissance and The Enlightenment, and ending with the revolutionary period (starting with the American Revolutionary War) at the turn of the 19th century.

The early days of the Age of Discovery marked the development of navigational science. Maps like the Hereford Mappa Mundi, which served the spiritual needs of the pre-modern era well, were not very useful in finding one's way across the Atlantic or around the Cape of Good Hope. Waldseemüller's map was one of the earliest attempts at bridging the divide between pre-modern religious and thematic maps, Ptolemaic maps, and a modern map describing the physical world. Building on Waldseemüller's work, later cartographers generated increasingly scientific and formulaic maps, introducing mathematically sophisticated projection systems ranging from cordiform, through gnomonic, to the all-important Mercator Projection.

Thus, the publication of the Universalis Cosmographia began a slow progression towards ever more accurate and realistic world maps. As global commerce, exploration, conquest, and exploitation increased, mapmakers received ever more valuable data. Hubs like Amsterdam and London, from which ships sailed to the far corners of the globe and returned with new information daily, became centers of cartography and printing.

Most cartographers from this period were not themselves navigators or explorers per se but rather mere compilers. It was their job to collect as much information as possible from as many sources as possible and codify it into map form. This was no easy task when much of the world was unknown and sorting the wheat from the chaff was often impossible. Cartographers would engage in lengthy correspondence with one another and with other luminaries throughout Europe in their attempts to fill the blank spaces on their maps. Through this correspondence, societies of learned men developed in major centers, like Paris, London, and St. Petersburg. These were the academies of sciences, where the greatest minds of the era would meet, present papers, and thrash out the mysteries of the world.

The rise of the Academies of Sciences marked a major change in the development of cartography. Earlier cartographers attempted to create accurate maps, but their maps were rarely subject to peer review. With the development of the Academies of Sciences, cartographers in the great mapmaking centers would meet regularly to argue questions of latitude, longitude, mountains, rivers, and arctic passages. The answers to these questions became highly politicized and certain cartographers sought prestige by gaining the ear of a king or other important noble. Nowhere was this more significant than in the French Royal Academy of Sciences.

By the beginning of the 18th century, the nexus of European mapmaking had shifted, largely because of the French Royal Academy of Sciences, from Amsterdam to Paris.

There, cartographers vied with one another to have both the most accurate information and to attract the attention of the political and economic elite. Therein lay their challenge. With much of the world still unknown, how could those empty spaces of the map be addressed? Some mapmakers developed sophisticated geophysical theories relating to global temperatures, geology, ice flows, currents, the presence or absence of mountain ranges, and other features. Others simply bowed to the political interests of the time. If, for example, the king and wealthy merchants wanted there to be an open Northwest Passage, then an enterprising cartographer, despite lack of hard evidence, would map that passage, or at least create a map that strongly suggested it must be there awaiting discovery. Similarly, a French cartographer, hoping to please his king might map French colonies as far larger than those of rivals Spain and England. This school became known as speculative or positivist cartography, and dominated the European mapping tradition until the end of the Early Modern Era when the successful expeditions of Captain James Cook (1728-1779), Jean François de Galaup, comte de La Pérouse (1741-1788), and Captain George Vancouver (1757-1798) definitively charted most of the world's previously unmapped coastlines.

The rise of the great Academies of Science in Europe brought together not only cartographers, but scientists of all types, many of whom worked together to interpret and understand the wealth of data flooding into Europe from exploration and colonial enterprises. Working hand in hand, cartographers and scientists also began to produce thematic scientific charts, descriptions of currents, geophysical theories, and more. These were the first significant thematic maps of the modern era. Their intention was not only to map the land, but also to express an idea or argue in favor of a particular scientific position.

Ultimately, the circle began to turn back upon itself, from the practical map of the Roman Empire, to the carefully constructed mathematical maps of The Renaissance, to thematic scientific maps, to fanciful moral, propaganda, and instructional allegory. It was not long before the convention of thematic mapmaking was coopted by other non-scientific agencies in the form of instructional moral, social, religious and political maps.

With the overall increase and popularization of cartographic knowledge in the 19th and 20th centuries, cartographers realized they could assume an underlying level of cartographic understanding. People instantly recognized the shapes and forms of countries, cities, and continents. With this strong general underpinning of geographical knowledge, mapmakers realized they could use maps to communicate powerful messages. Hence, they thus began to play with cartography, sublimating the geographical content to the message of the map – much as was done with the Hereford Mappa Mundi. Eventually, entire genres of cartography evolved wherein geography was fully fabricated to support a thematic message, as with some of the allegorical maps appearing in the final chapter.
Thus, the circle turns again.

POLE
ARCTIQUE

TERRES ARCTIQUES

Grande Terre Réc...
par les Russes
1723

80

90

80

70

Smith

Hornesond

don Cost

ENLAND

The Dawn of Cartography: From Peutinger to Kepler

Mapping is part of the human experience and examples of maps, or map-like objects, are an integral part of our historical record. Maps have been found inscribed on Babylonian cuneiform tablets, etched on ancient Egyptian papyri, described in ancient Greek philosophy, and embedded in ancient Roman mosaics. For the purposes of this work, our study of world maps will begin with the ancient Roman world as illustrated in the Tabula Peutingeriana, a cartographic document believed to trace its history back to the very foundation of the Roman Empire. The chapters will progress through Ptolemaic, medieval, early Renaissance, and middle Renaissance cartography. We will witness the development of the projection, and the earliest systematic applications of mathematical principles to cartography.

Much of the earliest cartography, such as those maps found on Babylonian tablets and those originating in ancient Rome, define the limits of what we, today, understand as a "map." Nevertheless, these maps lay the foundation for most subsequent cartography.

The first two maps we illustrate, the Tabula Peutingeriana and the Hereford Mappa Mundi, each express a pre-Ptolemaic model, one from Ancient Rome and the other from Europe's Middle Ages and each presenting a radically different worldview.

On the one hand, the Tabula Peutingeriana illustrates Rome's vast road network and its emphasis is commerce and global trade. While not built on a mathematical system, the Tabula Peutingeriana is a practical tool which, combined with the excellent Roman road system, could facilitate the movement of people and goods throughout the sprawling empire. From a modern perspective, the Tabula Peutingeriana is most analogous to a metropolitan rail transport map, which, although not to scale, provides a usable overview of routes, distances, and stations, enabling a traveler to navigate easily from one destination to another.

On the other hand, the Hereford Mappa Mundi is as much a map of the spiritual realm as it is of the Earthly. One of the hallmarks of the Middle Ages was the breakdown of the Roman road system. Travel was much diminished and often involved moving through small unfriendly fiefdoms on ill-maintained, often dangerous, tracks. The waystations, and the guarded, and well-paved roads of Rome were no more. Instead of traveling the physical network, people turned inward, towards spirituality and faith. Maps like the Hereford Mappa Mundi reflected this change and served as guides to spiritual growth.

Probably the most significant cartographic advancement of the early Renaissance was the rediscovery by Europeans of Ptolemaic mapping. Claudius Ptolemy was a 2nd century Alexandrian mathematician who laid down in his seminal work, the Geographia, the fundamentals of modern mapmaking, including meticulous instructions on how to "build" a map on a coordinate system and how to account for the Earth's curvature using a mathematical projection. Furthermore, his work consisted of a list of hundreds of coordinates that, using his system, could be laid down on a two-dimensional plane to produce a reasonably modern map.

Although Ptolemy's work dates from the Roman period, its significance is mostly associated with its European rediscovery in the early Renaissance. Ptolemy's Geographia was first translated into Latin, from Arabic, by Jacobus Angelus of Scarperia, an Italian scholar and humanist, in 1406. The work was a revelation to the humanists of Europe, not because it allowed them to travel the world, but because it allowed them to have a better understanding of ancient texts that they were then ardently unearthing. In this sense, early Ptolemaic maps served much the same purpose as the Hereford Mappa Mundi, and other similar maps, with the exception that, instead of being a spiritual guide, they were intellectual guides to the ancient world.

It was not until the events of 1492 that everything changed and suddenly, maps took on new and more immediate value. The major limitation of the Ptolemaic model was that it was confined to the world known to the ancients, the tri-part world consisting of Europe, Asia and Africa. When these early maps were only being used for intellectual purposes, this was not an issue. But, with Christopher Columbus' landing in the New World, and the subsequent influx of wealth and discovery, many turned to maps, for the first time since Ancient Rome, not merely as tools to understand the historical or spiritual world, but as a means to understand their expanding contemporary world.

Martin Waldseemüller was the first cartographer to take up the challenge of addressing the discoveries of Columbus in the context of established Ptolemaic geography. As a cartographer, Waldseemüller came from the Ptolemaic tradition and the great Waldseemüller Map is, for all intents and purposes, merely an extended interpretation of a Ptolemaic map. The traditional Ptolemaic map extended from the Canary Islands (Fortunate Isles) to the mysterious city of

Cattigara, probably the ruin known as Óc Eo on the western shore of southern Vietnam. To take into consideration the discoveries of Columbus and Vespucci, Waldseemüller had to more than double the number of degrees that the globe covered. To do so, he changed the Ptolemaic system into a cordiform projection which, centered on the Caspian Sea, greatly extended the scope of Ptolemaic cartography. Waldseemüller's new map revealed not only the discovered shores of America, but far beyond, extending to include a yet undiscovered ocean to the west of America!

Many cartographers immediately after Waldseemüller, such as Oronce Finé, embraced the cordiform projection, some even expanding it into a double cordiform to accommodate the dual hemisphere system on a single map. Throughout the course of the 16th century, there was a continual pattern of improvement, as more lands were discovered and cartographers embraced increasingly sophisticated mathematical models for their projections, yielding, as a result, ever more complex and accurate maps.

Of course, as strong as the current of progress was, there was also resistance to progress. While some cartographers forged ahead with new models of mapmaking, others retreated into medieval cartographic styles, such as the Hereford Mappa Mundi. One such example, among many, was Bunting's Clover Leaf Map. The more conservative religious world was slow to adopt new ideas of mapmaking for fear that they might have conflicted with established Biblical rhetoric. Nevertheless, as more and more ships embarked for the New World on voyages of discovery, conquest, and commerce, modern maps inexorably emerged.

Tabula Peutingeriana

The Peutinger map represents one of the earliest world maps ever discovered. Although this example is a 12th century copy produced by a monk in Colmar, France, the original is thought to date from the reign of the Emperor Augustus in the 1st century BC. That original map, now lost, was engraved on stone under the direction of Marcus Vipsanius Agrippa, a friend and confidant of the emperor.

The map itself consists of an enormous scroll some 6.75 meters long and 0.35 meters high. Although initially confusing, if one can accept the linear distortion, the map makes cartographic sense. It encompasses the then known world, extending from Mediterranean Spain to India, through the lens of the phenomenal Roman Road network. Although not modern in the sense that there is a no clear mathematical framework or projection, the map does identify major cities and bodies of water with distance measurements noted, so an ancient traveler, following it, could easily find his way from Rome to India. Scholars believe that there must once have been an additional map section, now lost, that extended further westward to just beyond the Straits of Gibraltar.

Today, the *Tabula Peutingeriana* is housed at the Austrian National Library at The Hofburg in Vienna. Unfortunately, due to the map's incredible fragility, it is not on public display.

Cartographer

Marcus Vipsanius Agrippa (64/62 BC-12 BC) was an ancient Roman consul, statesman, general, and architect. Agrippa was raised with Gaius Octavius and they became close friends. When Octavius became Augustus, the first Emperor of Rome, Agrippa stood at his side. Under Augustus, Agrippa was credited with many of the great engineering feats of Augustus' reign, including the renovation of Rome.

Piretis . X . Iouia . Sirotis . X . Bolentio . Veronis . ad pretor

P ad fines . XX . Siscia . Burnomila . XII

Itaure . R ab Itaure . N aserie . O . XI . V

X dorata . XIII . Hedino . Iardona . XII

XX

H . Imna . Castello firmana . Cupra Maritima . Castro trentino . Castro

Bolentia . fl . Misio . Sacrata . VI . effusor . fl . Timna . II . E . N . V . OR . amiterno

firmo viceno . E . X . fisternas . III . Nerulos . VII . Pitinum . XII . priserno . XII . VII

G . XV . aueia

arpicano . Interocrio . aque cutilie . VIII . Reate . ad nouas . XIII . Creto . XIII . fidenis . Nomento . VIII . A . ad aqua

II . ad martis . Palacrinis . foroecri . XII . VII . fl . XIII . uatum fana . ad aquas

Inter manana . XII . aquo salsico . XVI . fansar . ad ponte . Via salaria . viatibur . A . mia

ne Recine . X . nteramno . VI . aqua viua . ad duodecimu . XI . ad rubras . VI . Via fla mia . II . Via prenna . XX

VIII . Azios . VI . ad sextum . Via clodia . ponte adriani . salis . Via laucan . XII

Caias . VIII . Turres . VIII . ad scm̄ pe . TRUM . vatru . co . Via appia . X . Via latina . XII

VI . lyrgos . X . Ialsium . VI . Baebiana . Iomio . XII . VIII . Via Hostensis . Host

Via aureha

Gallum Galbianum . XV

A . XVI . Huburbimanus . III . Thuraria . XV . Cicisa . XIII . Cartagine colon . thum

III . Sicilbba . XIII . Inuca . II . ad mercurium . III . ad pertusa . XIII . XV . Vthica . XX

TH u . IIS . X . durita . V . Tuburbomaius . XV . Onellana . XVI . Bibae

Pisca . XIII . diula . VII . ad tipsidam . VI . Vhappa . VI

X . ggo . XIII . Thasarte . ad thasartho . sizesua milia . P

thiges . XXV . thusuros

In the 10th segment of the *Tabula Peutingeriana* one can observe Eurasia, namely Anatolia, the Black Sea and the island of Cyprus. It highlights Antioch, a city that for its military importance and its wealth became the true metropolis of the East: its patriarch, Metropolitan of the East, had the rank of those of Rome and Constantinople, and in fact in the *Tabula Peutingeriana* Antioch is equated, among the fortified cities, only to Rome and Constantinople.

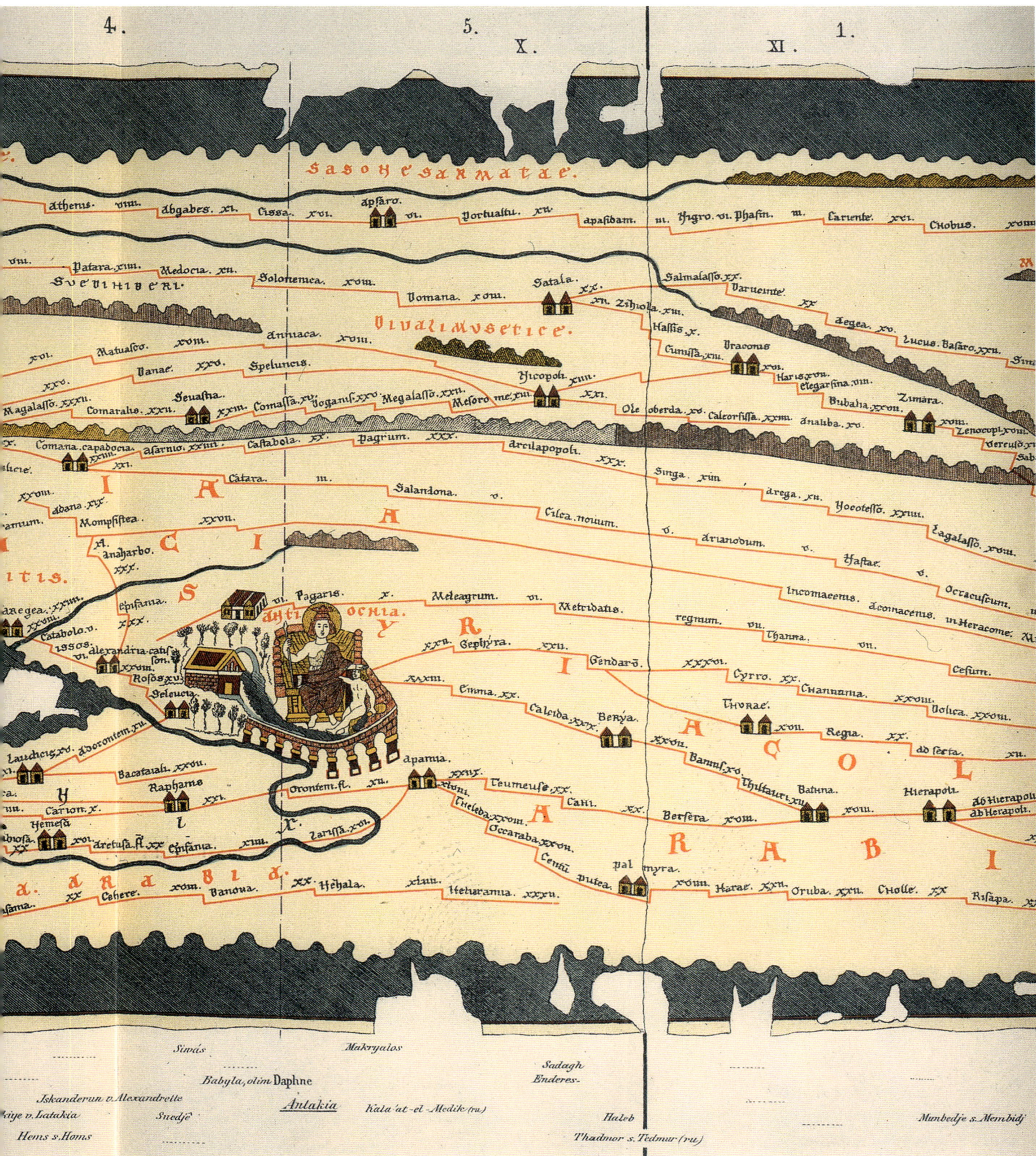

4. 5. X. XI. 1.

SASONES SARMATAE.

Athenis .VIII. Abgabes .XI. Cissa .XVI. Apsaro .VI. Portualu .XII. apasidam .III. higro .VI. Phasin .III. Cariente .XVI. Chobus .XIII.

VII. Patara .XIII. Medocia .XII. Solonenica .XIII. Vomana .XIII. Satala .XX. XII. Zihola .XIII. Salmalasso .XX. Varuente. Aegea .XV. Lucus Basaro .XXII. Sina.

SVEVI HIBERI.

XVI. Matuasto .XIII. Annica .XVIII. VIVALI MVSETICE. Hassis .X. Cumissa .XIII. Dracones. Haris .XVIII. elegarsina .VIII.

XXV. Danae .XXV. Speluncis Ole oberda .XV. Bubalia .XXVII. Zimara.

Magalasso .XXXII. Comaralis .XXII. Seuasta .XIII. Comassa .XIII. Yoganis .XXV. Megalasso .XXII. Mesoro me .XIII. XXI. Caleorsissa .XXIII. analiba. Zenocopi .XVII. Vereus .XI.

Comana capadocia .XIII. asarnio .XXIIII. Castabola .XX. Pagrum .XXX. arcilapopoli .XXX. Singa .XIII. arega .XII. Yocotesso .XIII. Sab.

Catara .III. Salandona .V. Lagalasso .XIII.

abana .XV. XXVII. Cilea nouum .V. arianodum .V. Octacuscum.

Mompsistea. incomacenis. aconacenis. in Heracome.

A. Anaharbo .XXX. Hastae .V.

arega .XXII. Epifania .XX. Pagaris .VI. ANTIOCHIA. Meleagrum .VI. Metridatis. regnum .VII. Thanna .VII. Cesum.

Catabolo .V. 19505. alexandria catisson .XXVII. Cephyra .XXII. Gendaro .XXXVI. Cyrro .XX. Channama .XVIII. Dolica .XXIII.

Rosos .XV. Seleucia. Emma .XX. Caleida .XXX. Berya .XXII. Thurae. Regia .XX. ad serta .XII.

Laudicia .XII. ad oronten .VI. Apamia .XXII. Bannus .XV. Thisauri .XII. Batna .XVIII. Hierapoli. ad Hierapoli.

Bacataiali .XXII. Orontem fl. .XII. Teumeuse .XX. Cahi. XX. Bersera .XVIII. ad Hierapoli.

Raphane. Theleda .XXIII. Occaraba .XXIII. Centu Putea .XXIII. Harae .XIII. Oruba .XXII. Cholle .XX. Risapa.

Cariom .X. I. Epifania .XIIII. Larissa .XXIII.

Hemesa. aretusa fl. .XX.

hosa. ARABIA. Cehere .XIII. Banoua .XX. Hehala .XIIII. Hetiarania .XXII. pal myra. ARABI.

Siuas. Makryalos. Sadagh. Enderes.

Babyla, olim Daphne

Iskanderun v. Alexandrette. Antakia. Kala'at-el-Medik (ru). Haleb. Munbedje s. Membidj.

kiye v. Latakia. Suedje. Thadmor s. Tedmur (ru).

Hems s. Homs

19

2. 3.

CAHHAFE. PSACCAHI. ararı.
Seracoe
ASPVRGIAHI.
Sarvetae
Monum. ILMERBE Lazi. EHIOCH
Sopatos.

Hermoca. Chimerium. B. ruam. Amyru. Macara Hale. Chritonis.
Humphi. Is. Achillis
Teagina

Chrisopolis. Iousort. xxv. ad promontorum xo. ad herbas. ft. xvi. Melena. artane. xviii. philum. xvii. Chelas. xxvii. Sagari ft. Hyppium
Calcedonia Luvista. xviii. Temp. Herculis x. Sagar. Manoris. xvii. Potonia. Cepora.
xxvii. xxviii. BITHINIA Hicomedia. xvii. Lateas. xvii. Solympum. xxx. Luliopoli.
Is. aytwchia Is. acarvas. xu. Demetru. xiii. Vusepro. Valoaton. x. fines.
SYHOSIHICOMEDICVS. Vadastana. xxviii. Pesinunte.
Pronetios. Eribulo. xu. Vorileo. xxviii. Mideo. xxviii. Tricoma. xxi.
Is. prauonessus. xxviii. Hicara xl. Cateabio. xiii. Dablis. xi. GAL Vocymeo. xxxvi.
Pylae. Labassou. ft. Sagari.
Hicara. tmo. Velo. Imte. Cranico. Priapos. xv. Pagrillo. PHRY xxx. Cocleo. Hacolea.
coria. Lythico. xxii. Cio. xv. prusad. olympum. Mileopoli. Agmoma. xvi. aludba. Claud
Lamasco. Lamasco. Prusias. Apollonia. xx. xxii. SI.
audo. viii. Pheme ruo. xx. Argelis. xxxv. Hadrianuteba. Pergano. Ger
Vardano. Alexandria. troas. Antandros. Corisanio. v. elana. xi. attalia.
Ilio. xvi. un. Sminthium. xv. assos. xxiii. Gargara. aderimtus. xo.
Litum. xvi. Inata. arcade. xxx. Blenna. xx. Hiera
rica. Monogam. Tapostri. Ermupoli.
VMS PEL A xxv. Serapeu. Yseum.
Cardu. xxxiii. Hemeseo. xiii. Calabathmo. xxviii. Melean. xvi. Haucrat. xlii. Yseum.
dratu. xxvi. Yesus. xxiii. Pretonio. xxiii. Philisc. xxiii. Tyconpoli. xii. Antano. xiii. hicru. Delta.
qui drudit asiam libiam. Hormucopto. xiii. Cenobosrio. xxiii. ananu. xvii. Panopoli. Ca monti. xx Celmi. xli. Memphi. Babilom
Spelei. xlii. Syene. xii. Ombos. xx. Tentra. xvi. Lato. xx. Viospoli. xxii. Phenice. xxiii. Affrodites. xx. Heradeo. vi. Casdri.
Ptolemaidonar. Sinoftu. venne.
Bydymos. xv. Conpasin. xii. Bios. xxiii. xeron. xxiii. philacon. xx.

PSACCAHI.

HERVAHI. ARSOAE. AMAZONES. CHIREOE.

CAVCASI.

e salinay hie salp scipiciur. SAHHIGAE. ARSOAE. ACHEII. PHRYS

CHISOE. Stratodis. Cepos. HERMOHASSA. Sindecae.

phamacorum.

V S E V X I N V S

euomsf. n. Zygum. fe. iii. Heraclea. xx. Tivon. xii. Mastrum. xx. Lycae. xv. Cereas. xv. Mileto. xoni. Snope. vii. Clopta sa. P Orgibate. Zacoria. xvi. Helega. xu. q

opolis. xxviii. Scylleum. x p Pompeiopolis. d f 2 a g xx. vii. Stefane. xxvii. Syrias. Y P amasia. Hauta

anabynata. xxxvi. Gangaris. amasia. xi. Cromen. vii. Cythero. viii. Egilan. xxvii. Carambas. xiii. Thoma. xxvii. Tauio. Tonea. xxx. Barsi. xx. xv. Palalce. xx

xxi. Otresa. xxv. Uralia. xi. Cromen. vii. Cocobriga. xxvii. Lassora. xvii. Stabiu. Tauio. Tonea. Rogmoy. xxxvi. degonne. xxxvi. ptemari. xxvii

Zagania. xvi. Mihago. xx. deitorihaco. xxxxii. Cocobriga. xxvii. Lassora. xvii. Stabiu. xvi. Tomba. xxii. Cogom. Sarako. xxii. Zama. xxxii. A

Rostola. xxiii. Amurio. Abrostola. xxxiii. Ysita Rho. affasi. xii. aspona. x. Garmias. xii. Corueunte. xxii. Salaberrina. xoi. Caena. xoi. Tracias.

Synnada. xxvi. Iullae. xxxv. Philomelo. xxvii. Tolosocorio. vii. Bagrum. xx. Verisso. xx. Egdaua. xx. Pegel la. xx. Congusso. xv. Petra. xx. Comitanasso. xii. Ubinnaca. xxii. aquas

G conn. ASYNHAVE IV FORBIO. Ml? xxii. Caballucome. xxxii. Congusso. Sabatra. xxii. Pyrgos.

Adelfia. Eucarpia. Tripoli. xii. Hierapoli. xv. Cumenia. Euforbio. ab euforbio. Abamea. Mil?. xxxvi. Apamea ciboton.

Tyatira. Hermon. fl. castur. Tralls. xxvii. Socrau. ix. Pella. A xx. ad uicum. xiii.

Mirinna. viii. Smyrna. ypepa. viii. anagome. Magnesia. Lvi. antochie. xii. Laudicium pilycum. Temissomo. Cormassa. Per

Cyme. xxvii. Chemnum. Metropolis. Leos. xx. lebedo. Colofon. xvi. Ephesum. Carura. xx. Miletum. xii. Lynce. Loi. Mande. Chidum.

CARIA. LYCIA.

G Pelusio. vii. Gerra. xxiii. Cassio. Ostracine. xxiii. Rinocorura. xv. INSVLA. RHODOS.

Serapeu. Heradeo. ascalone. Choton. x. Lamnia. xii. Ioppe. Apollomade. Cesaria. viii.

Suba. phacust. Rinocorura. Iuddis. xii. Thorax.

Senpho. Betogabri. amauante. Heapoli. xxvi. xx caporcoton.

Ierapeu. Ceperaria. Antea dicta Herusalem in heliacapitolin. xii. xii.

Siman. Desertum u quadraginta annis errauert filii isr'l ducente Moyse. Oboda. xxii. Elusa. Lxxi. Cofna. Herichonte. xii. arcelais. Coabis. xii.

Hic legem acceperunt i monte Syna. addrianam. Rasa. xvi. Cypsaria. xxvii. Lysa. xlvii. Oboda. Thamaro. Monsoliueti. Fl. IORDAHIS.

Mons. Syna. Haila n. fl. adio. Petris. Thanara. Bostris.

Veia. Lxxv. Phara. L. Hauarra. xx. Zadagatta. xxiii. Hegla. Thorma. xvii. Rababatora. Lxxi. Philadelfia. Tiantha. xxiii. abra. x

nonos. xxvii. Cabau. Cenonnydroma. xii. Pernicide Porhon. Hic cenocephali nascuntur. Gadda. xii. Hatita. ix. xl. RHOSE.

Hereford Mappa Mundi

This stunning manuscript from Hereford Cathedral, England, is the largest known example of a medieval world map. It was drawn on flayed calfskin around 1300 AD by Richard of Haldingham and Lafford, also known as *Richard de Bello*, a high-ranking cleric.

The Hereford Mappa Mundi is a near perfect example of a traditional medieval T and O (T-O) map, a Biblically inspired cartographic model popular during Europe's Middle Ages. The map is hard to interpret by modern standards as it is drawn with the spiritual rather than Earthly world in mind, but with some imagination, it does become clear. Jerusalem, the religious center of the world, appears at its center. East is at the top of the map and the furthest eastward point is the Garden of Eden, or the Earthly Paradise. Eden is walled off and appears to be an island, thus suggesting inaccessibility from the mundane world. The large body of water at the bottom center of the map is the Mediterranean, with the Straits of Gibraltar marking the westernmost point. Africa occupies the right-hand part of the map with the river Nile somewhat easy to identify. Europe appears in the lower left quadrant.

Most of the more specific locations on the map are Biblical rather than geographical references and are, typically, associated with episodes from scripture. The site of Noah's Ark, for example, is noted. Nevertheless, this being an English production, England, Ireland, and Scotland appear prominently in the lower left.

Today, as it has been for hundreds of years, the Hereford Mappa Mundi is housed at Hereford Cathedral in England. It is on display to the public.

Cartographer

Richard of Haldingham and Lafford (fl. c. 1275-1313) was an English clergyman and scholar. Also known as Richard de Bello, *he was a high-ranking cleric, possibly a treasurer, and later prebend, at Lincoln Cathedral in Lafford. He was reassigned to Hereford Cathedral in 1305.*

23

24

Universalis Cosmographia

Known as the Waldseemüller Map, this is one of the most important maps ever published. The map's greatest claim to fame is that it was the first map to use the term "America" to define the newly discovered continent. Apparently, Martin Waldseemüller, having read both the accounts of Columbus and the accounts of Amerigo Vespucci, found the Vespucci accounts so superior that he honored Vespucci by giving his name to the continent. It has since been dubbed as the "Birth Certificate of America." However, there is much more to this map than the naming of America.

Waldseemüller's greatest challenge in preparing this gigantic map was to increase the scope of known cartography, then limited to Ptolemaic maps, to include the recent discovery of the New World. The Ptolemaic model advocated a three-part world comprising Europe, Asia, and Africa. Waldseemüller took that a step further, considerably expanding the scope of his map to add a fourth part, the Americas. That was a monumental leap in geographic thought that transformed all subsequent cartography. Earlier Ptolemaic maps were not so much perceived as guides to the modern world, as they were guides to the ancient world – more useful to humanists and scholars than to travelers. Waldseemüller, by expanding the coverage of the Ptolemaic model, modernized it, and took a great leap forward towards the production of the first useful modern world map.

Evidence suggests that Waldseemüller issued 1000 copies of the map in 1507. Of these, only a single example survives today. It was discovered in the Schloss Wolfegg library of Prince Johannes zu Waldburg-Wolfegg in Württemberg, Germany in 1901. There it remained until 2001 when the United States Library of Congress purchased the map for a record ten million dollars. At the time, it was the highest price ever paid for a single historical map.

Cartographer

Martin Waldseemüller (1470-1520) was a German cartographer and humanist. He studied at the University of Freiburg and became a canon at the Gymnasium Vosagense of the Collegiate of the Church of Saint-Dié in Lorraine. Aided by Matthias Ringmann he produced several important maps, the most significant of which is this great 1507 map of the world.

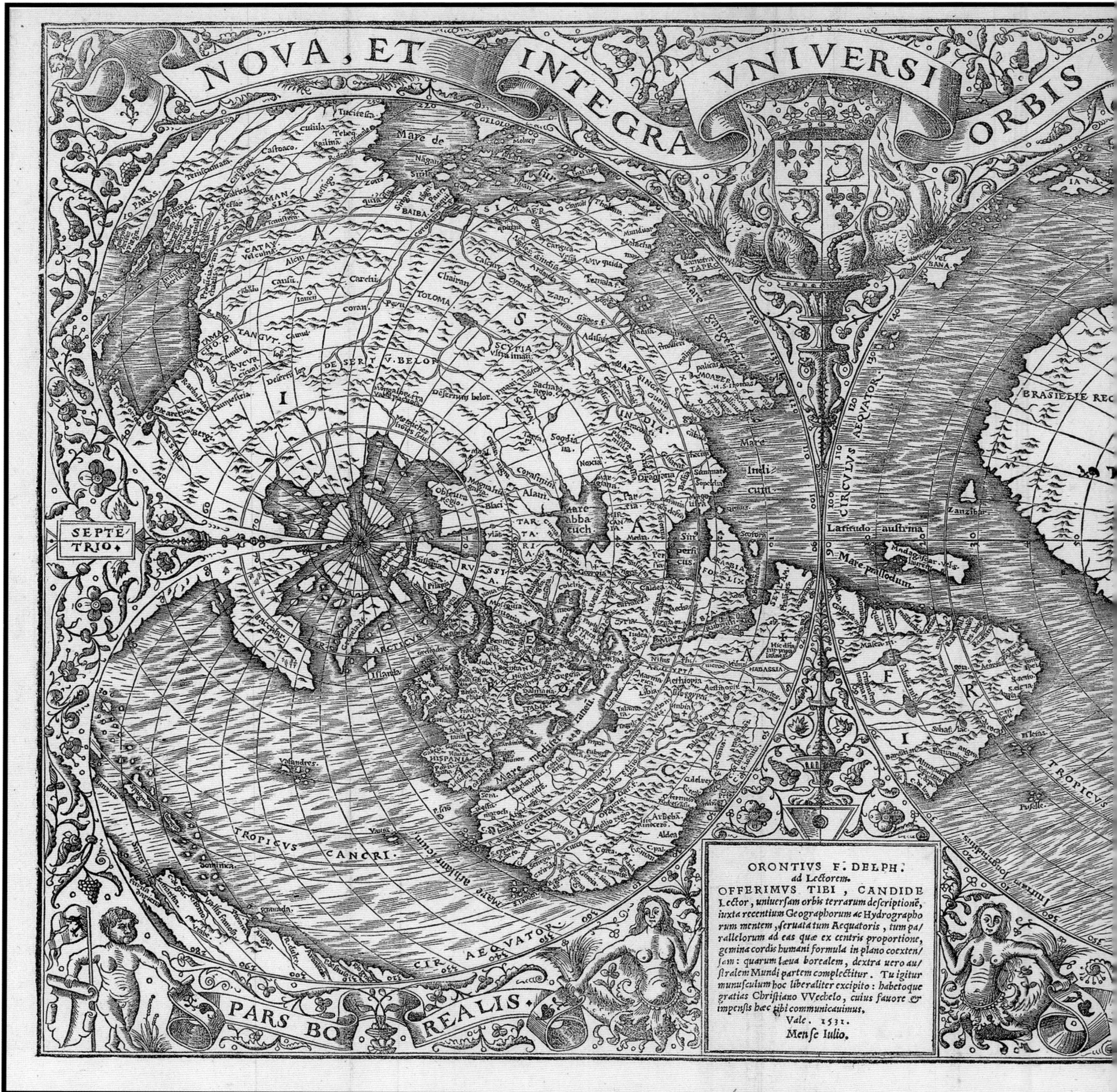

NOVA, ET INTEGRA VNIVERSI ORBIS

SEPTE/TRIO

PARS BO REALIS

ORONTIVS F. DELPH.
ad Lectorem.
OFFERIMVS TIBI, CANDIDE
Lector, uniuersam orbis terrarum descriptionē,
iuxta recentium Geographorum ac Hydrographo
rum mentem, seruata tum Aequatoris, tum pa/
rallelorum ad eas quæ ex centris proportione,
gemina cordis humani formula in plano coexten/
sam: quarum læua borealem, dextra uero au/
stralem Mundi partem complectitur. Tu igitur
munusculum hoc liberaliter excipito: habetoque
gratias Christiano VVechelo, cuius fauore &
impensis hæc tibi communicauimus.
Vale. 1531.
Mense Iulio.

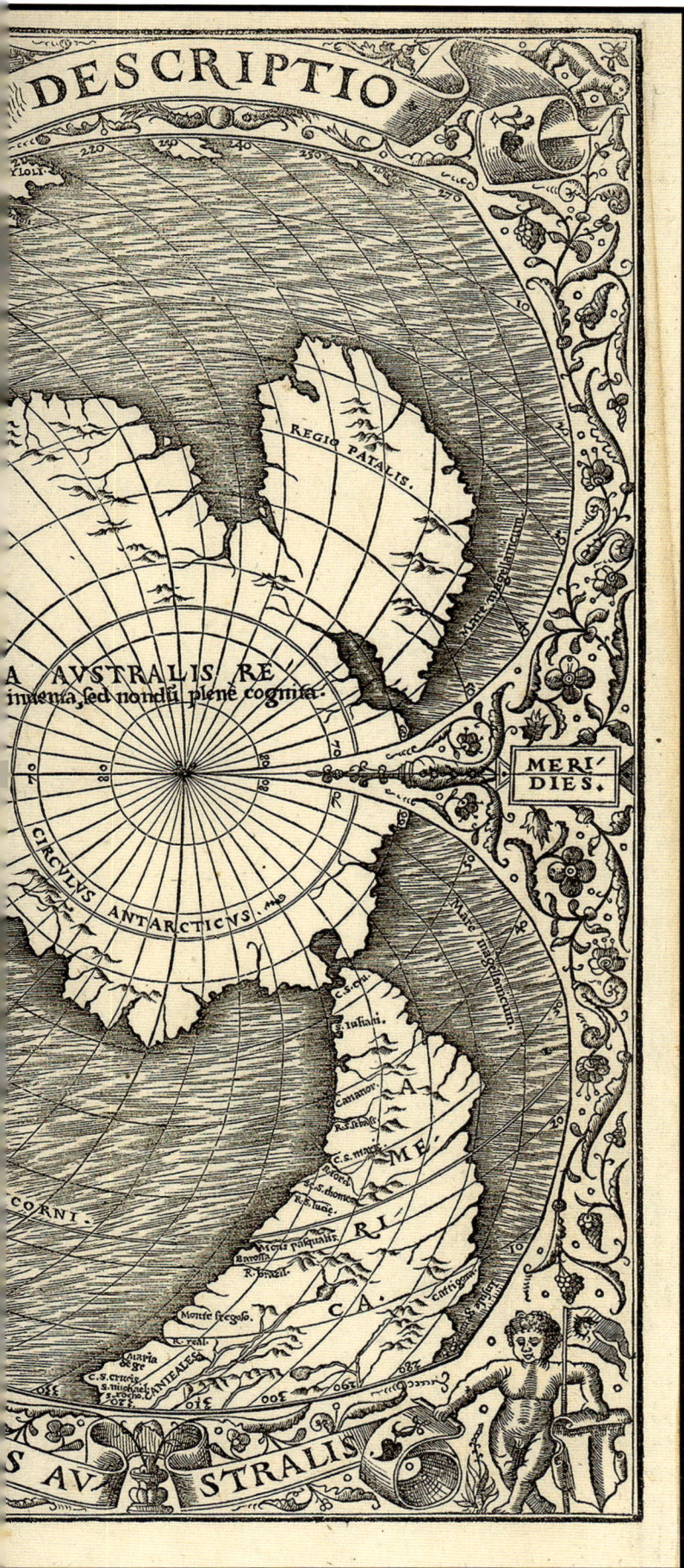

Nova, et Integra Universi Orbis Descriptio

A map of exceptional interest, this is the French cartographer Oronce Finé's 1531 woodcut of the world. The map is presented on a unique heart-shaped cordiform projection. With this model, Finé was attempting to apply mathematical principles to the problem of rendering the Earth's spherical surface on a two-dimensional plane. He is one of the first cartographers to do so making this map one of the earliest and most sophisticated maps to be based upon a projection system. The Finé Cordiform Model was embraced by several other cartographers, including Gerard Mercator.

Cartographically, the map follows on the discoveries of Christopher Columbus, Amerigo Vespucci, and Ferdinand Magellan. The left hand cordum illustrates Europe, Asia, North Africa, and what little was known of North America. The more arresting right hand cordum, while including parts of southern Africa and South America, is primarily dedicated to the vast speculative continent of *Terra Australis* with the annotation, in translation, "recently discovered but not yet explored." Here Finé is referring to the discoveries of the Magellan-Elcano Circumnavigation completed in 1522, just 10 years earlier. Passing through the Straits of Magellan at the southern tip of South America, it was initially assumed that Tierra del Fuego, the land south of the Straits, was attached to the mainland of *Terra Australis*, a continent that no one ever seen but most believed to exist. It was not until Sir Francis Drake's circumnavigation of 1577-1580, which passed to the south of Cape Horn and Tierra del Fuego, that the association with *Terra Australis* was abandoned. The assumption that *Terra Australis* existed, nevertheless persisted.

Cartographer

Oronce Finé (1494-1555), often referred to as Finnaeus, was a French physician, mathematician, and cartographer. He was born in Briançon and studied medicine at the Collège de Navarre in Paris. Despite being briefly imprisoned for practicing "Judicial Astrology," a technique for predicting future events considered heretical to the Catholic Church, he was, in 1531, appointed to a chair of mathematics at the Collège Royal of King Francis I and was the author of many books on mathematics. Today a lunar crater and part of Antarctica are named in his honor.

Altera Generalis Tab. Secundum Ptol.

Sebastian Münster produced this map in 1550 in order to illustrate the world as it was perceived using the Ptolemaic model most common prior to the Great Age of Discovery. Despite being published in the 16th century, this map offers a view of the world from the 2nd century. Münster's work followed the cartographic vision presented in Claudius Ptolemy's seminal work *Geographia*. Although many 'Ptolemaic' maps survive today, most are extrapolated from the text of the *Geographia*. It remains unclear if Ptolemy himself produced an actual map.

The "Old World" is somewhat limited from our modern perspective, covering only the areas from Indochina to the Atlantic Ocean and from the Equator to the Arctic. Europe, Arabia, and the Persian Gulf are recognizable. The Nile and the Niger are both visible in Africa. India is under-sized relative to "Tapobrana," an archaic name for the important spice-trading center of Sri Lanka. Note how Africa continues at the base of the map to connect with Southeast Asia. The Indian Ocean is thus fully enclosed, a belief that was common until Bartolomeu Dias sailed around the southernmost tip of Africa in 1488.

Also of interest is the way Africa clearly extends southward below the Equator but is not even conjecturally mapped. It was believed in Ptolemaic times that these lands, referred to as the Tepid Zone, were full of monsters and too hot to sustain human life.

Cartographers

- *Sebastian Münster (1488-1552) was a professor of Hebrew at the University of Basel, Switzerland. Münster had issued a call throughout Germany's academic communities for cartographic information, in preparation for putting together the* Cosmographia, *and the book's accuracy and scope were unprecedented. It sold well and went through 24 editions. The intricate woodcuts, by a variety of artists, were one of the reasons for its vast influence. It was produced for nearly 100 years. Most of Münster's work was published by his sons. He died in Switzerland in 1552.*

- *Claudius Ptolemy (100-170 AD) was a Greek Alexandrian astronomer and mathematician considered to be the "Father of Cartography." His most important geographical work, the* Geographia, *laid the foundation for modern geographical thought and included instructions on mapmaking and an extensive coordinate system. Ptolemy's work was thought lost until it was reintroduced to European scholars during the Renaissance by the Moroccan scholar Muhammad al-Idrisi.*

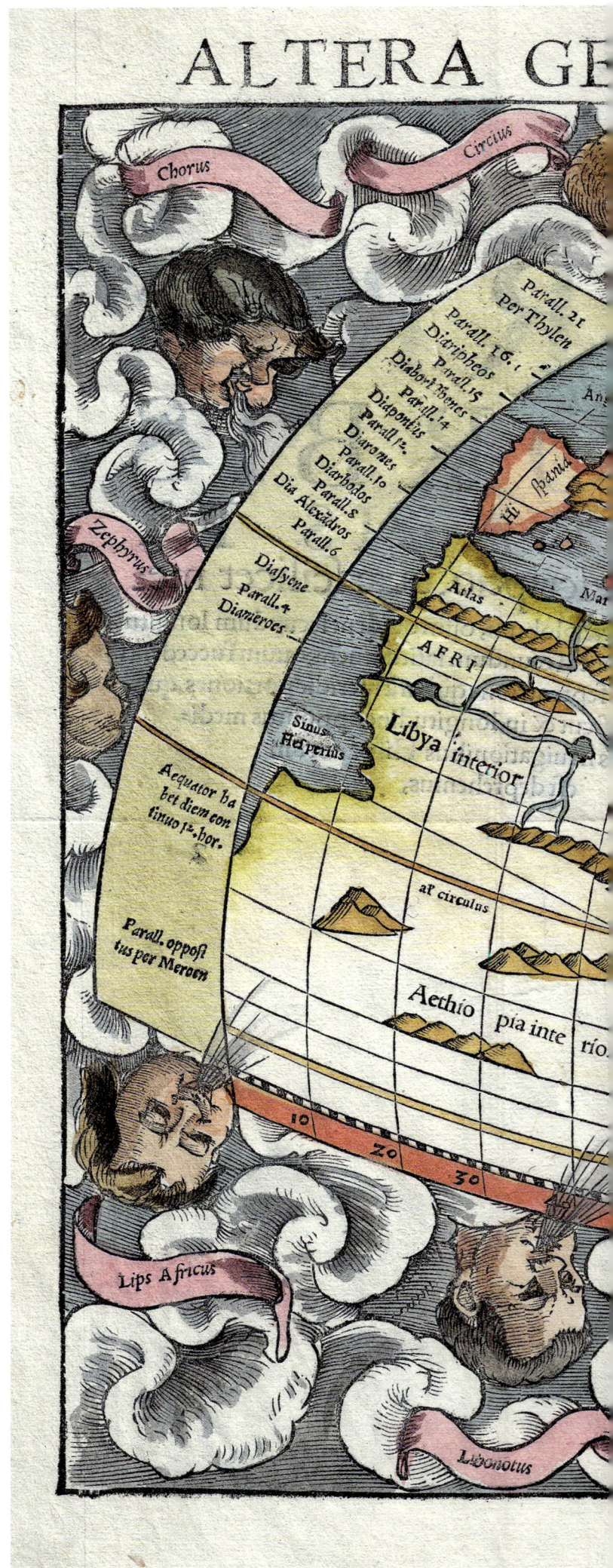

Septentrio

Aquilo

Caecias

Sub Solanus

Mare Glaciale

Septetrional Regiones

10 20 30 40 50 60 70 80 90 100 110 120 130 140 150 160 170 180

Ger mania

EV RO PA

Tanai

Rha. fl.

Scythia intra Imaum

Imaus mons

Sinarum regio

Scythia extra Imaum

Emodii môtes

ASIA

Graecia

Pōtus Euxi

Alia minor

Mare Caspiũ

traneum

Eufrates

Syria

Aegyptus

Sinꝰ Per ficus

Arabia Felix

India intra Gan gem

Ganges

INDIA extra Gangem

magnus Sinus

Sinus Gange ticus

Nilus fl.

Mare Rubrũ

Tapro bana

Mare Indicũ

Sinus Bar biaticus

Mare Prafo dum

Terra incogni ta fecun dum Pto lemeum

60 70 80 90 100 110 120 130 140 150 160 170 180

Vulturnus

Aufter

Euro aufter

29

Typus Orbis Universalis

Twelve wind heads, one for each direction, and multiple sea monsters enliven this famous map of the world. Well-known among educated Europeans of the 16th century, this map was included in one of the most popular and influential books of its time, Sebastian Münster's *Cosmographia*. Considered to be the first description of the world in the German language, it was later published in many other languages including Latin, French, Czech, English, and Italian.

Münster's map is considered to have been the first to identify the Pacific Ocean (*Mare Pacificum*). Here, North America, still largely an unknown land, is identified as *Terra Florida*. Africa is shown with the Nile prominently represented on the Ptolemaic two-lake model. Japan is identified as *Zipangri*, an archaic term referencing Marco Polo, and Asia extends and reappears just north of America. In South America, the Strait of Magellan and the Rio de la Plata are visible. Tierra del Fuego (Land of Fire) is oversized on the assumption that it must be connected to Plato's mythical southern continent. Europe is nearly connected to North America and Greenland by an Arctic land bridge.

Cartographer

Sebastian Münster (1488-1552) was a professor of Hebrew at the University of Basel, Switzerland. Münster had issued a call throughout Germany's academic communities for cartographic information, in preparation for putting together the Cosmographia, *and the book's accuracy and scope were unprecedented. It sold well and went through 24 editions. The intricate woodcuts, by a variety of artists, were one of the reasons for its vast influence. It was produced for nearly 100 years. Most of Münster's work was published by his sons. He died in Switzerland in 1552.*

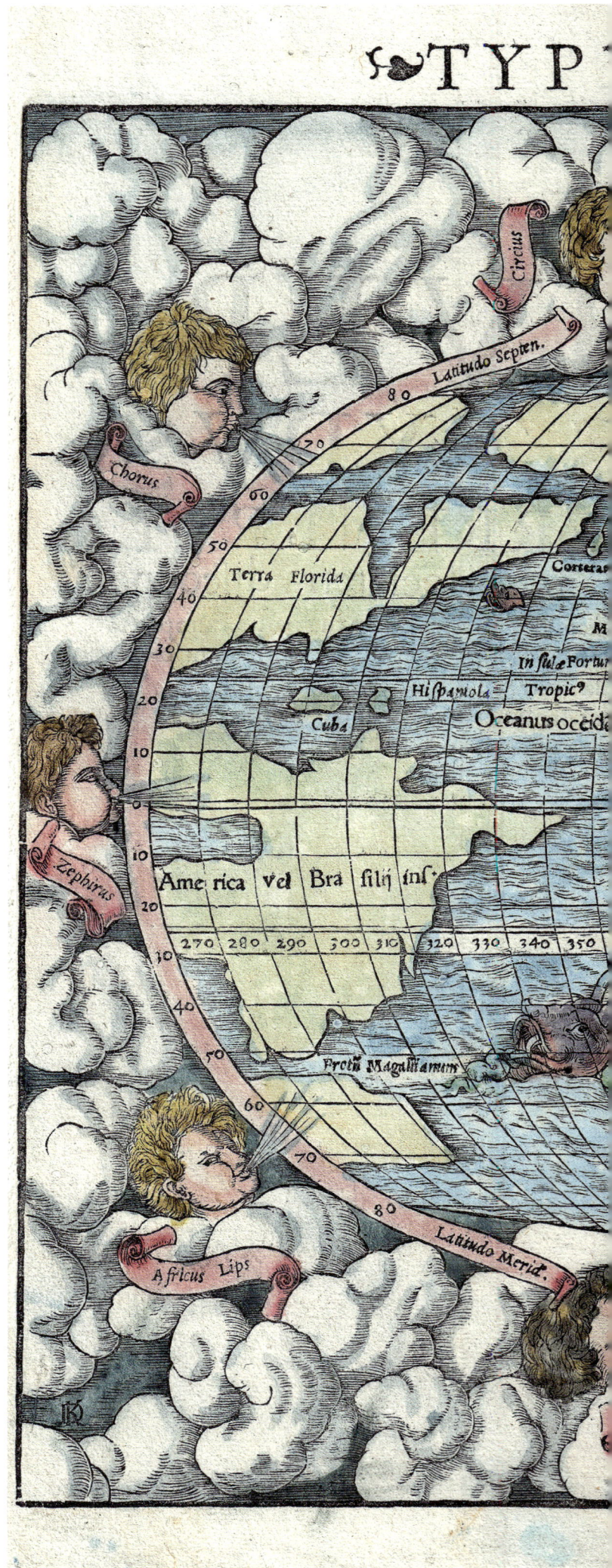

Septemtrio

Polus Septē.

Aquilo

Latitudo Septen. 80

70

60

Cecias

50

Tēmi fian

40

Isfand

Ca thai Re gio

30

Euro pa

mare Casp.

Asia

India

20

Mare mediterr.

10

Mauritania

Arabia

Oceanus oriētal

Zipangri

Cancri

Libya

Calicut

0

Africa

Aethiopia

Tro glodite

Aequino. iial Circul⁹
Madagascar

Tegura

Porne

Iaua

Giolo

Sub folanus

10

20

Tropicus Capricorni⁹

30

10 20 30 40 50 60 70 80 90 100 110 120 130 140 150 160 170 180 190 200 210 220 230 240 250 260

40

Zanzibar

Calen sua

Mare pacificum

50

In sulæ Gri simum

60

70

Latitudo Merid'

Eurus

80

Polus merid.

Eurolufter

Libonotus

africus

31

Die gantze Welt in einem Kleeberblat/Welches ist der Stadt Hannouer meines lieb-

SEPTENTRIO

Dennemarck Schwe=den

Engeland

ARMEN

Franckreich Saxen

MESOPO TAMIA Niniue 171.

Hispanien Deudschland

Lothringen Behemen Reussen

SIRIA Harau 110.

Meiland Polen

CHALDEA

EVROPA Vngern Moschaw

Antiochia 70.

Welschland Türcken

Damascus 40.

Vr 150.

ARABIA

Griechen-land

Roma 382.

IERVSALEM

Saba 312.

Das Rote Meer.

Das grosse Mittelmeer der Welt.

Alexandria 72.

Egypten

Cyrene 284.

LYBIA Meroe 14.

Morenland

AFRICA

Königreich Melinde.

AMERICA Die Newe Welt.

CAPVT BO-NÆSPEI

OCCIDENS.

MERIDIES.

Die ganze Welt in einem Kleberblat

Heinrich Bünting's thematic map of the world in the form of a cloverleaf was first issued in 1581. The map is drawn in the T-O style, a Biblically-based cartographic model that was popular prior to the rediscovery of Ptolemaic mapping in the 12th century. It is revelatory of just how slowly early discoveries and cartographic advancements made their way into regular usage that Bünting continued to embrace the T-O model more than 70 years after Waldseemüller's advancements, and several hundred years after the rise of the Ptolemaic model.

The religious interpretation of the three-part world is the essence of the T-O model. Typically, as here, Jerusalem, as the heart of the world, appeared at its center, with Europe, Asia, and Africa radiating outward. In Europe, Rome was given precedence and was the greatest city on the map outside of Jerusalem. In Asia, there are many cities, most of which like Babylon, Persepolis, and Damascus, were known to Europeans from Biblical tradition. India is identified as the farthest eastward point. Africa has only three cities, Meroe (Sudan), Cyrene (Libya), and Alexandria (Egypt). Curiously, England, Scandinavia (including Denmark), and the New World are divorced from the main body of the map, suggesting that Bünting was struggling to reconcile modern cartographic knowledge with his religiocentric values.

Cartographer

Heinrich Bünting (1545-1606) was born in Hanover, Germany. He studied at the University of Wittenberg. Graduating in 1569, after studying theology, he became a Protestant pastor. He retired to Hanover in 1600 after a dispute about his teaching. His book "Travel Through the Holy Scripture" (Itinerarium Sacrae Scripturae)*, which consisted of several maps printed in woodcut, became very popular and was reissued multiple times.*

Des Erdtrichs theilung fahen wir Europeer an/nach der lenge/im Occidentischen Meer hinder Spanien vnd Gallien/ vollstrecken sie gegen Orient/ durch das Indianische Meer zum halben theil/ der begreifft in sich Europen vnd Asien ge gen Orient: aber gegen Mittag Africen vnd Papagoier land: das ist/ Psitacorum regio.

SEPTENTRION

MARE SEPTENTRIONALIS

Nova Zembla

Estotilandt

Gronland

Jlland Schne

Nona Francia

Dän

Russia

Tartaria

ANIAN Regnum

CIRCVLVS ARTICVS

INDIA VEL ARMERICA NOVA

EVROPA

Gallia

Grecia

Mare Casp.

Quinta Regnum

Hispania

OCEANVS OCCI

ASIA

Granata

Florida

IVDÆA

Hispannia nova

Tropicus Cancri

BARBARIA

AEGIPTVS

ARABIA

ARCHIPELAGO

Mexico

Cuba

Span

AGISVBA

AFRICA

NVBIA

CIRCVLVS AEQVINOCTIALIS.

190 200 210   220 230 240 250 260 270   280 290 300 310 320   340 350 360   10 20 30   40 50 60 70 80 9

Cari Hana

MARE

Manconoa

Melu de

Nova Gui nea

S. Petro

Peru

Bruſily

ÆTHIOPICVM

S. Laver

America

TROPICVS CAPRICORNI

MARE PACIFICVM

Chile

Chica

Ca: Bona ſpei.

Magellanica Regio

CIRCVLVS ANTARCTICVS.

Fretum Magellia nium

Terra del fugo

Prom.

Prom. TERRÆ AVSTRALIS

PSITACORVM REGIO

TERRA AVSTRALIS   NONDVM   COGNITA

MERIDIES

Den andern halben theil der Erdtagel nemmen wir von Orient vnd dem Indianischen Meer/ wider herumb gegen Occident/ der begreifft in sich vom Aequinoctial gegen Septentrion/ new Spanien/ new Indien/ new Francien: ge gen Meridien Peru/ Americen/ vnd Braſilien/ die alle new erfundene landt ſindt.

OCCIDENS

Monçol

Cathaio

Ahina

Quinpan

INDIA ORIENTALIS

Japen

Calecut

ORIENS

e INDICVM

Sumatra

Iaua

Beach Iaua Minor

LVCAOH

MALETVR

Die erst General Tafel

This impressive early woodcut map was produced by Sebastian Münster in 1588. In this sophisticated work, the modern world was beginning to emerge. North America, South America, Africa, Europe, and Asia are recognizable although not without error. Note how the mythical southern continent, *Terra Australis* was attached to both a proto-Australia and to Tierra del Fuego. Other anomalies include the curious lump on the southwestern corner of South America, an elaboration that was removed in subsequent versions of this map. The Arctic was divided into four insular regions on the Mercator model, with navigable passages in between as well as an open and navigable Arctic Sea. Even though the shores of the world were taking on a recognizable shape, most of the inland world outside of Europe, except isolated colonies, remained unknown.

Münster was frequently admired for his prolific use of sea monsters to illustrate his maps. This is not purely decorative. While most of Münster's monsters may seem odd to us today, they represented reality to early scholars and navigators who studied this map, illustrating, for example, rich cod and whale fisheries and dangers not to be ignored. This map was published posthumously by Münster's heir and son-in-law, Heinrich Petri.

Cartographers

• *Sebastian Münster (1488-1552) was a professor of Hebrew at the University of Basel, Switzerland. Münster had issued a call throughout Germany's academic communities for cartographic information, in preparation for putting together the* Cosmographia, *and the book's accuracy and scope were unprecedented. It sold well and went through 24 editions. The intricate woodcuts, by a variety of artists, were one of the reasons for its vast influence. It was produced for nearly 100 years. Most of Münster's work was published by his sons. He died in Switzerland in 1552.*

• *Heinrich Petri (1508-1579) was the son-in-law of the famous cartographer Sebastian Münster. He and his son, Sebastian Petri, were printers in Switzerland. Their firm,* Officina Henricpetrina, *was known for publishing several seminal works in the field of cartography.*

Noua Orbis Terrarum Delineatio

This graphically-rich map represented major changes in cartography from the vague and religious cartography of earlier generations to a far more scientific model. The map was engraved by Philip Eckebrecht at the request of his friend Johannes Kepler. Kepler spent much of his career compiling and completing the astronomical tables of his predecessor in the post of Imperial Mathematician, Tycho Brahe. In the process, he discovered and codified Kepler's Laws of Planetary Motion, for which he is most remembered today.

The map typically accompanies editions of the *Tabulae Rudolphinae*, the publication containing the Kepler–Brahe Tables, used for predicting astronomical events. In addition to astronomical tables the volume also consisted of a table of cities with latitude and longitude noted. To illustrate this useful secondary table Kepler hired Eckebrecht to compile a new map of the world referencing his calculations. The rich detail, fine engraving, longitude, and latitude lines correspond to the scientific underpinnings of the map. Unfortunately, because of Kepler's death in 1630, the map was set aside and not published until rediscovered in 1658.

Of course, the most striking feature of the map is the stunning janiform Hapsburg Eagle used as part of the map's dedication to Leopold I (1640-1705), the then Holy Roman Emperor, by whose predecessor Rudolph II, Kepler was employed. The map itself, we must note, was published posthumously. Kepler died in 1630. The map plates must have remained uncompleted in Eckebrecht's offices until 1658, when the Leopold I dedication was added.

Cartographer

Philipp Eckebrecht (1594-1667) was a merchant in Nuremburg, Germany and a hobbyist astronomer.

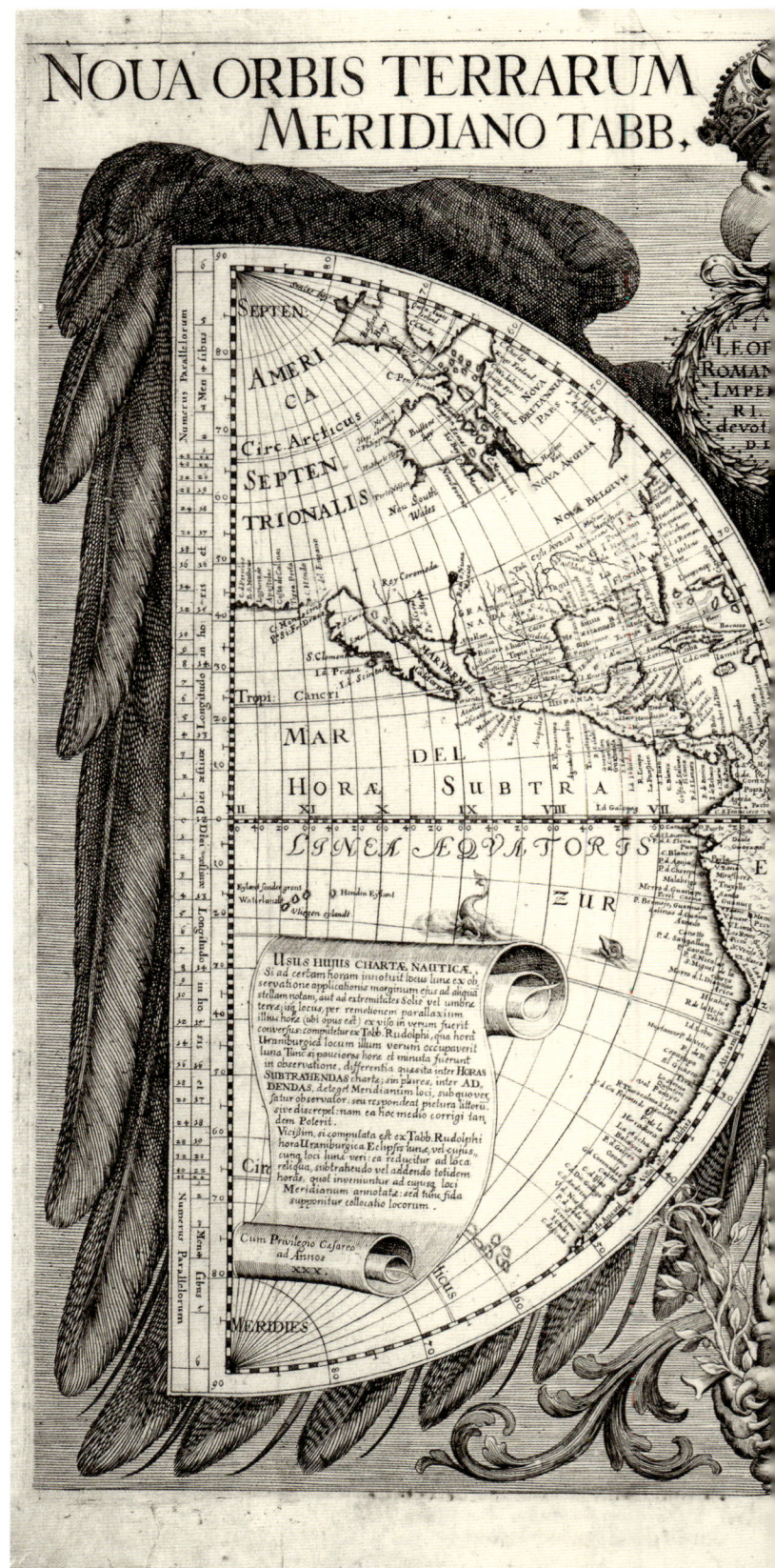

Courtesy of Library of Congress

The Dutch Golden Age
The Rise of the Modern Map

In the final days of the 16th century and throughout the subsequent 17th century, nowhere in Europe was more vibrant than the Dutch Republic. During this period, known as the Dutch Golden Age, Dutch science, art, and industry flourished. Dutch navigators and merchants followed in the paths of explorers like Christopher Columbus and Bartolomeu Dias to found global empires based upon trade and commerce. Bolstered by rich merchant princes who needed maps to better understand their global business empires, ship captains hungry for nautical charts to the Indies, a sophisticated printing industry, and a wealth of new information flooding daily into the Republic's busy ports, the cartographers of the Dutch Golden Age revolutionized commercial cartography.

No two figures were more influential in the early days of Dutch cartography than Abraham Ortelius and Gerard Mercator. Ortelius and Mercator were contemporaries, friends, and competitors. Ortelius is credited with publishing the world's first modern atlas, the Theatrum Orbis Terrarum, *or "Theater of the World," and Mercator is credited with creating the term "Atlas" to apply to a book of maps.*

Ortelius and Mercator met in 1554 at the Frankfurter Buchmesse (Frankfurt Book and Print Fair) where the elder Mercator, already a man of influence in the map trade, inspired Ortelius to pursue a career as a scientific geographer. Today, we are fortunate that much of Ortelius' remarkable subsequent correspondence as a geographer, over 500 letters, survives in library archives. Through his correspondence, we can understand the incredible research and scholarship that early Dutch mapmakers invested in compiling their maps. Ortelius' correspondence is vast, reaching to luminaries, including scholars, priests, and other mapmakers throughout Europe. His correspondents included not only other cartographers like Gerard Mercator and Arias Montanus, but also figures like John Dee, Francis Drake, and Richard Hakluyt, among many others.

The correspondence typically seeks answers to geographical questions: What lies at the North Pole? Is this an island or a peninsula? What manner of people inhabit this land or province? Are these open or frozen seas? How can we account for compass variation to magnetic north? These questions and those like them plagued early geographers, who were trying to find a way to map a world that remained mostly unexplored. Answers came in the form of scientific theories, educated speculation, interpretation of Biblical or classical writing, and, from time to time, interpretation of evidence from actual exploration.

In addition to a vast network of correspondents, the cartographers of the Dutch Golden Age were particularly blessed with daily merchant ships that left and arrived at the docks of Antwerp and Amsterdam. Each of these ships brought new information from the far corners of the world. While there was an active attempt on the part of the Dutch East India Company (VOC) and other powerful concerns, to keep this information secret, much of it, through tavern gossip among sailors and a network of coveted informants, filtered into the hands of cartographers like Ortelius and Mercator. They used these reports to compile increasingly accurate charts. Maps typically went through multiple editions, often with extensive revisions, as new information emerged and geographical theories changed.

This exchange went both ways. Cartographers used information drawn from the experience of pilots and navigators to produce ever more accurate charts, these in turn were passed back to the sailors, who, armed with more accurate information, could, with increasing confidence, navigate the world more safely. The most significant innovation of the Dutch Golden Age with regard to navigation was without doubt Gerard Mercator's construction of his namesake projection.

The Mercator Projection addressed one of the fundamental problems of 16th century navigation, accounting for the curvature of the Earth when setting a course at sea. Earlier projections, while scientifically sound, did not correspond to the navigational experience in that a straight line on the map did not necessarily equate with a straight line in the real world. Quite the opposite in fact as navigators setting a course by an earlier map could, after several hundred kilometers at sea, easily find themselves wildly off course. In his 1569 wall map, Nova et Aucta Orbis Terrae Descriptio ad Usum Navigantium, *Mercator was able to address this issue through applied mathematics. By distorting distance proportionally in those parts of the map closer to the poles, he created a projection wherein a straight line on the map equated to a straight line in the real world. These lines of bearing, which were later incorporated into maps by Mercator himself and other cartographers, came to be known as "rhumb lines" or "loxodromes." Today, rhumb lines are part of the iconic imagery we associate with maps of all types, but at the time they served a very practical purpose in navigation. Mercator's Projection remains in use today.*

In addition to scientific and mathematical improvements to maps, the Dutch Golden Age was noteworthy for producing some of the most beautiful and luxurious maps ever issued. This era corresponded with the evolution of the Baroque ethic in Europe. Baroque art, which rose to prominence in the late 16th century and dominated much of the 17th century, used exuberance and grandeur, often combined with classical forms, to produce opulent and resonant artworks.

The Baroque ethic was most often associated with painting, music, and architecture, but maps too were the recipients of Baroque design elements. These included the introduction of magnificent surrounds with rich allegorical imagery related to classical mythology and Biblical doctrine. The decorative work surrounding Dutch Golden Age maps was not merely intended to beautify the maps, it also had a message for the reader and, while, today, this imagery is seemingly complex and arcane, it represented themes and tropes that would have been familiar to the educated 16th or 17th century European.

Typus Orbis Terrarum

"Who can consider human affairs to be great, when he comprehends the eternity and vastness of the entire world?" Marcus Tullius Cicero's famous words support the bottom of this iconic map.

This remarkable map appeared in Ortelius' *Theatrum Orbis Terrarum* or "Theater of the World," considered to have been the first modern atlas. This particular map was of fundamental importance to the field of cartography and was the first world map to be included in a standard atlas.

Pre-dating the official discovery of Australia by 36 years, the western Australian coast represented here is thought to have been drawn from secret Portuguese maps. In Asia, Korea and The Great Wall of China are conspicuously absent. Japan is mapped (with capitol Miaco), and Borneo and the East Indian Islands are mentioned. When Ortelius drew this map little was known of America and, as a consequence, much of the cartography is speculative and even a little wishful, including, among other things, several apocryphal 'kingdoms of gold' including "Norobega" on the Atlantic Coast and "Quivara" on the Pacific.

Nevertheless, some exploration had occurred and this filtered back to Ortelius' workshop in the Netherlands. Hernando de Soto and Francisco Vazquez de Coronado's discoveries of American Indian centers, east and west of Texas, are shown along with colonial centers in Mexico and the West Indies. In South America, the Amazon is shown along with Caracas, Quito, Cusco, and Lima.

Cartographer

Abraham Ortelius (1527-1598) was a Dutch cartographer active in Antwerp and Amsterdam in the late 16th century. He has been credited with the production of the Theatrum Orbis Terrarum, *generally considered to have been the world's first modern atlas. On his death on July 4, 1598, Ortelius' body was buried in St Michael's Præmonstratensian Abbey, Antwerp, where his tombstone reads,* Quietis cultor sine lite, uxore, prole *(served quietly, without accusation, wife, and offspring.)*

SEPTENTRIO.

Groelant
Estotilant.
Noua
fran
cia.
Milaga
Flori
da.
La Bermuda
Noua
zembla
Nortiegia
Suedia
EVROPA
Tartaria
Taïata
Mongol.
Naiman
Mongul
Cathaio
China
Turcheltan
Natolia
Persia
Coraïan
Arabia
Guzarate
India orien
talis
AFRICA.
Agi
ymba
Aegyptus
Nubia
Abissi
ni

TROPICVS CANCRI
MAR DEL
NORT
Caribana
Peru.
Amazones.
Brasil
Tisnada
Chica.
Rio de la Plata
Chile
Terra del Fuego

OCEANVS AE
THIOPICVS.
Manicon
go.
Mel
inde.
MAR DI INDI

Plitacorum regio.
sic à Lusitanis appellata ob in
credibile earum autem studem
magnitudinem.

Lantchidol
mare.
BEACH
LVCACH
MALETVR
Vastissimas hic esse
regiones ex M. Pauli Ven. et
Lud. Vartonianni scriptis pe=
regrinationibus constat.

270 280 290 300 310 320 330 340 350 360 10 20 30 40 50 60 70 80 90 100 110 120 130 140 150 160 170 180

A V S T R A L I S   N O N D V M   C O G N I T A.

MERIDIES.

Franciscus Hogenbergus sculpsit

Pars Orbis

This finely engraved, important map may very well be the first printed map to include Australia. South of Java, an unnamed landmass appears rising out of the waves. The official discovery of Australia, by the Dutch, was in 1606, over 30 years later. Before that time there were vague Italian missionary reports of people, to the south of Java, who 'navigated by the stars.' This most likely referred to the navigation practices of indigenous Australians. Marco Polo, the famous Italian explorer, had also described 'an extensive and rich province' that he speculated formed part of an unexplored southern mainland.

Aeoli or Wind Heads surround the map proper and blow storms upon the sailing ships and monsters that inhabit these oceans. A curious land bridge, uniting northeast Asia with America's Pacific Northwest, attempts to reconcile new discoveries with Biblical traditions.

This map was also one of the first to include Tierra del Fuego (Land of Fire) as an island on the southern tip of South America. Abandoning Aristotle's theory of complementary landmasses balancing the Earth, this was one of the first maps to remove the massive, speculative continent of *Terra Australis* previously connected to Tierra del Fuego.

This map was designed by Benedict Arias Montanus for inclusion in the *Antwerp Polyglot Bible*, which included text in Greek, Latin, and Hebrew. Sadly, most examples of this map's first printing were destroyed when the ship carrying them was lost at sea.

Cartographer

Benedict Arias Montanus (1527-1598), also known as Benito Arias Montano, was a Spanish orientalist and polymath active in Spain during the second half of the 16th century. Montanus attained a high rank early in his career, becoming Royal Chaplain to Philip II of Spain. Nevertheless, the inclusion of rabbinical references in his Antwerp Polyglot Bible led to censure by both the Roman and Spanish inquisitions.

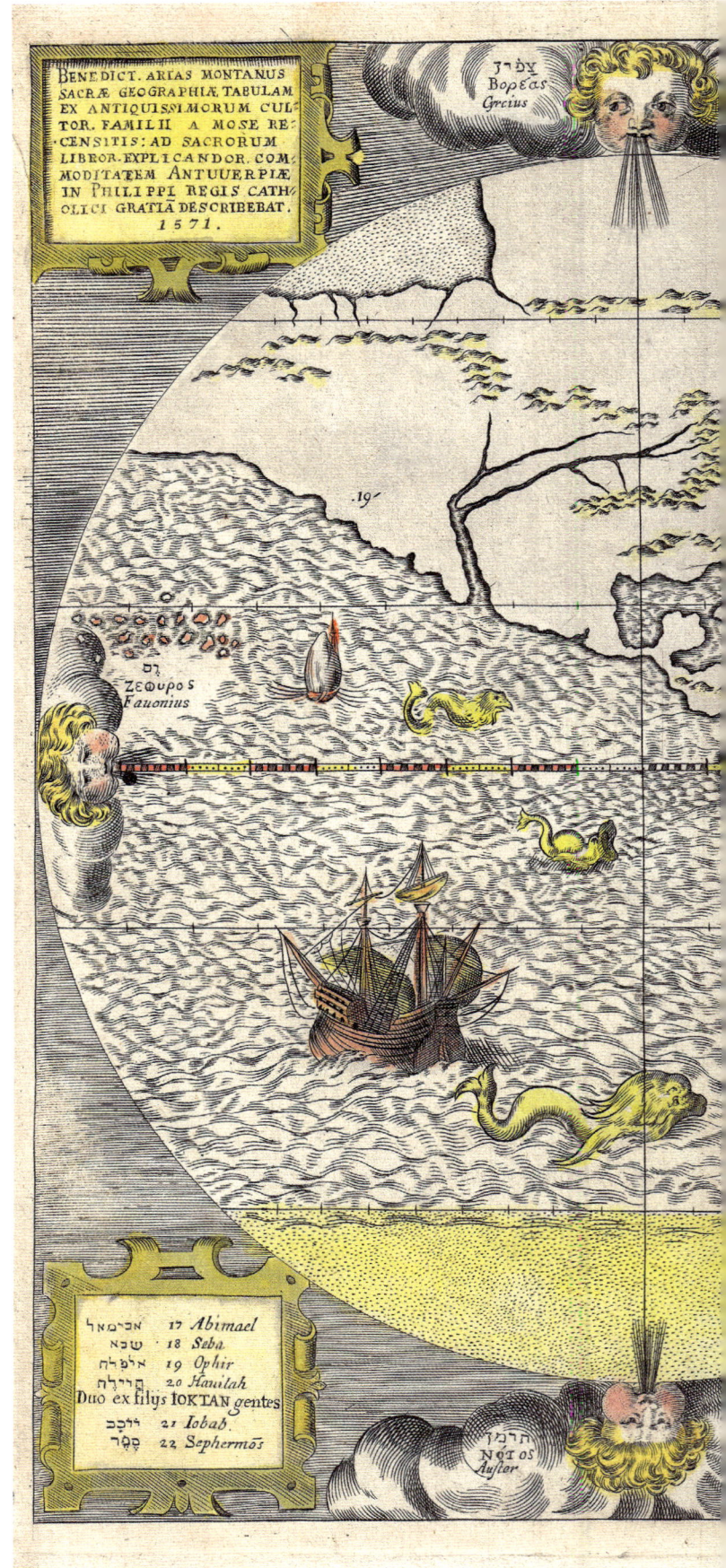

PARS ORBIS

IAPHETH FILIOR.		FILIOR. GOMER SEDES.
גֹּמֶר	I	Gomer
מָגוֹג	II	Magog
מָדַי	III	Madai
יָוָן	IIII	Iauan
תֻּבָל	V	Thubal
מֶשֶׁךְ	VI	Mesech

IAPHETH SEDES
FILIOR. GOMER SEDES.
תִּירָס VII Thirax

Duorum qui occiduas partes incoluerunt
nomina, & sedes incertis parentibus

סְפָרַד XV Sepharad
צָרְפַת XVI Sarphat

FILIOR. GOMER SEDES.		
אַשְׁכְּנַז	VIII	Ascenaz
רִיפַת	IX	Riphath
תֹּגַרְמָה	X	Thogarma

FILIOR. IAVAN SEDES.
אֱלִישָׁה	XI	Elisa
תַּרְשִׁישׁ	XII	Tharsis
כִּתִּים	XIII	Kithim
דֹּדָנִים	XIIII	Dodanim

Βορέας
Cyrcias
צָפוֹן

Εὖρος
Fauonius
מַעֲרָב

Ζέφυρος
Subsolanus
יָם

Εὖρος
Subsolanus
קָדִים

Νότος
Auster
תֵּימָן

FILIOR.
CHAM
SEDES.
כּוּשׁ	A	Chus
מִצְרַיִם	B	Misrai
פּוּט	C	Phut
כְּנַעַן	D	Chanaan

FILIOR. Chus nomina & sedes.
סְבָא	E	Seba
חֲוִילָה	F	Sabtha
רַעְמָה	G	Raghmah
סַבְתְּכָה	H	Seba
דְּדָן	I	Dedan
Nimrod	

Loca a NIMROD occupata cum filijs Chus
בָּבֶל	L	Babel
אֶרֶךְ	M	Arach
אַכַּד	N	Achad
כַּלְנֵה	O	Chalne
אַשּׁוּר	P	Assur

FILIOR. MISRAIM SEDES.
לוּדִים	Q	Ludim
עֲנָמִים	R	Ghanamin
לְהָבִים	S	Lehabim
נַפְתֻּחִים	T	Naphthuthim
פַּתְרֻסִים	V	Petrusim
כַּסְלֻחִים	X	Chasluhim
פְּלִשְׁתִּים	Y	Pelisthim
כַּפְתֹּרִים	Z	Caphthorim

SEDES FILIOR. SEM.
עֵילָם	1	Elam
אַשּׁוּר	2	Assur
אַרְפַּכְשַׁד	3	Arphaachsad
לוּד	4	Lud
אֲרָם	5	Aram

SEDES FILIOR. ARAM.
חוּל	6	Hul
גֶּתֶר	7	Gether
מַשׁ	8	Mes

FILIOR. IEKTAN SEDES.
אַלְמוֹדָד	9	Almodad
שָׁלֶף	10	Seleph
חֲצַרְמָוֶת	11	Hassermaueth
יָרַח	12	Iarahh
הֲדוֹרָם	13	Hadoram
אוּזָל	14	Vzal
דִּקְלָה	15	Dikla
עוֹבָל	16	Obal

Appendix Col. 553

43

LA HERDIKE ENTERPRINSE FAICT PAR LE SIGNEVR DRAECK D'AVO...

La vraie description du voiage du S. fransoys draech
Cheualier lesquel estant acompaigne de cinq nauires deux
desquel il brula rug aultre sen retourna et la quatri
fuit peris il partit dang.r Le 13 desembre 1577 passa
oultre et fit le sirquit de toute la terre et retourna audict
royame le 26.e septembre 1580

TERRA   ART   NO

GROEN LAN
premieremёt descouuert par le signeur drack
sainct iulian 1579 fut le sig.e courone roy
par les habitans dudict païs duex diuerse...

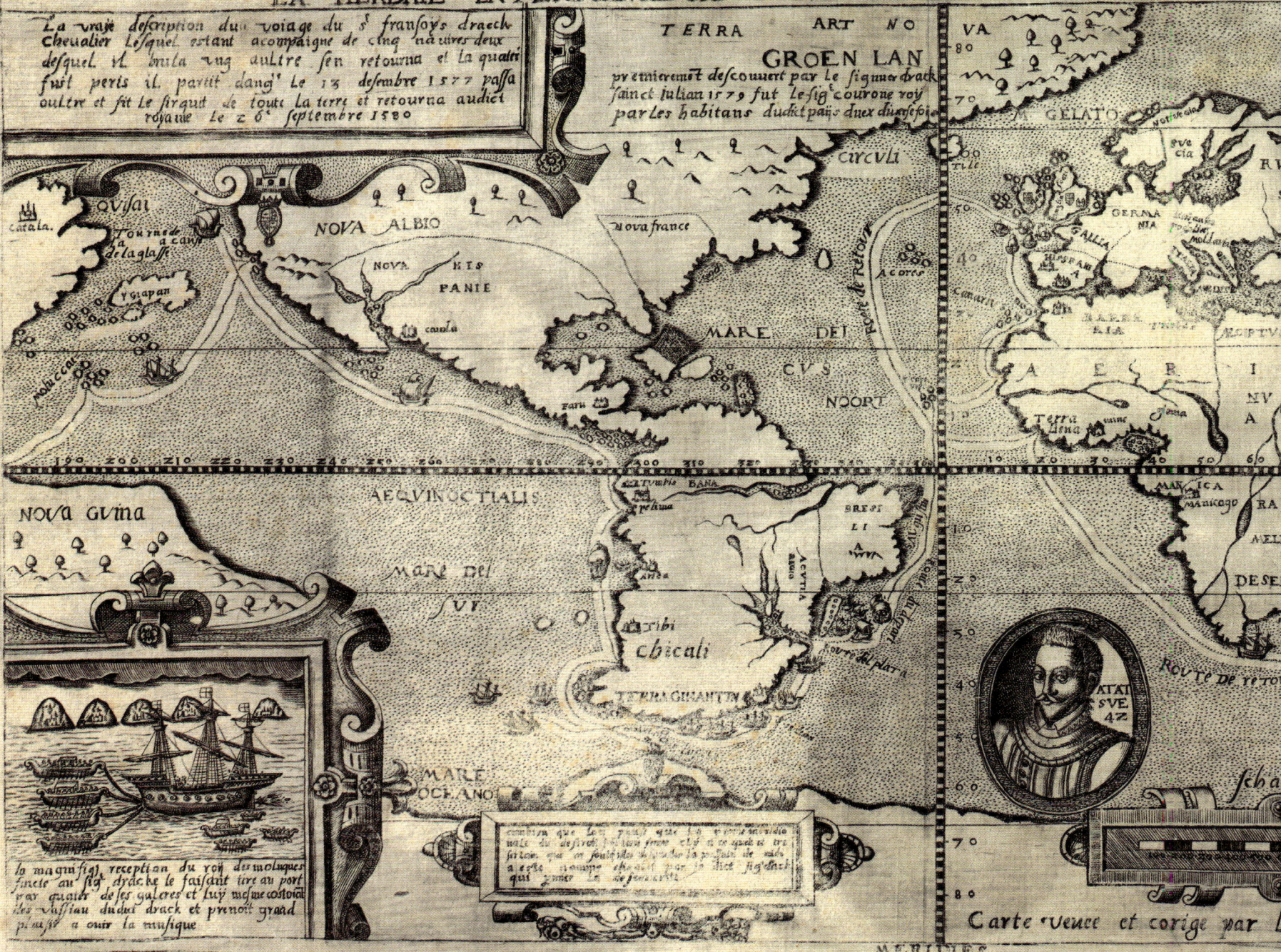

QVISAI
Catala.

TONRNE
a d'cana
de la glasse

NOVA ALBIO

Nova france

circuli

GELATO

SVE
CIA

RV

GERMA
NIA
GALLIA
SPANI
A

YGIAPAN

NOVA
HIS
PANIE

caula

MARE   DEL
CVS
NOORT

Acores

BARBA
RIA

Route de retour

A   F   R   I

NV

Terra
flua   Jema

AEQUINOCTIALIS

NOVA GVINA

Mare   del
Svr

BANA

BRESI
LI

MANICA
Manicago

RA

MELI

DESER

Caribi
chicali

TERRAGIRANTE

ATAT
SVE
42

ROVTE DE RETOV

MARE
OCEANO

la magnifiq. reception du roy des moluques
sincle au sig.r dyacke le faisant tire au port
par quatre de ses galeres et luy mesme costoiot
des vaisseau dudict drack et prenoit grand
plaisir a ouir la musique

combien que l'on pance que la terre meridio
nale du destroit de mira fome chi si ce quele si tra
fortun que on foulsidit d'sproduir la profuit de cels
a este nouupe chacell par le dict sig'dack
qui prmer la descouuerte

schät

Carte veue et corige par l...

MERILIES

Courtesy of Library of Congress

44

La Herdike Enterprinse faict par le Signeur Draeck

This early 1581 Dutch map of the world by Nicola van Sype was drawn to illustrate and celebrate Sir Francis Drake's circumnavigation of the globe. It is considered by the map historian H.P. Kraus as "One of the Greatest Cartographic treasures of the Elizabethan Era." This map is the first published document to illustrate Drakes' voyage and most likely is based upon the lost Whitehall manuscript.

Drake himself appears at center as a handsome rakish English gentleman in the prime of his life. The Drake circumnavigation, between 1577 and 1580, marked only the second full circumnavigation of the globe. Although Drake's circumnavigation occurred more than 50 years after Magellan circumnavigation (1519-1522), it was arguably the more successful voyage.

Drake's course is easy to follow as it is marked by a clear break in the stippling used to illustrate the seas. Starting from England, Drake traveled through the Atlantic, skirting the coast of South America and, bypassing the Straits of Magellan, passed south of Tierra del Fuego (not shown here), the North along the American coast, where he harassed Spanish shipping. As Drake passed north of Mexico he continued to skirt the coast of North America. He and his crew wintered at an unknown bay, called Drake's Bay, somewhere north of San Francisco, in the processes claiming this land for England as New Albion, shown here as 'Nova Albio.'

Although not definitively proven, some scholars argue that Drake was the first to discover Vancouver Island, Graham Island, Prince of Wales Island, and Chichagot Island, which may be rendered here as four small islands on the coast. If so, his voyage must be considered an achievement of even greater significance than currently assumed. Unfortunately, although Drake kept meticulous voyage notes, they were politically suppressed shortly after the voyage and did not become mainstream – which is why it is remarkable that they are rendered here, suggesting that Sype must have had direct contact with Drake, or at least leaked access to Drakes suppressed records, when composing this map.

Cartographer

Nicola van Sype (fl. c. 1589-1612) was a Dutch cartographer active in Antwerp during the late 16th and early 17th centuries. Little is known of Sype and his corpus is small, but his maps are significant, being the first to illustrate the circumnavigation of Sir Francis Drake.

Orontius Fineus

Auriculas asini

Ô Caput elle=   boro dignum

Hic est
mundi punctus et materia gloriae nostrae, hic sedes, hic honores gerimus, hic excercemus imperia, hic opes
hic tumultuatur humanum genus, hic instauramus bella, etiam civilia. Plin.

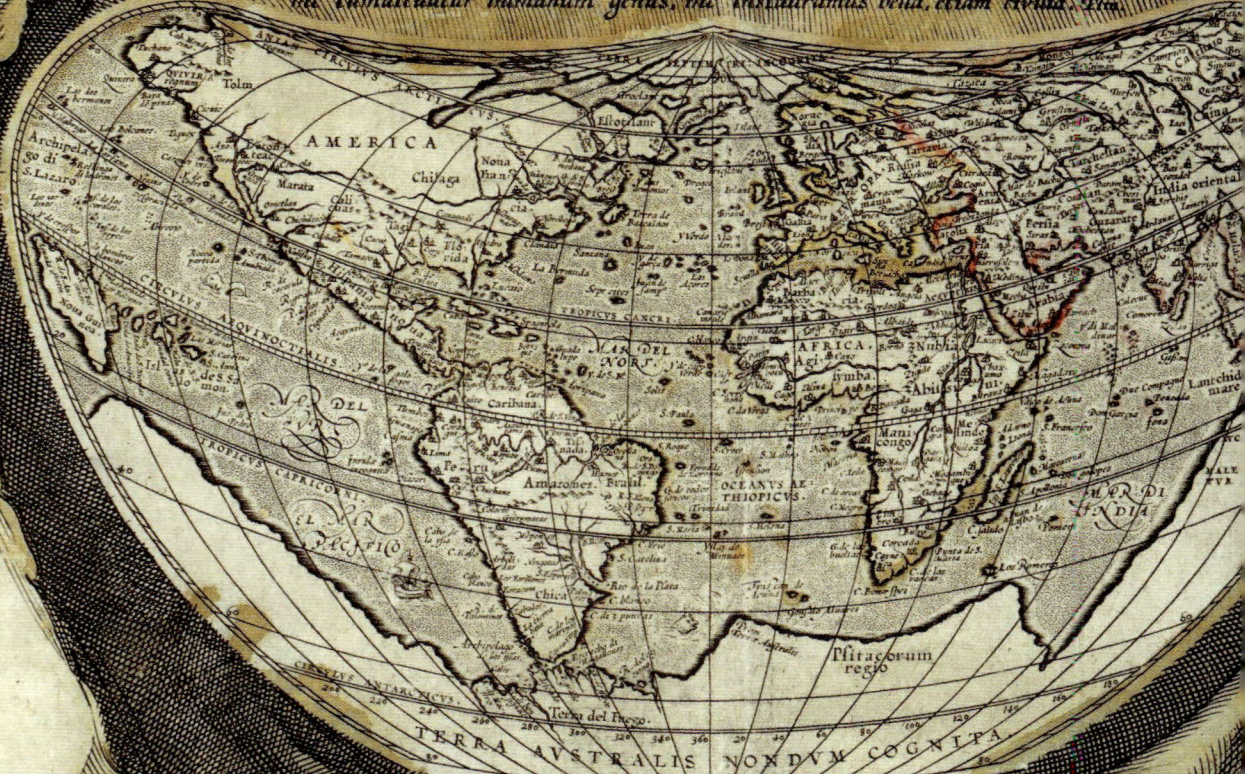

Democritus Abderites
deridebat;
Heraclitus Ephesius
deflebat;
Epichthonius Cosmopolites
deformabat.

Stultorum infinitus
est numerus
Salomon

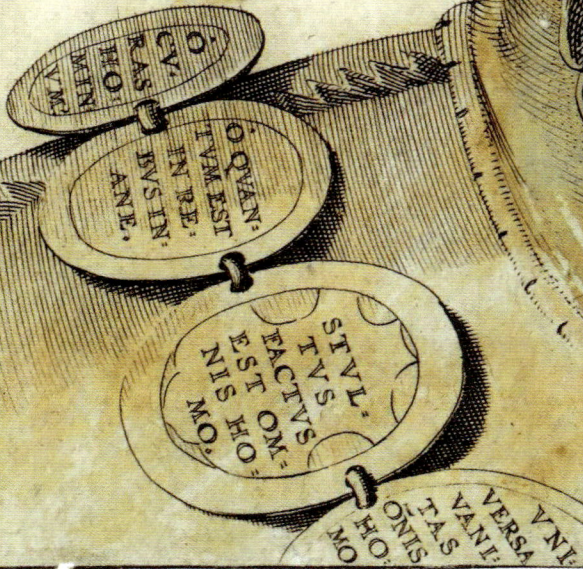

O Caput elleboro Dignum...

In 16th century Europe, when kings held absolute power, the court jester enjoyed a unique position. He alone, through the vehicle of comedy and mockery, could contradict the king, poke fun at his policies, and openly criticize royal decisions. The jester here is the world itself and the message clear, "kings and men make plans, at which god laughs." The acts of kings are thus made small by the unpredictability of the world itself. The Latin quote above the map, attributable to Pliny the Elder, sums this up: "… for in the whole universe the earth is nothing else: and this is the substance of our glory, this is its habitation, here it is that we fill positions of power and covet wealth, and throw mankind into an uproar, and launch even civil wars…"

This map is not unique, but is in fact a larger and more refined version of a 1570 map by Jean de Gourmont. Even so, this map's maker is a matter of considerable mystery and debate. In the upper left corner, the name, Orontius Fineus (Oronce Finé) appears. Finé was a well-known 16th century cartographer, but he died some 30 years before this map was issued. Some have argued that Finé is actually the butt of the maps ridicule for his practice of judicial astrology, a forecasting art dependent upon calculations of celestial forms relative to the Earth. Others attribute the map to a Christian sect called the *Familia Caritatis*, of which the Dutch mapmaker Abraham Ortelius, whose engraving work resembles this map, may have been a member. The map itself bears a note, in the left cartouche, ascribing the map to one *Epichthonius Cosmopolites*, a Latin expression that literally translates to "everyman."

Cartographer

The cartographer is unknown.

Veritable Representation des Premieres Matieres ou Elements

Eight concentric circles of the elemental spheres are illustrated with baroque grandeur. At the center is the fiery core of the universe, where angry souls burn and are tormented by demons in what can only be the Christian hell. Above this is the physicality of the Earth, a great earthen sphere with underground caves, waterways, mines (complete with miners) and deposits of precious metals. On the surface, the world of man is full of activity, including farming, traveling mining, and sailing as well as natural phenomena such as trees and volcanoes. Next, there is a map, which takes the form of a polar projection from the North Pole. This map is derived from De Jode's 1593 *Hemispheriu Ab Aequinoctiali Linea*. The map covers roughly from the Mediterranean and Florida south to the Equator. Following this are three zones of air corresponding to Aristotle's climatological treatises. Within these zones we can find observable weather patterns (such as rain, snow, and hail), and cosmic events, including the 1577 Great Comet. These are in turn embraced by the final sphere – the hermitic purifying realm of empyrean fire, where salamanders and phoenixes frolic.

Saliba's world is both ordered and chaotic, spiritual and temporal, familiar and fantastical. His work attempts to reconcile Christianity with Greek philosophy, the Ptolemaic world view, Renaissance science, and mythology.

Cartographers

• *Antonio Saliba was a Maltese cartographer, astronomer, theologian, and philosopher. Litte is known of his life.*

• *Cornelis de Jode (1568-1600) was a Dutch cartographer based out of Antwerp. De Jode was the son of Gerard de Jode, another cartographer of note. He studied at the Academy of Douai and, in 1591, took control of his father's map published business. Cornelis completed and published his father's great atlas, the* Speculum Orbis Terrae. *Unfortunately, faced with more innovative and sophisticated competition in the form of the Ortelius firm, and others, De Jode's cartographic enterprises met with little success.*

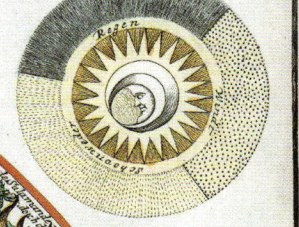

SEPTENTRIONALIUM Terrarum descriptio.
Per Gerardum Mercatorem Cum Privilegio
POLUS ARCTICUS
OCEANUS SCYTHICUS qui et Mare Tabin
California regio sola fama Hispanis nota
Anian regnum
Bergi regio
El streto de Anian
Circulus Arcticus
OCEANUS SEPTENTRIONALIS
GROENLAND
ISLAND
NOVA ZEMBLA
PETZORKE MARE
Scetland insulæ
Farre in: sulæ
Frisland insula

Septentrionalium Terrarum Descriptio

This revolutionary 1606 Arctic projection by Gerard Mercator was considered the world's first map of the North Pole. This map had its roots in Mercator's great 1569 wall map of the world wherein he introduced the Mercator Projection. The Mercator Projection is not suited for polar mapping, so that to accurately depict the polar regions, a map would need to be infinitely tall. To address this issue, Mercator created this separate map.

Why map a part of the world that is both fully unexplored and fully inaccessible? It was not perceived as such at the time. Scholars believed that the North Pole was most likely navigable and free of ice. Drawing on Arthurian legend and reports from the few explorers (Gorge Best, Martin Frobisher, and James Davis) who had made their way northward, Mercator developed a theory that the northern polar regions were composed of four large islands divided by great rivers, and surrounding an open polar sea. To these islands he added other features, such as populations of female Pygmies and tropical vegetation.

Mercator also used this map to address mathematical and scientific theories he had been working on. One was the true location of Magnetic North. Attempting to account for the phenomenon of magnetic variation, Mercator theorized that true magnetic north was not at the North Pole, but rather a great magnetic island. That island is mapped here as a giant rock between Asia and America.

The example here is the 1606 second edition of Mercator's *Septentrionalium Terrarum Descriptio*. The first edition, 1595, included four complete polar islands. This edition, edited and reissued by Jodocus Hondius in 1606, features updates to account for new discoveries. The polar island north of Europe has thus been partially erased to accommodate Spitzbergen. This illustrates beautifully the nascent conflict between medieval and renaissance cosmographical perspectives. Like many of Mercator's maps, the present example was published posthumously by Mercator's heir, Jodocus Hondius.

Cartographer

Gerard Mercator (1512-1594) was a seminal figure in the history of cartography. His achievements are many, but none was more significant than his introduction of the Mercator Projection. The Mercator Projection was a mathematical solution for the navigational problem of the Earth's curvature. On earlier maps, if a navigator sailed in a certain direction his point of arrival may not have been where the map suggested. Using the Mercator Projection, on the other hand, a ship would arrive roughly where anticipated.

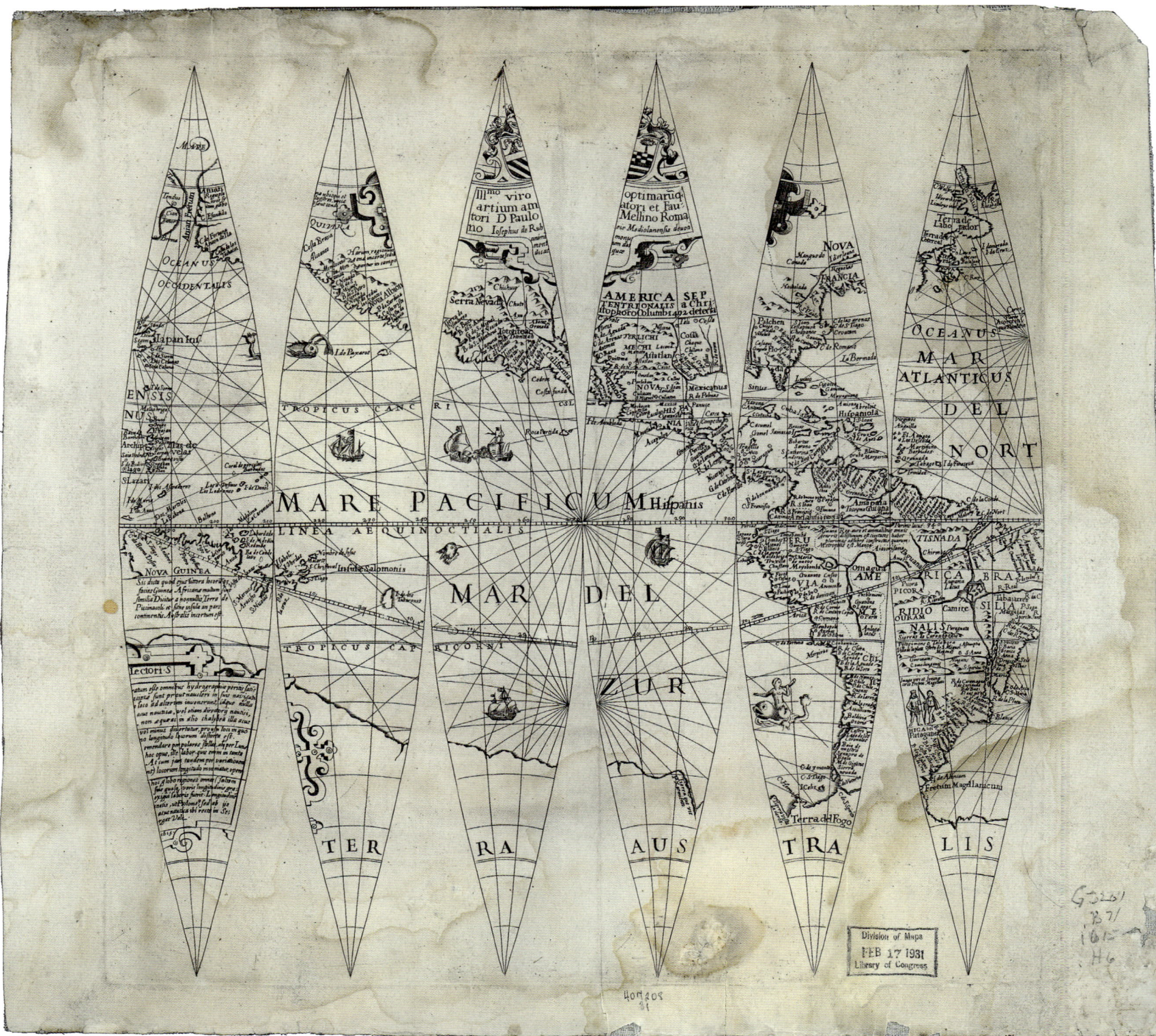

Terrestrial Globe Gores

Cartographer

Jodocus Hondius (1563-1612) was an important Dutch cartographer. Hondius inherited the 16th century plates of Gerard Mercator and republished them well into the 17th century, reviving the Mercator brand. His maps were far from slavish copies of Mercator's map and included numerous important revisions. Even so, the significant influence of the Hondius firm cemented many outdated ideas into cartographic canon.

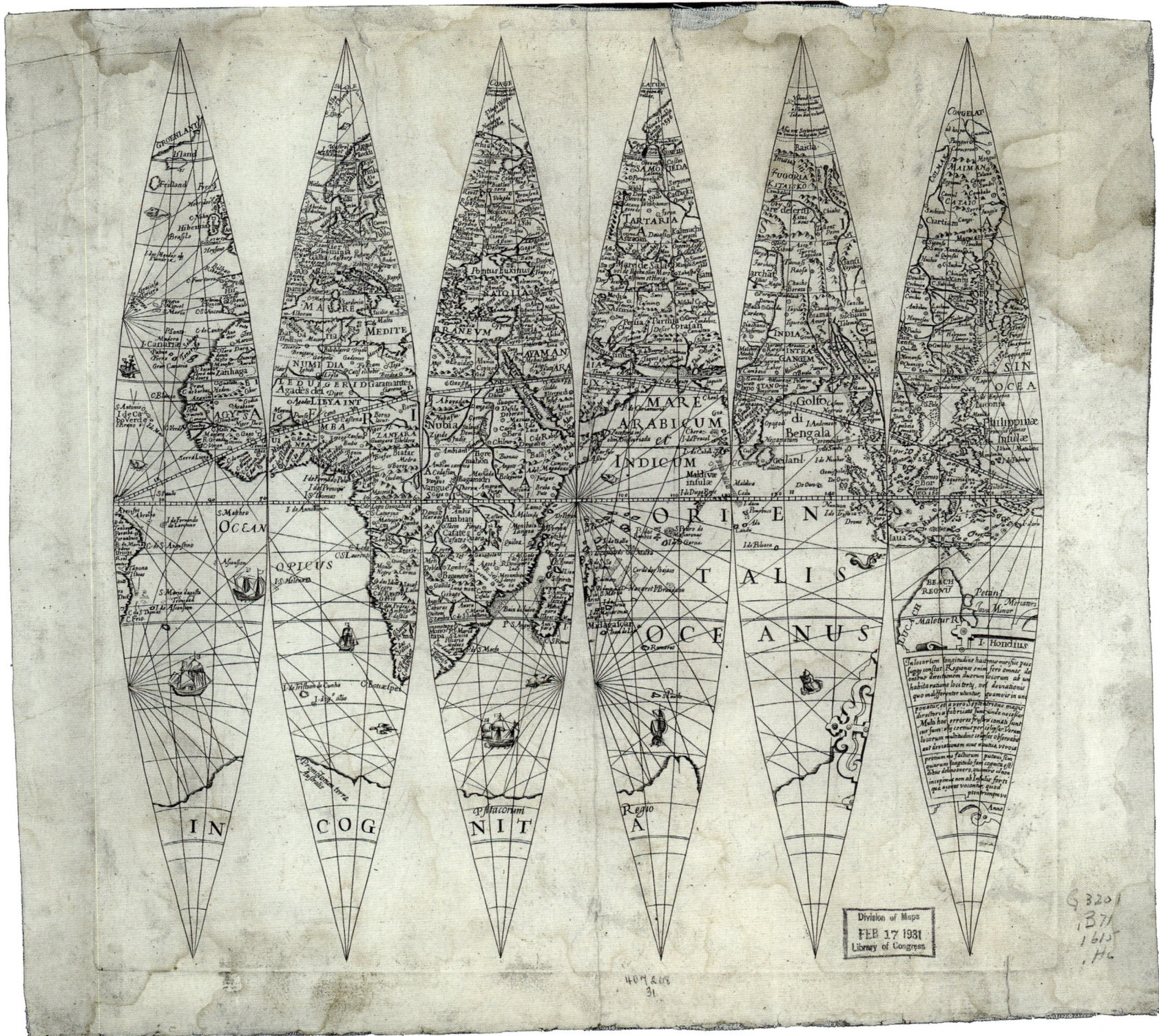

This remarkable set of globe gores was prepared by Jodocus Hondius in 1615. Gore sets like this were issued both for conversion to actual globes and, as here, separately issued as parts of books and atlases in the place of a more traditional projected world map. Gore sets could be easily cut out and wrapped around a wooden or glass sphere to form a proper globe. Typically gore sets also include northern and southern cap plates, but in the current example, due to its small size, about 19 cm in diameter, the gores extend from pole to pole. Although small, this map exhibits the exuberance and baroque ornamentation of Dutch Golden Age globes. The gores feature the most up to date cartographic information of the period that, at the time, was streaming into Dutch ports via trading empires such as the Dutch East India Company (VOC). The cartography offers much of note, including an embryonic mapping of Cuba, considerable accuracy in the East Indies due to VOC activity, and an insular rendering of Korea. The globe's most arresting feature is its illustration of northern Australia. Australia was first encountered by Dutch VOC navigator Willem Janszoon in 1606, about 9 years before these gores were engraved. Janzoon had little inkling of the magnitude of his discovery and it was slow to appear on subsequent maps and globes. Nontheless, Australia here appears definitively, a broad but empty land south of Java. The nomenclature, including 'Beach Regnu' and 'Maletur Regnu' reference the journals of Marco Polo, who described such regions but provided little substantial content. Polo was commonly used by cartographers to give structure to the Asian and Southeast Asian part of their maps, but, as history has proved, much of his cartography was inaccurate and lacked sufficient detail to definitively associate with factual locations.

Orbis Terrae
Novissima Descriptio

Jodocus Hondius and Jean Le Clerc's rare 1633 map of the world in two hemispheres features many of the cartographic curiosities evident in world maps at the outset of the 17th century. For example, in the north we can see the polar regions following Gerard Mercator's apocryphal four-island system. The island above Europe was notably extended to include the discovery of Nova Zembla, thus reconciling earlier cartographic speculation with the dawning age of discovery.

In North America, there appeared a great inland sea in the Canadian arctic. This was the Lago de Conibas and provided a good example of how mapmakers struggled to adapt unclear and incomplete reports from explorers and navigators into valuable cartographic data. When the French explorer Jacques Cartier (1491-1557) explored the St. Lawrence River in the 1530s, he noticed that the Native Americans used a strange currency: polished shells in long strings, probably an early type of *wampum*. The Natives referred to them as 'Conibaz,' claiming they came from a great inland lake where, to acquire them, a man was killed before being lowered into the water where the body was left overnight. The next morning, the corpse would be found covered with the shells, which were then gathered, polished, and strung. Cartier duly recorded this in his journals and, finding the story intriguing, subsequent cartographers added the Lake of Conibas to their maps. It is probable that the Native Americans were referring to one, or all, of the Great Lakes, but of course, we can only speculate. Although we can trace the map and the engraving to the work of Hondius and Le Clerc, this map was published posthumously by Le Clerc's heir, Jean Boisseau.

Cartographers

• *Jodocus Hondius* (1563-1612) was an important Dutch cartographer. Hondius inherited the 16th century plates of Gerard Mercator and republished them well into the 17th century, reviving the Mercator brand. His maps were far from slavish copies of Mercator's map and included numerous important revisions. Even so, the significant influence of the Hondius firm cemented many outdated ideas into the cartographic canon.

• *Jean Le Clerc* (1560-1621) was a French bookseller, engraver, and publisher based in Paris. He worked with the Dutch cartographer Jodocus Hondius to produce several important continental and world maps. After his death, Le Clerc's work passed into the hands of Jean Boisseau.

RRAE NOVISSIMA DESCRIPTIO

TRAMONTANA
MAESTRO · GRECO
PONENTE · LEVANTE
GARBINO · SIROCO
AUSTRO

Nomina ventorum in Mari Mediterraneo

MAR DEL NORT

TROPICVS CANCRI

MAR DI INDIA

BRASIL

OCEANVS AETIOPICVS

AEQVINOCTIALIS Linea

TERRA AVSTRALIS

Circulus Antarcticus

Polus Antarcticus

Septentrio

Meridies

Authore Gerardo Mercatore, nuperrimè verò iuxta
recentiores Cosmographos aucta et recognita
I. Hondius sculp.   I. le Clerc excu. 1633.

Quinque zonae, in
quibus cursus Solis per ea signa patet:

FRIGIDA
Circulus arcticus
TEMPERATA
Tropicus Cancri
TORRIDA
TOR.
Tropicus Capricorni
TEMPERATA
Circulus Antarcticus
FRIGIDA

TERRA ET PLENITVDO EIVS, ORBIS TERRARVM ET VNI
ITANT IN EO. QVIA SVPER MARIA FVNDAVIT EVM, Etc. PSAL 24

55

EUROPA

IULIUS CÆSAR | AUGUSTUS | TIBERIUS | CALIGULA | CLAUDIUS

NOVA TOTIUS TERRARUM ORBIS GEOGRAPHICA AC HYDROG

ROMA

EUROPÆI

AMSTERDAM

ASIATICI

IERUSALEM

AFRICANI

TUNIS

AFRICA

GALBA | OTHO | VITELLIUS | VESPASIANUS | TITUS

ZONA FRIGIDA · ZONA TEMPERATA · ZONA TORRIDA · ZONA TEMPERATA · ZONA FRIGIDA

America primum detecta à Christophoro Colombo a° 1492 az ab Americo Vesputio latius retecta a° 1499 deq, suo nomine eam dixit hinc a°1540 à Ferdinando Magellano. Fretum quod de nomine sui Magellanicum dictum, Traiectum est. Idem preteristu Franciscus Draco a° 1579 Thomas Candisch a° 1587 Oliverius à Noort a° 1600. Sebaldus de Weert à 1600 Georgius Spilberg a° 1615. Commodius vero à totius freturn deprehensum a° 1616 à Iacobo le Maire, quod ab ipsius nomine dictum, fretum le Maire.

MARE CONGELATUM

GROENLANDIA

MARE GLAC

OCEANUS

SEPTENTRIO

Circulus Arcticus

AMERICA SEPTENTRIONALIS

TERRA DE LABRADOR

MARE ATLANTI

CUM

MEDITERRANEUM

MAR DEL

NORT

Tropicus Cancri

MAR DEL

ILHAS DE LADRONES

Circulus Æquinoctialis

OCEANUS PERVSA

ZUR

AMERICA MERIDIONAL

ÆTHIOPI

CUS

Tropicus Capricorni

NVS

MARE

PACIFICUM

CHILIS

Rio de la Plata

Fretum Magalanicum

Fretum le Maire

AMERICA SEPTENTRIONALIS

Promontorium terræ Australis

MAGALLANICA SIVE

Circulus Antarcticus

TERRA AUSTRALIS INCOGNITA

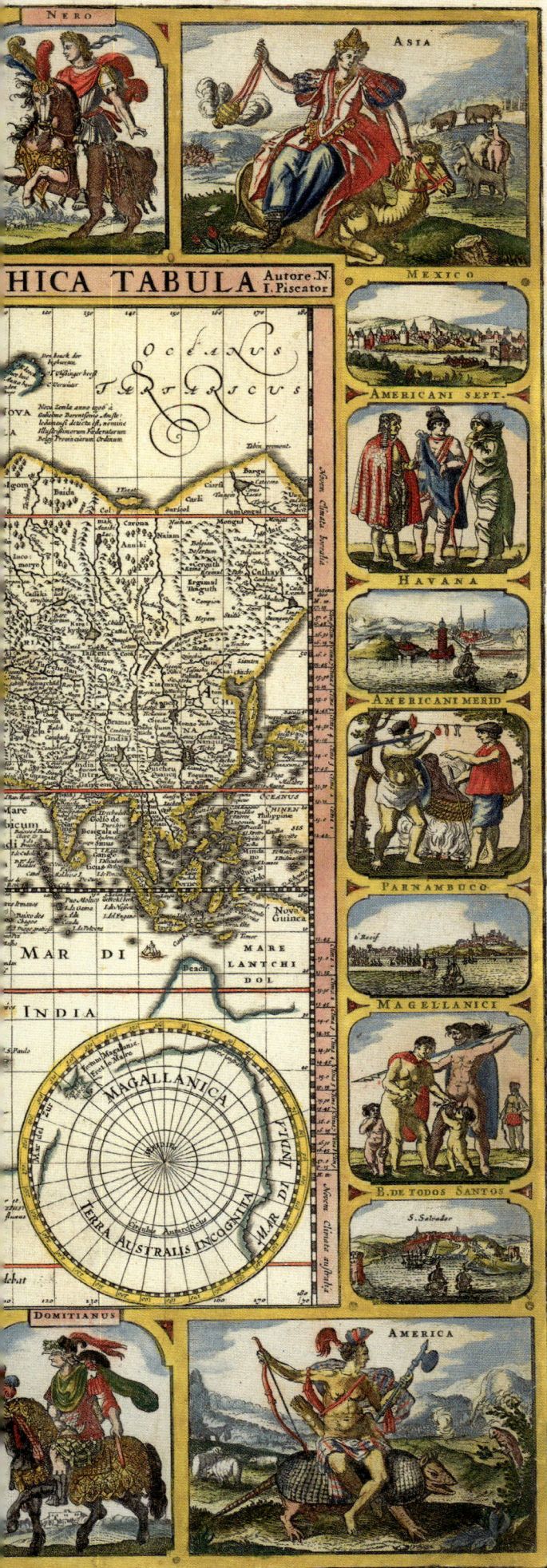

NERO

ASIA

HICA TABULA   *Autore .N. I. Piscator*

OCEANUS TERRICUS

MEXICO

AMERICANI SEPT.

HAVANA

AMERICANI MERID

PARNAMBUCO

MAR DI LANTCHI DOL

MAGELLANICI

INDIA

MAGALLANICA

TERRA AUSTRALIS INCOGNITA   MAR DA INDIA

B. DE TODOS SANTOS

S. Salvador

DOMITIANUS

AMERICA

Nova Totius Terrarum Orbis Geographica ac Hydrographica Tabula

Known as the Twelve Caesars Map, this 1552 world map by Claes Visscher was prepared on a Mercator Projection. Stylistically, the map followed the work of Blaeu and Hondius who pioneered the decorative surround as seen here. This style was uncommon for Visscher, who, in nearly forty years of mapmaking, only produced four world maps that included illustrated border panels. In addition to images of twelve Roman Emperors ready for battle, views of eight cities appeared on either side, including Amsterdam, Rome, Havana, Mexico City, and Jerusalem. Traditional costumes were depicted by region, including stylized images of Europeans, North Americans, South Americans, Africans, and Asians. Each corner featured an allegorical female personification, riding fabulous beasts, from one of the four known continents.

Cartographically, *Terra Australis*, the mythical southern continent, was present, although here its speculative shores were broken in several places, suggesting that doubt about the continent was beginning to emerge. In North America, there was as yet no trace of the Great Lakes but place names, mostly speculative, began to appear all along the west coast as far as the presumed Strait of Anian. Across the world, in Asia, Korea appeared in its insular form. A proto-form of Australia appeared connected to the mythical southern continent and was identified, based upon the account of Marco Polo, as "Beach."

Cartographer

Claes Jansz Visscher (1587-1652) was the founder of the Visscher cartographic dynasty. Visscher established the firm in Amsterdam near the offices of fellow map publishers Pieter van den Keer and Jodocus Hondius. It has been hypothesized that Visscher may have been one of Hondius's apprentices. Visscher often published under the name Piscator (fisherman), a Latinized version of Visscher, and incorporated the image of an elderly fisherman into his maps.

NORT

AFR
Sarra

CA

OCEANUS

ÆTHIOPICUS

AMERICA MERIDIONALIS

GUIANA

BRASILIA

CHILIS

Fretum Magellanicum
Fretum le Maire
Statenlandt

Rio de la Plata
Buenos ayres

I. de Cabo Verde

S. Helena

TERRA AV
COG

C. de Bona
Esperanca

POLUS ANTARCTICUS

Luna
Terra
Orbis Lunæ
Orbis Mercurii
Orbis Veneris
Orbis Solis
Orbis Martis
Orbis Iovis
Orbis Saturni
Stellarum fixarum quod et Primum mobile

Werreldt Kaert

This gorgeous world map is a striking example of Dutch Baroque cartography. The borders are lavishly illustrated with allegorical imagery from classical mythology including Zeus with his chariot, Poseidon with his followers, Demeter receiving offerings, and Persephone being attacked. The map was created for the 1682 version of the Keur Bible by Nicolaas Visscher.

Visscher was a proponent of the insular California theory and, indeed, California is included here as an island. The idea of an island called "California" was initially proposed in a 1510 work of fiction by Rodriguez de Montalvo. In his romance novel, *Las Sergas de Esplandian*, he wrote, "Know, that on the right hand of the Indies there is an island called California very close to the side of the Terrestrial Paradise; and it is peopled by black women, without any man among them, for they live in the manor of Amazons."

Following Francisco de Ulloa, Hernando Cortez traveled to Baja California shortly after its discovery and immediately claimed the 'Island of California' for the Spanish crown. It was not long after that it became clear that it was not an island. Nevertheless, recorded history and actual reality rarely march hand in hand. Francis Drake had sailed up the western coast of America and claimed 'New Albion' near Vancouver, and Washington State for the English crown. The influence of the Spanish crown, and the desire to maintain its claim on California, caused a resurgence in the insular California theory in the late 17th and early 18th centuries.

Elsewhere on the map, in an expansive Asia, Silk Route cities are noted including Kashgar, Tashkirgit, Samarkand, and Bukhara. South America and Africa have interiors that are almost entirely speculative, often filled with hopes and dreams. Many Europeans, for example, believed that King Solomon's mines were hidden in South Africa. The Kingdom of Monomotapa, most often associated with the legendary mines, maintained an active trading network with India and Asia and did indeed have rich gold mines.

Cartographer

*The **Visscher family** were prominent Dutch map publishers for nearly a century. The patriarch of the family was Claes Jansz Visscher (1586-1652) who, around 1620, established the firm in Amsterdam near the offices of Pieter van den Keer and Jadocus Hondius. Visscher meant "fisherman" and the family incorporated this icon into many of their maps, often signing maps "Pescador." The firm was passed down successive generations of the Visscher clan until eventually sold to Peter Schenk.*

Septentrio

AME RI CA

Circul Articus

SEPTENTRIO

NALIS

MAR

DEL

NORT

Tropicus Cancri

Circulus Æquinoctialis

MAR DEL

OCEANVS

PERVVI ENSIS

ZUR

Tropicus Capricorni

MARE PACIFICVM

AME RI CA MERI DIO

TERRA

Circulus Antarcticus

AVSTRA LIS

INCOGNITA

Meridies

POLVS A

Nova Totius Terrarum Orbis Tabula

This rare map by Joachim Bormeester was published in 1685. Bormeester presented the world in four hemispheres, two main hemispheres, augmented by smaller hemispheric projections for both the Arctic and Antarctic regions. Striking allegorical imagery drawn from classical mythology decorated the elaborate border, including Poseidon romancing a beauty, Demeter offering gifts, Persephone being kidnapped, and Apollo with his chariot. Polar projections were presented in smaller spheres above and below the main map.

Bormeester's map offered several interesting advancements, but most importantly introduced the mapmaking convention of leaving unexplored areas blank. European cartography was slowly moving away from the era when cartographers would fill in unexplored parts of the globe with ideas extracted from myth and legend. With merchant ships and exploratory missions leaving the busy ports of Europe, such as Amsterdam, daily, striving for accuracy was becoming increasingly the norm. Consequently, the unexplored areas were obvious throughout for their emptiness: The Pacific Northwest of America, the southern and eastern shores of Australia, the high Arctic, the islands of Polynesia, and of course, the southern polar regions. In particular, *Terra Australis*, Aristotle's apocryphal southern continent, had at last been removed from the map.

Cartographer

Joachim Bormeester (1620-1702) worked as a printer, publisher, and engraver in Amsterdam. His work is scarce and, in addition to this map, includes one of the most beautiful wall maps of the 17th century.

POLUS ARCTICUS

POLUS ANTARCTICUS

The French
Positivist Cartographic Imaginings

*T*he Dutch Golden Age began to wane by the second half of the 17th century. As centers of power and influence shifted, so too did the centers of scholarship and, for cartography and many other sciences, the new hub was Paris. The first great French cartographer to present serious competition to Dutch mapmakers in both quality of engraving and accuracy of information was the geographer Nicolas Sanson (1600-1667).

Sanson was born in Abbeville, Hauts-de-France, and trained in mathematics by Jesuits at Amiens. He exhibited an early mastery of mapmaking, drawing the attention of Cardinal Richelieu and Louis XIII for one of his earliest maps of Gaul, for which, in 1630, he was appointed Géographe Ordinaire du Roi. Sanson's maps combined scholarship and scientific principles to a degree not seen before, yielding maps that were more accurate and sophisticated than comparable Dutch maps, which, by the mid to late 17th century, were increasingly derivative. His work established new standards for mapmaking and, for this, he spearheaded the "Golden Age of French Cartography," for which he is considered the "Father of French Cartography."

Toward the end of Sanson's life, in 1666, the French Académie Royale des Sciences was founded in Paris with a mission to encourage French scientific research and discovery. It was one of the earliest such organizations in Europe. While for the first 30 years or so of its existence the Académie remained somewhat informal, at the end of the 17th century, in 1699, Louis XIV, the Sun King, laid down a structured path and rules for the society. It was the subsequent rise of the Académie, under Louis XIV's royal patronage, that attracted many of the great European luminaries to Paris in the early days of the 18th century.

Around that time, following in the footsteps of Sanson, Claude de L'Isle and his sons, Louis, Joseph Nicolas, and Guillaume, emerged as important French mapmakers. In aggregate, the work of the de L'Isle family was a tour de force previously unseen in the cartographic field. While each of the de L'Isle brothers made significant contributions to cartography, the true star of the family was Guillaume. Guillaume de L'Isle joined the Académie Royale des Sciences at 27, a sure indication of his genius. Unlike earlier cartographers in Amsterdam and in other parts of Europe, who had to carry on lengthy correspondences with distant centers of scholarship to develop their geographical theories, Guillaume, and his contemporaries, would meet regularly at the Académie to argue over their ideas. These geographical debates, which centered on the presentation of theoretical or reactionary papers, were a combination of genuine scholarship, wild speculation, enormous egos, and political maneuvering. Consequently, debates often grew heated, and bitter rivalries developed. Despite warring factions within the Académie, there was a great deal of pressure, scientific, economic and political, to produce the most accurate maps, with the hope that some might draw the King's attention and result in a royal appointment. These positions, such as Guillaume de L'Isle's title, Premier Géographe du Roi, not only brought prestige, but frequently included a heathy stipend that could provide a mapmaker's family with a life of ease.

In their desire to outclass one another, French cartographers at the Académie, including the de L'Isle family, Jean-Baptiste Nolin, Philippe Buache, Gilles Robert de Vaugondy, Jean Baptiste Bourguignon d'Anville, and others, spun out a host of geographical theories, some baseless, and others quite prescient.

Their maps filled the unknown parts of the globe, places such as the Pacific Northwest, the Arctic Regions, the heart of Africa, the Pacific, and the Far East, with educated speculations based upon scientific theories, the journals of dubious explorers, and theories they thought might appeal to the king. This was the birth of positivist or speculative cartography, in which maps were prepared, often in small limited editions, to illustrate competing ideas on the floor of the academy.

Many of the conventions established by the positivist cartographers of the Académie Royale would live on long after their deaths, or be appropriated and adapted to the ideas of other, competing cartographers. Among the cartographic ideas born of the French Positivist school were the 'Sea of the West,' a mythical inland sea in the western part of North America; the open polar seas postulated by Buache; numerous versions of the Northwest Passage; the River of the West, a supposed river route to the Pacific; the Lago de Xarayes, a paradisiacal lake known as the gateway to the Amazon; and Fusang, a legendary Chinese colony on the west coast of America, among many others.

If the Golden Age of French cartography began with Sanson, it ended with the great voyages of discovery led by Captain James Cook, Jean-François de Galaup comte de La Pérouse, and George Vancouver. These exploratory expeditions into the unknown, completed between 1768 and 1795, definitively and progressively answered the questions that, for the better part of a century, had fueled debate at the Académie Royale.

With the diminution of French cartographic schools, and the coming of the French Revolution (1789-1799), the center of cartographic innovation transitioned from Paris to London, thus ending the Golden Age of French Cartography.

Mappe-monde Geo-Hydrographique

This map of the world was made by Nicolas Sanson for the King of France, Louis XIII, and published in 1691. Dolphins, a symbol of the French crown, figure prominently in the map's impressive decorative cartouche. Below the map proper, powerful mer-men, suggestive of lordship over land and sea, officially present the world, on a double hemisphere projection, to the King. This map is elaborately decorated and the extensive use of gold foil, which can be seen here throughout both hemispheres accentuating elements and denoting cities, is almost exclusively found on maps commissioned for royalty or other high nobility.

Cartographically, there is much of interest. Sanson was considered to be among the first of the "scientific" cartographers, who attempted to use science and real-world reports from explorers and navigators to complete their maps rather than rely on myth and established convention. Nevertheless, the map's most striking feature, a gigantic continent embracing the southern polar regions, stands out. However, this is not Antarctica. Antarctica had yet to be discovered. Instead, it is the mythical southern continent of *Terra Australis*, speculated by none other than Aristotle as a counterbalance to the mass of Asia. Aristotle's influence on cartographic thought was so great that hundreds of years after his death, the ideas remained the underpinning of European scientific thought. This map was published posthumously by Sanson's heir Alexis-Hubert Jaillot (c. 1632-1712).

Cartographer

Nicolas Sanson (1600-1667) is considered as the "Father of French Cartography."
He championed the value of scientific observation over historical cartographic convention.
This practice resulted in less embellishment of geographical imagery, as was common in
the Dutch Golden Age maps of the 16th century, in favor of standardized cartographic
representational modes. Sanson's corpus of some 300 maps influenced European cartography
for over 100 years.

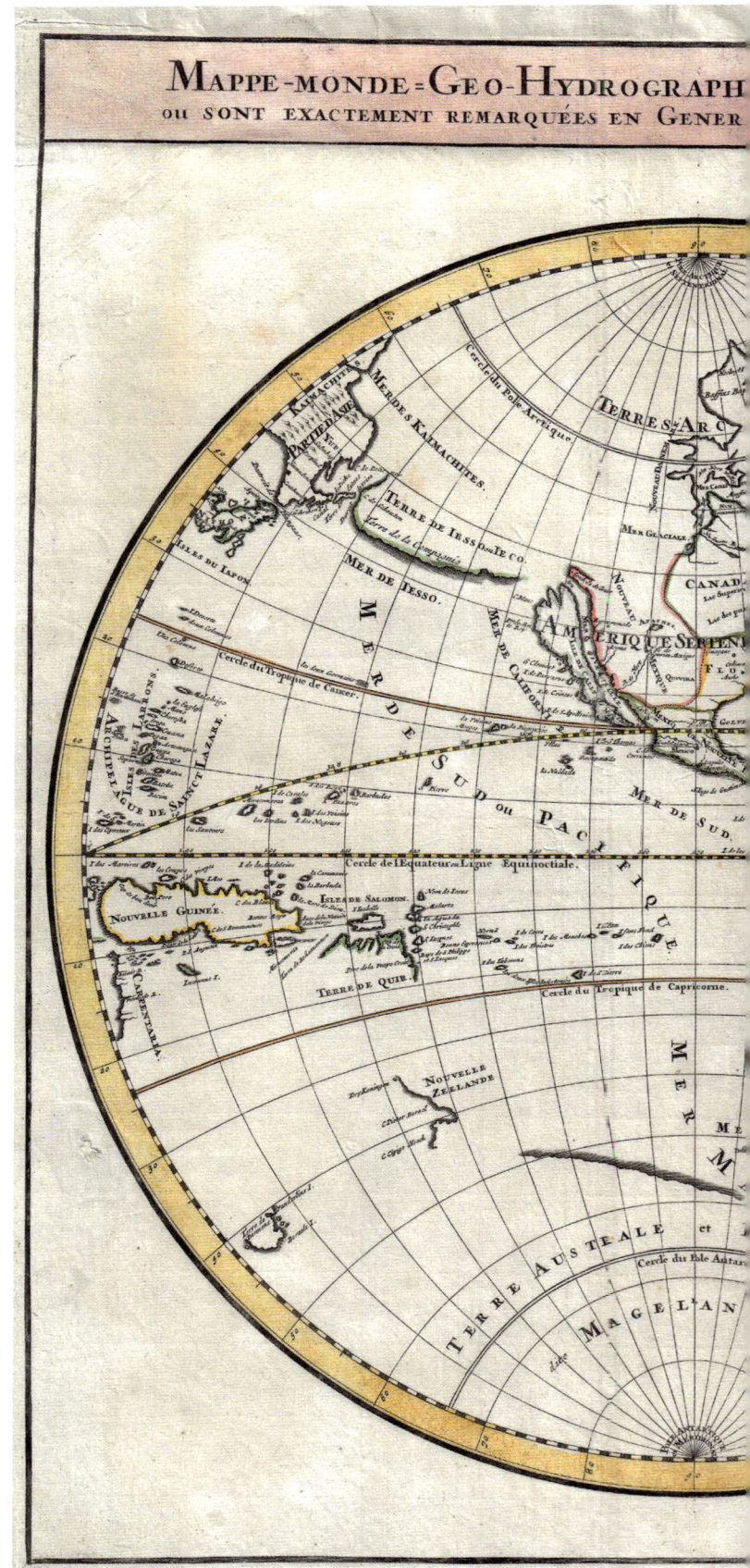

ou DESCRIPTION GENERALE DU GLOBE TERRESTRE ET AQUATIQUE EN DEUX-PLANS-HEMISPHERES.
OUTES LES PARTIES DE LA TERRE ET DE L'EAU, SUIVANT LES RELATIONS LES PLUS NOUVELLES. Par le S:SANSON Geographe Ordinaire du Roy 1691.

OCEAN OCCIDENTAL

OCEAN SEPTENTRIONAL GLACIAL ou SCYTHIQUE

MER DE TARTARIE

GRANDE TARTARIE

OCEAN ATLANTIQUE ou OCCIDENTAL

MER MEDITERRANEE

ASIE

OCEAN ORIENTAL ou

ARABIE

AFRIQUE

OCEAN INDIEN

MER DE GUINEE

Equateur ou Ligne Equinoctiale

MER DE CONGO

AMERIQUE MERIDIONALE

MER DE BRESIL

PARAGUAY

OCEAN MERIDIONAL ou ETHIOPIE

MER DES CAFRES

Cercle du Tropique de Capricorne.

HOLLANDE

NOUVELLE

Terre de Nuits

TERRE AUSTRALE et INCONNUE

MAGELLANIQUE

Cercle du Pole Antarctique

MER DE NORT

MER DU CAP VERD

Presenté
A MONSEIGNEUR LE DAUPHIN,
Par son tres-humble, tres-Obeissant, et tres fidele seruiteur,
Hubert Iaillot.

67

Le Globe Terrestre Répresenté en Deux Plans-Hémisphères

This extraordinarily graphic wall map is Jean-Baptiste Nolin's great 1708 double hemisphere map of the world. This map is notable as the high point of French map engraving and baroque allegorical expression. The finely engraved spheres of the Earth are supported by Atlas-like titans, but these are no gods. Despite impressive musculature, they are men, farmers and scholars, whose work, product, and tools lie scattered at their feet. At each corner of the map, and at center, God, reminiscent of a Michelangelo painting, takes and active role, flying through the firmament in the act of creation.

From a cartographic perspective, Nolin's great wall map is strongly in line with early 18th century cartographic conventions in terms of the form of the continents, the presence of Terres Australes, and the rendering of unexplored shores. Note the clear and open Northwest Passage, then known as the Strait of Anian, extending from the west coast of America to the Hudson Bay – a hoped for but ultimately apocryphal trade route. Also of note is the unexplored eastern shore of Australia, which joins both Van Diemen's Land (Tasmania) and New Guiana to the continental mainland.

This map is the first of a series of grand five wall maps covering the world and the continents (Europe, Africa, Asia, and America) issued by Nolin and his son, also Jean-Baptiste Nolin, between 1708 and 1740. The present map is undoubtable the work of the father, but was published by the son. The other maps in the series, while derived from the elder Nolin's work, were mostly the product of the son. Such wall maps, also known as parlor maps, were common in the great sitting rooms of Europe, where rich merchants and powerful nobles could pontificate on the complexity of the world.

Cartographer

Jean-Baptiste Nolin (1657-1725) was a French cartographer active in Paris. Nolin mastered mapmaking under his father of the same name. When the elder Nolin died in 1607, the younger took over his father's business and republished many of his father's maps. Unlike most 18th century mapmakers, the Nolin firm enjoyed exceptional financial success, largely due to strategic partnerships with other cartographers and the production of highly decorative beautifully engraved work.

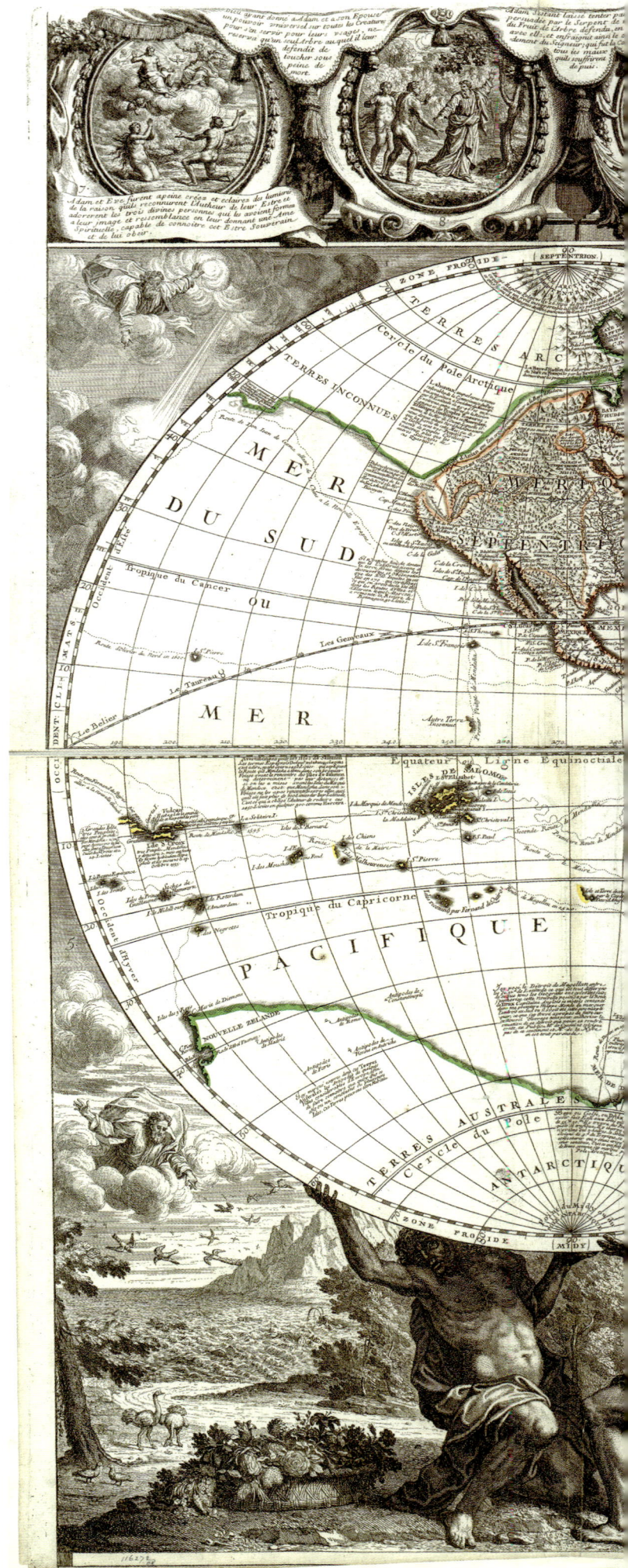

LE GLOBE TERRESTRE
REPRESENTE EN DEUX PLANS-HEMISPHERES

Dressé

Sur la Projection de M.r de la Hyre
sur plusieurs Routiers et Mémoires des
le tout rectifié et calculé selon
et Dédié
les dernieres observations

A M.r L'ABBE BIGNON CONSEILLER
D'ETAT ORDINAIRE

Par

A PARIS

MER GLACIALE

SEPTENTRION

MER de TARTARIE

OCEAN

MER DU NORD

ASIE

AFRIQUE

OCEAN ORIENTAL

Tropique du Cancer

Equateur ou Ligne

Equinoctiale

OCEAN ETHIOPIEN ou MER MERIDIONALE

MER DES INDES

NOUVELLE HOLLANDE

Tropique du Capricorne

TERRES AUSTRALES et INCONNUES

Cercle du Pole Antarctique ou ANTARCTIQUE

MIDY

69

I. de S. Pierre

Mariages
des
Canadiens

Terre Ve
non con

Leurs festins qu'ils nomment
Vin où ils se font servir
par leurs Femmes

Moulins pour
Separer les Metaux
de la Terre

Danse du
Calumet

Aguacate

Decentes
des
Mines

LA VILLE DE MEX
tiée au Milieu et entre d
Cortez Espagnol sur M
Les Guerres qu'elle a sou
grande Ville. On la Rebatie e

Les Environs de l'Embouchure de la Riv.re du MISSISIPI Decouverte par Mr. de la Salle en 1683. et Reconnuës par Mr le Chevalier d'Iberville en 1698. et 1699.

R. Guyoui loppezi
Sacellum
Imperiale

Rivier
Rouge
les Machitoche

les Tchome
Desert ou Anciennes Habi-
tations des Mobiliens
Riv. ou Yagnenga ou
petite Riviere

Santa Fee
Tacubaya

Village ou Portage
des Nomas Portage
de la Croix à 2 Lieues

la Mobile R.

S. Angel

Rivier aux Boeufs
Ancienes Habitations

Tasquaoula R.

les Mobiliens

Chasmen ou Conchaques R.

S. Marie
Pietatis
S. Aug.in
de las Cuevas

Chasse du Buff

Village ou sont aujour-
dhuy les Tainslas

Pascagoula

NATION DES CHICACHA

Animas

Lac de Maurepas

Escort ou sont au-
jourdhuy les Tonkas

Lac de Pontchar-
train

Churubusco
Istapalapa

Portage du Sucur

Baye St. Louis
I. et Fort de
Miloxi
Russe
Baye des
Pascagoula

Baye Espagnole

Cuyoacan

Portage du Piloxi

Baye des
Pascagoula
Baye des
Pascagoula

Pinsaco

Istacua

Lac d'

Sr.
Echelle de 20. Lieües.

GOLFE DE MEXIQUE

les Espagnols
Frontiere de
les Espagnols
à l'Escalette

Anguilar

rtices

le Detour de
l'Anglois

Ancien Fort
Mississipi Ra

I. de la
Chandeleur

BALDIVE ville Considerable du Perou, sur la Mer du Sud.
Elle est habitée par les Espagnols qui extire de l'Or des Mines qui sont proches, et qu'y font Scier quantité des Planches
qu'on transportes à Lima et ailleurs.

Pointe de Mardigras

I. au Breton

Entrée ou
Embouchure
du Mississipi

Melons d'Eau

Ville et un Port de
Mer du Sud. Situeé
agne Fort commode
qui fusse le com

Cocos

St. Lazare

LIMA

Asagou

Moro Selaz Peroquet

la Madelaine

ncs,

Grand Gozier

Gennes

BALDIVE

Isle de
Constantin

Perou, on la nomme
aussi la Ville des Reys,
on l'ort se nomme
Caillau. L'Archeveque
y Reside et est Primat. d
Chili et du Perou. Il ne Pleut
jamais aux environs de ce lieu
et neanmoins le Terroir est
si Fertile qu'on y recceuille
le Froment Deux fois
l'année

ros Ycacos

Prairies

Poule d'Eau

Port de
Nobla

oulco

Claudolle de
Caillau

Natureis du Perou

Port del
Marques

Port de Caillau

Poule
Pintada

Entrée de
la Riviere
de Baldive

MER DU SUD

Isle de Caillau
ou de Lima

Moro de Boniface

El Bouqueron

SUD

MER DU SU

route de Magellan en 1520.

Tropiqu

Prisonniers de Guerre destinés à être Sacrifie

Grand Temple de Mexique

Magiscatzin le Premier du Mexique qui reçoit à sa Mort le Batesme

la plus grande et la plus Riche Place de l'Amerique elle etoit si- ...ituée d'eau douce et d'eau Salée, elle fut prise par Ferdinand ...rnier Empereur l'an 1521. ...*nondation qu'y arriva en 1629. ayant presque détruit cette ...t aujourd'hui sur les Bords de ces mêmes Lacs.*

Jacuba ...chimi la Ville des S... Ville ...s Marquis Ossanguacalco Altemies Guauhtlan Villa Villa

Sea l

Grande Place

Villa Villa

Mont Chiquihuithle

S. Isabel

Mont Crasus S. Christoval

Villa

Douce

LA CONCEPTION

Cortez fait abatre les Idoles de Mexique

Bon Mouillage

Baye de la Con

LA CONCEPTION, Ville ... Mer du Sud sur les Côtes ... Gouverneur de cette Provi- ...dence. Il y a une forte Garni... les environs de cette Place a...

Indigo

Annanas

Baye de la C

Roix Musque

Quinquine l'...

Opassum

Pointe de la Herradoura MER DU

Carte Très Curieuse De La Mer Du Sud

One of the most spectacularly decorative maps of the 18th century, this magnificent work was sumptuously engraved and centered on the American continent. Innovative for his time, Chatelain combined fine artwork with scholarly studies of geography, history, ethnology, heraldry, and cosmography. This map was graphically rich with a wealth of lush inset maps and vignette illustrations. It was issued in Chatelain's Atlas Historique and was the finest map to be found in the whole of Chatelain's work. It included insights on local traditions, flora and fauna, political commentary, and notes on trade.

With Niagara Falls as a backdrop, Chatelain illustrated the astounding American fur trade and the seemingly boundless cod fisheries off the Grand Banks. The vignettes included images of tribal life, overflowing hunting grounds, native industry, rich mines, and whale fisheries. Dangers, too, were included in the form of vicious animals, hostile natives, and a grizzly image of human sacrifice before a stylized Aztec pyramid. Importantly, this was one of the first maps to question the popular convention of rendering California as an island.

This map was issued just as the world was being opened up to international commerce. Here both the Atlantic and Pacific oceans were remarkably foreshortened, suggesting that passage between these widely divided continents might be a matter of ease. The routes of the many explorers who made these passages were noted, with their ships illustrated, including Columbus, Vespucci, Magellan, Drake, Schouten, La Salle, and Dampier. The rich imagery also detailed the Spice Islands (Moluques), the Isthmus of Panama, and the bustling ports of Acapulco, Baldivia, Veracruz, Conceptión, Buenos Aires, Havana, and San Sebastián.

Cartographer

Henri Abraham Chatelain (1684-1743) was a Huguenot pastor of Parisian origins. He was best known as a Dutch cartographer and specifically for his contribution in the seminal seven volume Atlas Historique.

CARTE TRES CURIEUSE DE LA MER DU SUD, CONTENANT DES REMARQUES NOUVE

Mais auſſy ſur les principaux Pays de l'Amerique tant Septentrionale que Meridionale, Avec les Noms & la Rou

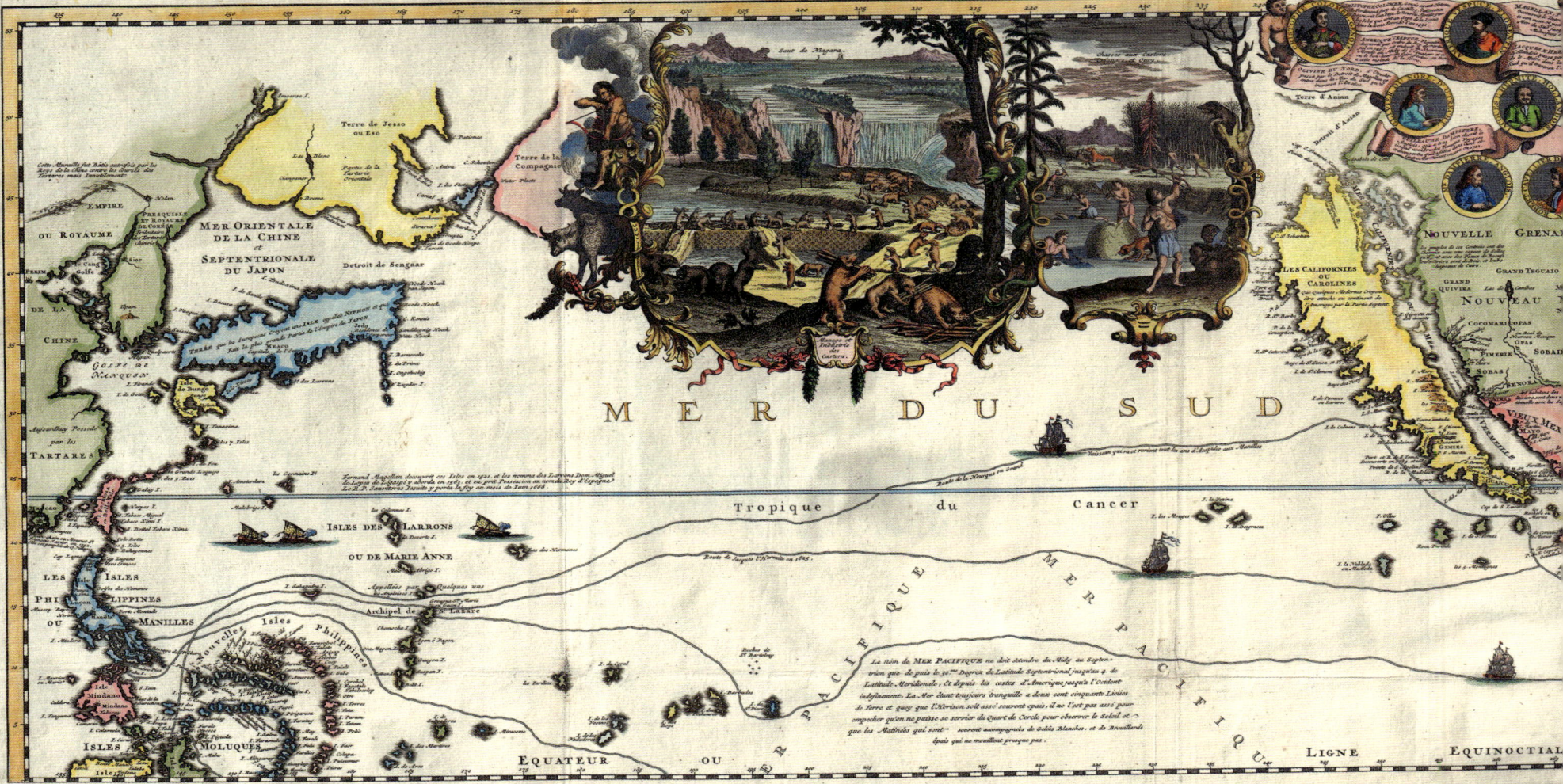

MER ORIENTALE DE LA CHINE et SEPTENTRIONALE DU JAPON

Terre de Jesso ou Eso

Terre de la Compagnie

EMPIRE OU ROYAUME

DE LA CHINE

GOLFE DE NANQUIN

DE LA TARTARIE

LES ISLES PHILIPPINES OU MANILLES

Isles Philippines

ISLES MOLUQUES

MER DU SUD

ISLES DES LARRONS OU DE MARIE ANNE

Tropique du Cancer

MER PACIFIQUE

MER PACIFIQUE

EQUATEUR OU LIGNE EQUINOCTIAL

NOUVELLE GRENAD

LES CALIFORNIES OU CAROLINES

NOUVEAU

GRAND QUIVIRA

VIEUX MEX

Celebes

ISLES MOLUQUES

Nouvelle Guinée

Papous ou Nouvelle Guinée

MER DE LANTCHIDOL

TERRE DE QUIR

NOUVELLE HOLLANDE

Terre d'Eendracht ou de Concorde

Terre de Wit ou Terre Blanche

Terre d'Edels

Terre de Leuwin

MER

MER DU NORD

MER DU SUD

MER DU SUD

MER DU SUD

MER DU SUD

MER DU

Les Isles de Salomon

Isle Guadalcanal

Port de Acapulco

Port de Callao

Lac d'Eau Douce

GOLFE MEXIQUE

NATION DE CHICACHA

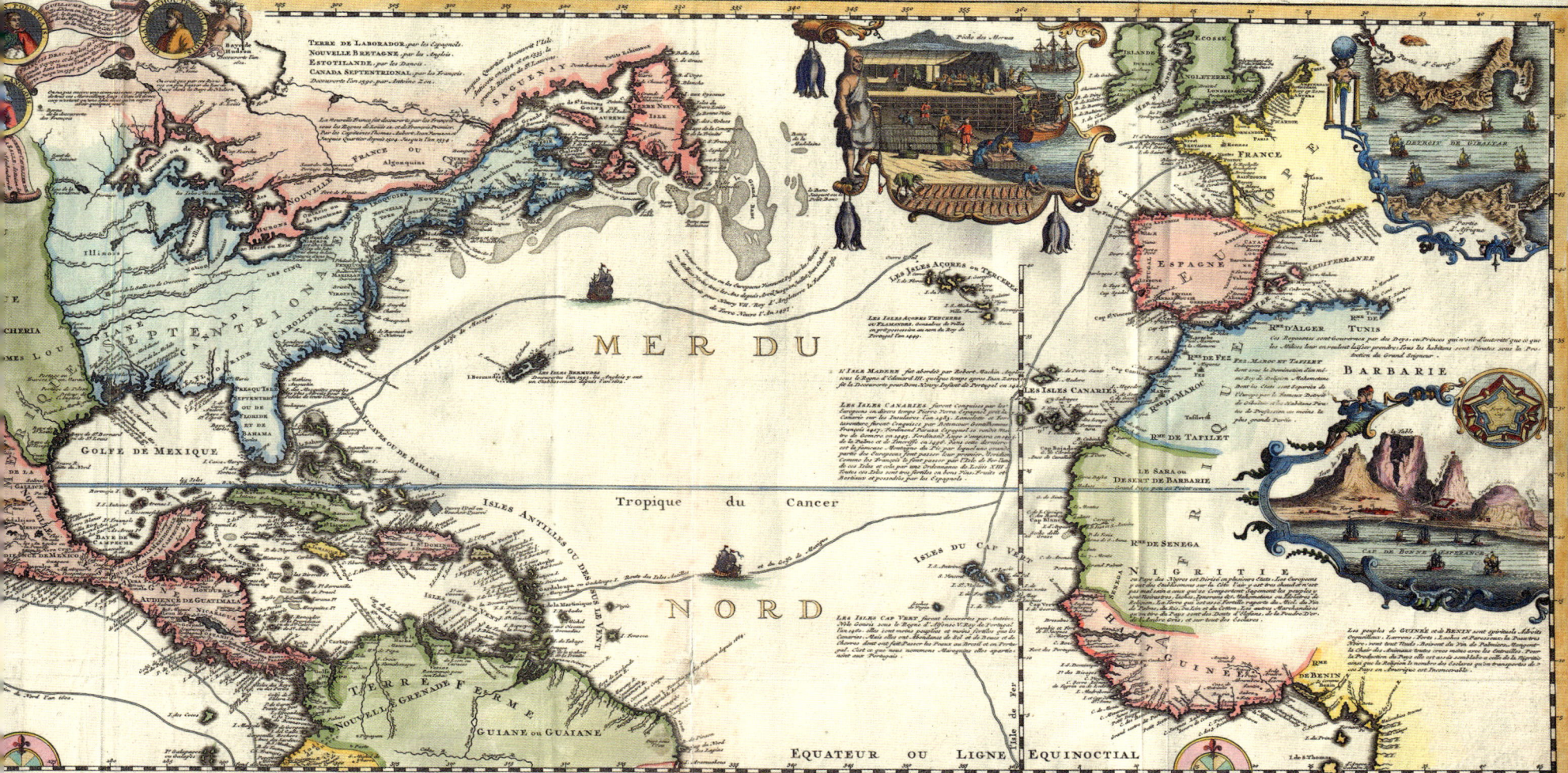

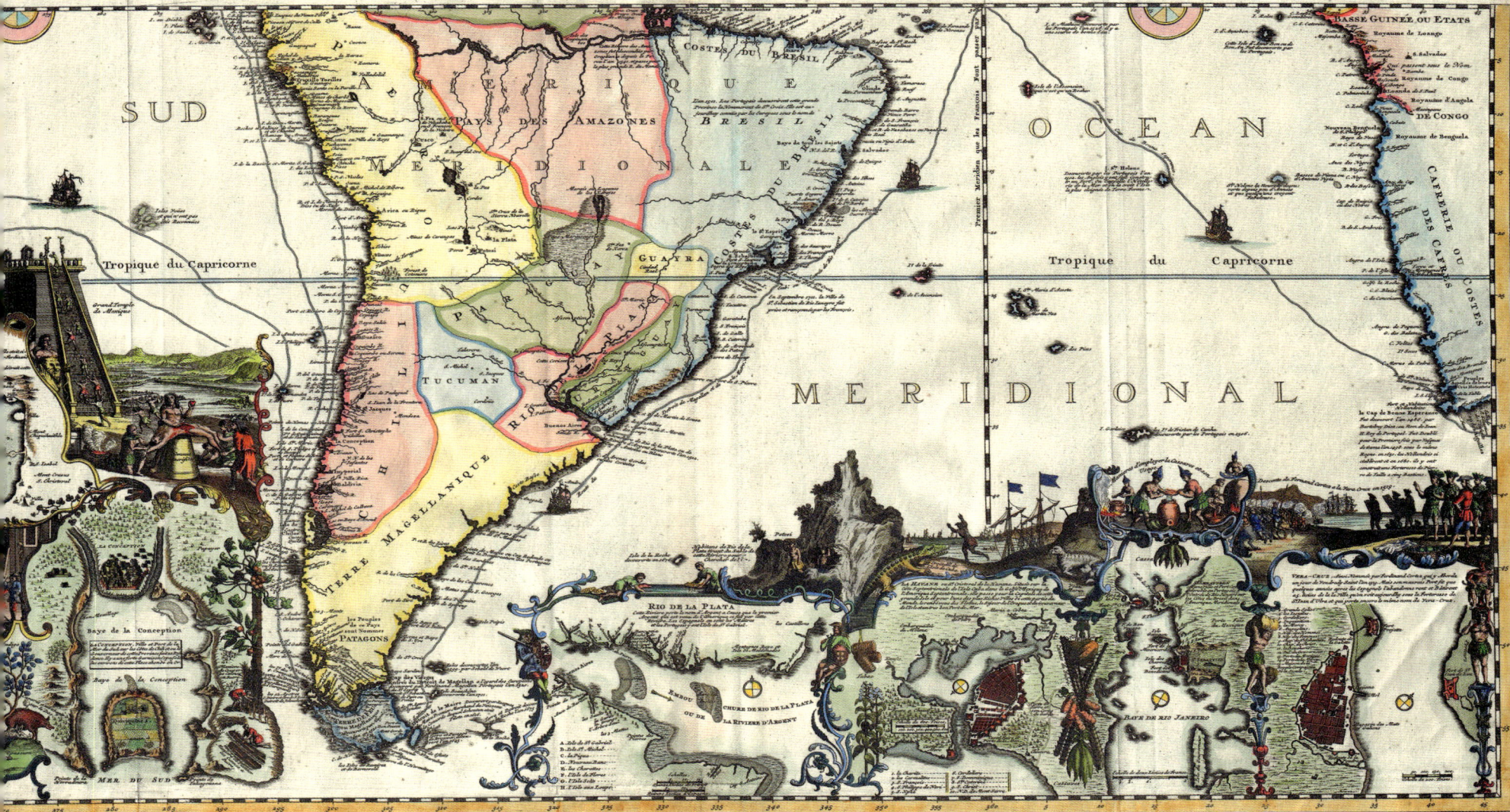

Le Globe Terrestre Representé en Deux Plans-Hemispheres

This exceptional 1742 double hemisphere map of the world by Jean Nolin was augmented by no less than ten additional sub-maps. Nolin was attempting to condense the history of global cartography into a one double folio. Among the smaller maps surrounding the main chart are illustrations of the world as understood before and after the discoveries of Christopher Columbus in the New World. In addition, there are maps showing alternative ways of viewing the globe ranging from northern and southern hemispherical projections to a cordiform projection.

This map presents an information-rich stylistic convention rarely seen in earlier maps. The density of data throughout responded to general enthusiasm for scientific discovery. In the subsequent century, such maps became increasingly common and often even more elaborate. Even so, the cartography presented here by Nolin is generally vague and speculative. This is, for example, one of the last published maps to represent California in its insular incarnation. Also apparent are guesswork mappings of Australia and the South Pacific. Note how, rather than fill in unknown areas with speculative cartography, Nolin chooses to leave unexplored shores undefined with supplementary textual annotation describing that region's state of discovery, what was known, and what was unknown.

Cartographer

Jean-Baptiste Nolin (1686-1762) was a French publisher and cartographer. He inherited the successful firm of his father, also Jean-Baptiste Nolin (1657-1725). The younger Nolin, like his father, was a canny businessman, who, unlike many mapmakers, prospered financially.

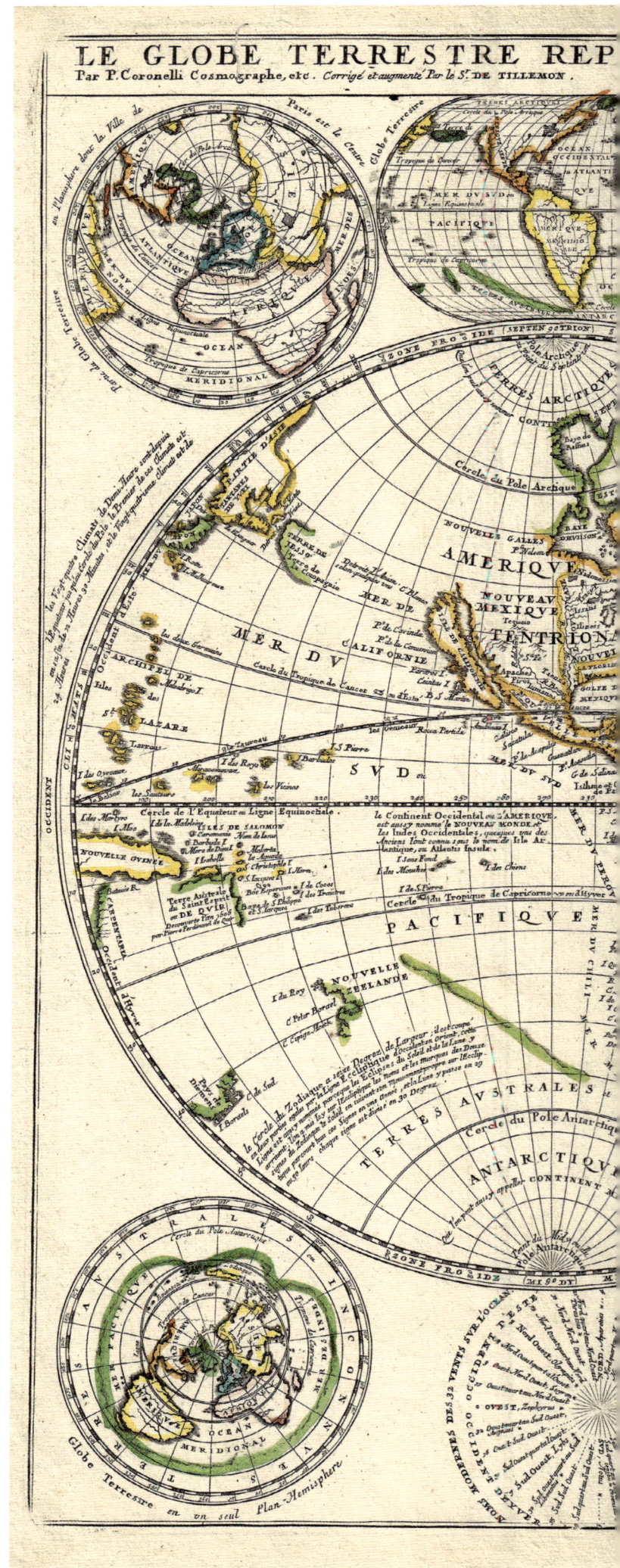

SENTE EN DEVX PLANS-HEMISPHERES, ET EN DIVERSES AVTRES FIGVRES.

A PARIS *Chez I.B. NOLIN sur le Quay de l'Horloge du Palais proche le Pont-Neuf a l'Enseigne de la* PLACE DES VICTOIRES. *Avec Privilege du Roy.*

EVROPE

AFRIQVE

ETHIOPIE

GRANDE TARTARIE

OCEAN INDIEN ou MER DES INDES

NOUVELLE HOLLANDE

OCEAN ETHIOPIEN ou MERIDIONAL

TERRES AVSTRALES et INCONNVES

Cercle du Pole Antarctique

ANTARCTIQVES

MER DV NORD

AMERIQVE MERIDIONALE

MER DV PARAGVAY

MER PACIFIQVE DV SVD

GRANDE OCEAN MER

OCEAN ATLANTIQVE

75

MAPPE MONDE NOUVELLE

Dediée

A Monseigneur le Comte de Maurepas Ministre
et Secretaire d'Etat.

Par son tres humble et tres Obeissant Serviteur,
le ROUGE, Ingenieur Geographe du Roi.

A PARIS.
Ruë des Augustins vis a vis le panier
Fleuri
1744.

POLE ARCTIQUE

TERRES ARCTIQUES

GROENLANDE

AMERIQUE SEPTENTRIONALE

NOUVELLE FRANCE

MER DU NORD

Tropique du Cancer

Ligne Ecliptique

GOLFE DU MEXIQUE

Isles Lucayes

Cap Verd

GRANDE MER DU SUD ou PACIFIQUE

EQUATEUR ou LIGNE EQUINOCTIALE

TERRE FERME

OCEAN

PAYS DES AMAZONES

AMERIQUE MERIDIONALE

BRESIL

Isles Salomon

PARAGUAY

Tropique du Capricorne

ANTIPODES

NOUVELLE ZELANDE

Chili

MAGELLANIQUE

D.

TERRES AUSTRALES ou ANTARCTIQUES

Cercle Polaire

ANTARCTIQUE POLE

OCEAN OCCIDENTAL

DESERT DE BARBARIE

ETHIOPIE

GUINEE

AFRIQUE

EQUATEUR

CAFRERIE

HOTTENTOT

Tropique du Capricorne

MERIDIONAL

TERRES

Remarque

Dans cette Mappe, les Côtes et les Isles
de l'Ocean Oriental, Meridional, Occidental,
de la Mer du Sud, et Mediterranée aussi bien que les Nouvelles Decouvertes en Amerique
sont tirées des Cartes Marines dressées
au Depôt par Ordre de Monseig.r le C.te
de Maurepas; le Cap de la Circoncision
est Placé Suivant les Raports, des Marins
de la Compagnie des Indes. J'ay ajoutée les
Nouvelles Observations des Moscovites, depuis
le 180.me Degré de Longitude, jusquau 210.me Contenant
le Kamtschatka, le Païs des Jakutes, des Tunkusiens, des Coriakins, et le
Cap Glacé... ce qui a été Obmis, dans les Anciennes Mappes

LE MONDE TERRESTRE

est de trois sortes
POLAIRE, NOUVEAU, ANCIEN,
le Monde Polaire Consiste en TERRES ARCTIQUES
et ANTARCTIQUES, le Nouveau Monde est L'AMERIQUE,
l'Ancien Monde Comprend trois Grandes Part.ies L'EUROPE, L'ASIE, et L'AFRIQUE,
les Terres Arctiques Sont.   les Terres Antarctiques Sont.
l'Estotilande; la Groenlande; Uslande;   la Noul.le Guinée.; les I.les de Salomon; la Noul.le Zelande;
le Spitzberg: le Cap Glacé.   la T.re de Feu; la Noul.le Hollande; le Cap de la Circonction.

Renvoy
Dangers
Roches
Herbes flotantes

A Paris chez le S.r le Rouge ruë des grands Augustins vis a vis le panier Fleuri.

Les Indes sont corrigées par M. Dapreis Capitaine des

76

Mappe Monde nouvelle

This highly decorative map of the world was published by George Louis Le Rouge in 1744. From the upper right of the map the sun of scientific achievement, represented by mathematical and astronomical equipment, enlightens the map. By contrast, the decorative work in the lower right features terrors of nature, including roaring lions and violent rapids.

The darkness before the dawn, this map appears just before the great discoveries of Cook, La Pérouse, and Vancouver in the late 18th century. With so much yet to be explored, cartographers struggling to understand the world turned to educated guesses and speculation. The great unknowns of this era included the Arctic, the Pacific Northwest, the South Seas, Australia, and the southern polar regions, as well as the interiors of Africa, east Asia, America, and Australia. Separating fact from fiction was no easy task with so many pieces of the puzzle missing.

While this map offers much of interest, one anomaly stands out. A great whirlpool or maelstrom is set in the middle of the Atlantic Ocean between the Equator and the Tropic of Cancer. Other diligent and well-respected cartographers, like Guillaume de L'Isle, who likely drew directly from mariners' accounts, described similar occurrences. It is only recently, with satellite imagery, that modern scientists have indeed discovered two massive occasional whirlpools in the South Atlantic. Lasting months before dissipating, these modern maelstroms may have at last proven to science what early cartographers already knew.

Cartographer

George Louis Le Rouge (c. 1712-1780) was a Paris-based map publisher. Born as Georg Ludwig in Germany, he Francophied his name after relocating to France. Le Rouge produced thousands of maps, many of which were based upon English prototypes, and was eventually awarded the title of Geographer to the King. He also worked with Benjamin Franklin to produce the influential 1769 Franklin/Folger Map of the Gulf Stream.

Carte General Des Découvertes De L'Amiral de Fonte

This is one of the most interesting maps ever published and perhaps the most influential map from the French golden age of positivist or speculative cartography, c. 1710-1783. In this map, Joseph Nicolas de L'Isle attempted to incorporate and reconcile numerous speculations about the region between the Siberian coasts in Asia and the Pacific Northwest of America. Note the gigantic territory extending southward from the North Pole, the large island east of Kamchatka, the peculiar network of inland seas and rivers in North America, and most astoundingly the gigantic sea, identified as the "Mer de l'Ouest" filling the western part of America.

This was not the first published mapping of the Sea of the West, but it was the most influential. The concept was developed by Guillaume de L'Isle. Reference to this development survives today only in manuscript form as Guillaume did not, apparently, have much faith in the idea. Guillaume died in 1726 and the manuscript was discovered by his younger brother Joseph Nicolas de L'Isle who proved a more enthusiastic champion of the Sea of the West theory. The idea had great appeal among the French and English who imagined that the sea might represent a practical outlet by which the wealth of their New World colonies could be transported to the rich markets of Asia. This map, and the theory behind it was presented by Joseph Nicolas de L'Isle and Philippe Buache, in a document called *Considerations,* to the French Royal Academy of Sciences in 1753.

Cartographer

The **de L'Isle family** *(fl. c. 1700-c. 1760) (also written Delisle) were, in composite, a mapmaking* tour de force *who redefined 18th century European cartography. The de L'Isles were proponents of the school of positivist or speculative geography, an ethic of mapmaking wherein the unknown parts of the world were mapped based upon geographical theories, extrapolation from known information, and pure guesswork. Of the 12 de L'Isle brothers, Guillaume (1675-1726), Simon Claude (1676-1726), Joseph Nicolas (1688-1768) and Louis (1690-1741), all made significant contributions to cartography.*

CARTE GÉNÉRALE DES DÉCOUVERTES De l'Amiral de Fonte Et autres Navigateurs Espagnols, Anglois et Russes, pour la recherche du Passage a la MER DU SUD. Par Mr. De l'Isle de l'Académie Royale des Sciences et Professeur de Mathematique au College Royal a Paris Septembre 1752.

Dediée A M. ROUILLÉ Chevalier Comte de Jouy, &c.
Secretaire d'Etat ayant le Département de la Marine.

Echelle de Lieues Marines de France, et d'Angleterre de 20 au Degré.
10 20 40 60 80 100 200 300 L.

Echelle de Lieues d'Espagne de 17½ au Degré.
25 50 75 100 125 150 175 L.

BAYE DE BAFFIN

Isle de Cumberland et de James

Baye de Cumberland Decou. 1587

LABRADOR

Montagnes de Glace

Detroit de Frobisher

Detroit de l'Aldermand

Detroit de Jacques Lancastre

Grande Terre decouverte en 1723. ou s'enfuient les Tzutzy lorsquils sont poursuivis par les Russes qui ne les ont pas encore Soumis.

B. de Repulse dec. en 1742

Eau de Wager dec. en 1746

Detroit d'Hudson

Lac que le Capitaine Bernarda a parcouru l'espace de 436 Lieues

LAC BERNARDA

de l'Amiral de Fonte

ses Capitaines en 1640

L. Basset

BAYE D'HUDSON

Decouvertes

Tzutzy

Cap Chalaginskoi

Cercle et de Polaire

Olutorski

Terres vûes par M. Spanberg en 1728. frequentées a present par les Russes qui en apportent de tres belles fourures.

Cette Riviere a 3 Cataractes

Isle Bernarda

Presqu'Isle de Combasset

R. Bernarda

LAC VALASCO

On trouve dans ce Lac depuis 23 jusqu'à 60 Brasses d'eau

Grande Isle très peuplée

LAC DE FONTE

8. Cataractes qui font en tout 32 pieds de hauteur

Terres veües par les Russes en 1741 ou le Capitaine Tchirikow perdit sa Chaloupe armée de 10 hommes.

LAC BELLE

CANADA

Baye de Haro

Cataracte

LAC

Archipel St. Lazare

R. de Los Reyes

MER DE L'OUEST

Decouv. par J. de Fuca en 1592 et parcourue par J. de Fuca en 1592

Il y a dans cette entrée une Isle avec une haute Montagne en forme de Colomne

Entrée desouv. par Jean de Fuca en 1592

Entrée decouv. par Martin d'Aguilar en 1603 Cap Blanc de St. Sebastien

CALIFORNIE

C. Mendocino

B. de Pinos Port St. Francois

B. de Nieuwe P. de Monterey Pte de Carmae P. de la Conception

Longitude du premier Meridien de l'Isle de Fer.

Retour de l'Amerique au Kamtchatka de la Croyere en Juin et Juil. 1741.

par Mrs Tchirikow en Septembre 1741.

Capitaine Tchirikow et Mr. De l'Isle en Aout et Septembre 1741.

NOUVEAU MEXIQUE

Sioux l'Ouest

Maha Tintons

Quivira

Padoucas blancs

Padoucas noirs

Teguio

Moqui Zuni Acoma

Yunas

R. del Coral

Casa Grande

Sta Maria de Grado

Sta Fe

79

Mappe-Monde
ou Description du Globe Terrestre

Crowned with elaborate Baroque cartouche work, this beautiful map was drawn by Jean Janvier for Lattre's 1762 *Atlas Moderne*. The map offers much of interest including one the first appearances of Hawaii on a European map, a curious mapping of the American Pacific Northwest, and an unusual presentation of Australia.

In the Pacific Northwest, the Muller Peninsula, suggested by German geographer Gerhard Muller, roughly takes the form of Alaska even though that land, at the time of this map's production, not yet been visited by European navigators and was mostly speculative. Further south a magnificent inland sea, known as Sea of the West (Mer de l'Ouest), fills the northwestern section of the modern day United States. Based upon American Indian stories, and questionable reports from the explorer Juan de Fuca, the Sea of the West was popular in its day among the French and the English, who were hoping for the existence of an inland water route to the Pacific.

In South America, the Lago de Xarayes is another speculatively mapped inland body of water at the northern extension of the Paraguay River. Known today as the Pantanal, this area is a vast flood plain, which was, not unreasonably, misidentified by early explorers visiting during the annual inundation as a vast inland sea. Hopeful explorers considered the Pantanal, or Xarayes after one of the indigenous tribes in the region, to be the gateway to the Amazon and possibly the Earthly Paradise.

Cartographers

• **Jean or Robert Janvier** *(fl. 1746-1776) was a Paris-based cartographer active in the mid to late 18th century. Janvier's true first name is a matter of debate, as it often appears as either Jean or Robert. More commonly, Janvier simply signed his maps as "Signor Janvier." By the late 18th century, Janvier seems to have been awarded the title of "Geographe Avec Privilege du Roi" and this designation appears on many of his later maps.*

• **Jean Lattre** *(fl. 1743-1793) was a Paris-based bookseller, engraver, and map publisher active in the mid to late 18th century. Lattre was an ardent defender of his Privilege and he was known to have brought plagiarism charges against several fellow cartographers.*

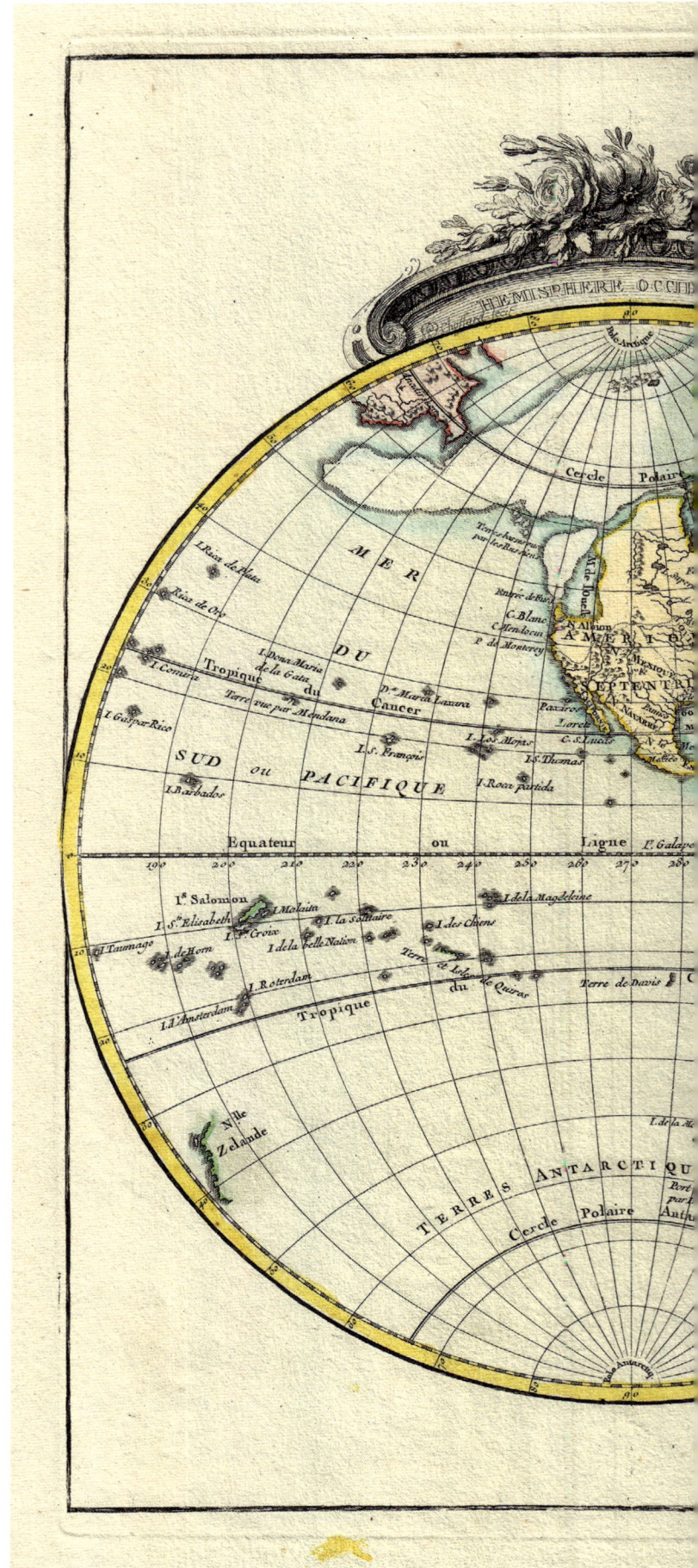

MAPPE-MONDE
ou
DESCRIPTION DU GLOBE TERRESTRE,
Assujettie aux Observations Astronomiques
Par le S.ʳ Janvier Géographe
Avec Privilege du Roi.
1762

HEMISPHERE ORIENTAL.

A PARIS
chez Lattré Graveur
rue S.ᵗ Jacques, au
dessus de la Fontaine
Saint Severin a
La Ville de
Bordeaux.

MER GLACIALE

EUROPE

ASIE

TARTARIE

CHINE

AFRIQUE

NIGRITIE

ETHIOPIE

GUINEE

Desert de Sahra

BARBARIE

MER DU NORD

Tropique du Cancer

ISLES DU CAP VERD

MER DU SUD

Isles Marianes

Philippines

Nouvelles Carolines

Isles Palas

Bornéo

MERIQUE MERIDIONALE

OCEAN

ISLES ACORES

Equinoxiale

ANTILLES

TERRE FERME

MER DES INDES

Tropique du Capricorne

N.lle Hollande

Terre de Diemen

Carpentarie

Terre du S.t Esprit

Nouvelle Guinée

N.lle Bretagne

Terre haute

Moluques

TERRES AUSTRALES

TERRES ANTARCTIQUES

Cercle Polaire Antarctique

Cap de la Circoncision

Isles Maldives

Ceylan

Bengale

Pondichery

Comorin

Madagascar

Zanguebar

Monomotapa

C. de Bonne Esperance

Banc des Aiguilles

Hottentots

S.t Paul Amsterdam

I.sle Bourbon

I. de France

I. S.te Helene

Grande Ascension

I. S. Mathieu

MAGELLANIQUE

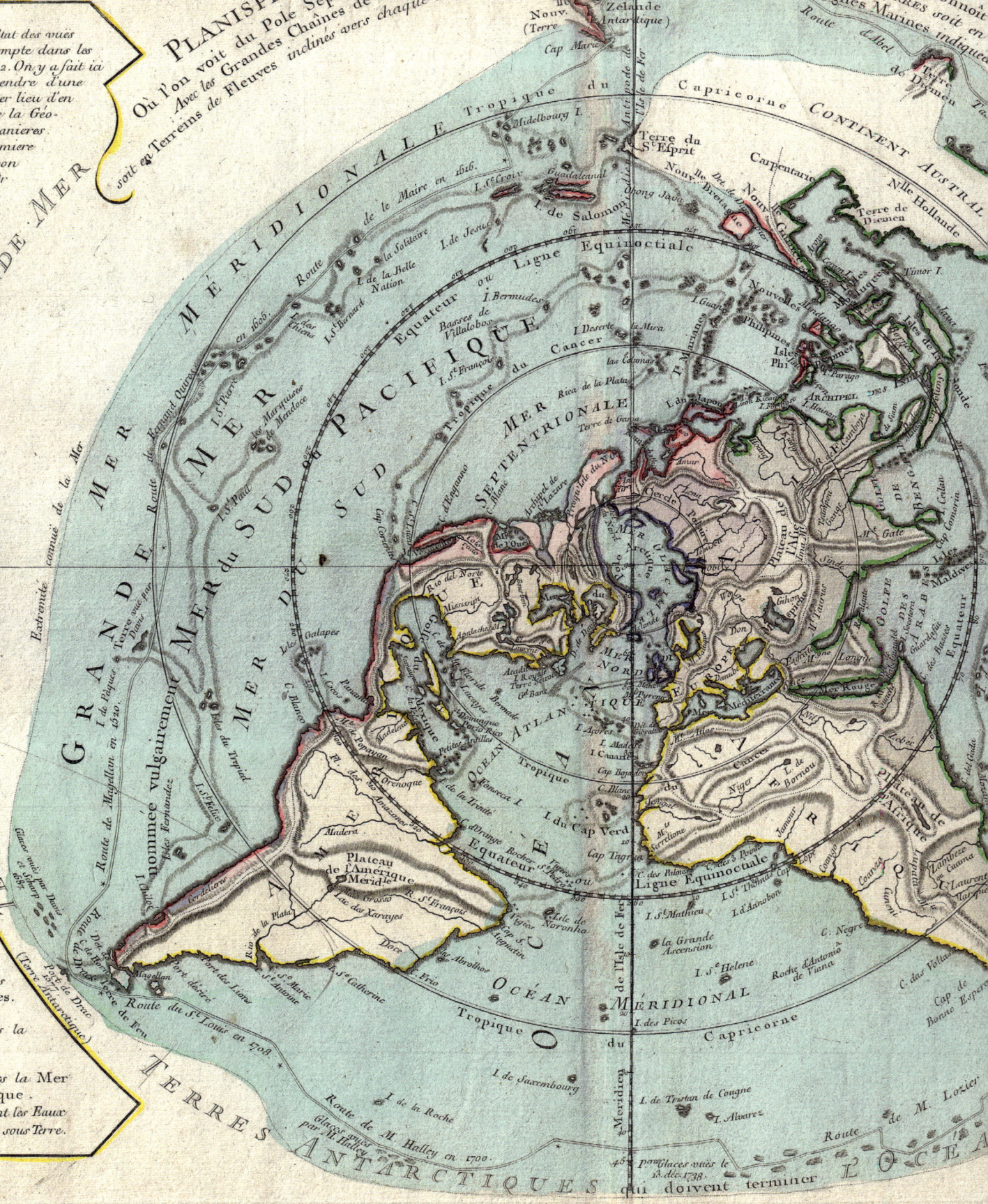

PLANISPHERE

Où l'on voit du Pole Septentrional
Avec les Grandes Chaînes de Montagnes, qui traversant le Globe, divisent naturellement les TERRES soit en
ce que l'on connoît
PHY
sont les Terreins de Fleuves inclinés vers chaque MER, et partagent les Mers par une suite de Montagnes Marines indiquées

CE PLANISPHERE est le résultat des vuës Physiques dont on a rendu compte dans les Mem. de l'Ac. des Sciences de 1752. On y a fait ici diverses additions, pour le rendre d'une utilité plus générale et donner lieu d'en faire application à l'étude de la Géographie. Car de toutes les manieres de considerer la Terre, la première doit être celle qui examine son état Naturel ou Physique; Or on voit dans ce Plan qu'indépendamment des Terres Antarctiques qui ne nous sont pas connuës, elle est divisée par les Chaînes de Montagnes (exprimées par un liseré blanc) en quatre parties, inclinées vers chacune des quatre Mers; et que ces Mers sont naturellement partagées par les Chaînes Marines, qui continuent sous les eaux, et dont les Isles sont les sommets. Cette seconde espece de Montagnes, que l'on a indiqué par une suite de hachures à travers les Mers, fait la liaison des Continents.

Ce Plan donne encore la division méthodique des Fleuves, qui se rendent dans chaque partie de ces Mers, depuis les Chaînes de Montagnes, dont les Terreins les plus elevés qui en sont comme les clefs, sont ici appellés Plateaux.

Explication des Couleurs.

- Terreins inclinés vers l'Océan.
- Terreins inclinés vers la Mer des Indes.
- Terreins inclinés vers la Grande Mer.
- Terreins inclinés vers la Mer Glaciale Arctique.
- Terreins inclinés dont les Eaux des Fl: se perdent sous Terre.

LA GRANDE MER qui doivent borner

TERRES ANTARCTIQUES

TERRES ANTARCTIQUES qui doivent terminer L'OCÉA

MER MÉRIDIONALE

GRANDE MER

MER DU SUD ou nommée vulgairement MER du SUD ou PACIFIQUE

Équateur ou Ligne Équinoctiale

Tropique du Capricorne

Tropique du Cancer

MER SEPTENTRIONALE

OCÉAN ATLANTIQUE

MER NORD

OCÉAN MÉRIDIONAL

CONTINENT AUSTRAL

Tropique du Capricorne

Ligne Équinoctiale

Équateur

Tropique

AMÉRIQUE MÉRIDIONALE
Plateau de l'Amérique Méridle

AFRIQUE

82

Pl. II.

Le point de vuë de la TERRE qui se présente ici du Pole Septentrional, s'étend régulièrement jusqu'à l'Équateur; mais l'Hémisphère Inférieur ne se voit que par un développement supposé, où l'on a eü attention a ne pas défigurer les Terres. C'est pour cela que l'on n'a pas crû devoir suivre absolument les voies Géométriques a cet égard.

La Route qui termine nos connoissances vers le Pole Antarctique, n'a été faite en entier par aucun Navigateur; et ce n'est que le Résultat des différentes parties de Routes faites par les plus célebres Marins qui se sont le plus avancés de ce côté. On les reconnoîtra par des Etoiles qui indiquent chaque partie de ces Routes, avec le nom des Navigateurs et les années.

Les Glaces considérables que plusieurs y ont trouvé, prouvent qu'il y a dans les Terres Antarctiques, une suite de hautes Montagnes et de grands Fleuves avec une Mer intérieure, d'où viennent les Glaces, dans une certaine proportion avec ce que l'on connoit du côté du Pole Arctique.

Cette Carte Physique de la Terre.
Dressée par Phil. Buache et publiée avec l'approb.on et sous le Privilège de l'Académie des Sciences,
Se trouve avec ses détails et les Tables Analytiques qui y sont relatives, à Paris, Chez DEZAUCHE, succ.r des S.rs De l'Isle et Buache et avec tous les Ouvrages Géographiques de Guill. Delisle. Rue des Noyers, près celle des Anglois.

Gravé par Desbruslins

Planisphere Physique

Rendered with the North Pole at its center, this 1781 map by Jean-Nicolas Buache de la Neuville is unusual both as a polar projection and for being a primarily real (rather than political) map. Although projected from the North Pole, the map embraces considerably more than the hemisphere extending south beyond Australia, Cape Horn, and New Zealand. The cartography is distinctly pre-Cook, with such ephemeral conventions as the Sea of the West and an unmapped eastern shore of Australia evident.

The focus of the map is physical geography, particularly the interplay of mountain ranges, river systems, and oceans. The striking color-coding corresponds to the oceans into which the rivers of each continent drain. Red represents the Pacific Basin, Yellow the Atlantic Basin, Green the Indian Ocean Basin, and Purple the Arctic Basin. This particularly is of note, as Buache's geophysical theories advocated for a warm ice-free polar sea. In his *Essai de Géographie Physique*, Buache claimed, not without reason, that the Earth's great river systems were influenced by both terrestrial and undersea mountain ranges that forced drainage into one oceanic basin or another. To confirm his theory, he added mountain ranges to this map where necessary, such as in South America as a channel for the Amazon River, and in Africa to channel the Nile, Congo, Niger, and other great rivers. He also incorporated the exploratory routes of Magellan, Quiros, and others, whose discoveries, he argued, confirmed the theories he advocated.

This map was originally published by Phillipe Buache in 1752. The present example was issued posthumously by his heir and nephew Jean-Nicolas Buache de la Neuville and the publisher Jean-Claude Dezauche.

Cartographer

Phillipe Buache (1700-1773) was a French cartographer and publisher.
He began his career as an assistant to the famous cartographer Guillaume de L'Isle.
Upon Guillaume de L'Isle's death, he married de L'Isle's daughter and took over the business.
Buache was appointed Geographer to the King and often served as tutor to the young Dauphin,
a position of privilege that he took advantage of to secure additional royal appointments later
in his career. After his death in 1773, Buache's business passed to his nephew, Jean-Nicolas
Buache de la Neuville (1741-1825), who continued to publish updated versions of his maps.

Mappemonde ou Description du Globe Terrestre

This 1783 Robert de Vaugondy map of the world celebrated the accomplishments of Captain James Cook in his three historic expeditions. The routes of Cook's voyages were identified with dated annotations so that scholars browsing this map could fully appreciate the extent of his voyages. The beautiful title cartouche, complete with trumpeting angels, was designed by the artist Charles Cochin. This map was prepared by Robert de Vaugondy for inclusion in his masterpiece, the grand *Atlas Universel*.

Geographers of this period were involved in a vigorous academic debate regarding the cartography of the American Pacific Northwest. Despite the fact that Cook's historic voyages were completed and much of the confusion regarding that part of the world would soon be lifted, his official results had yet to be published and the debates in Paris remained lively. In this map, Vaugondy expressed much of this confusion and attempted to reconcile what little he knew of Cook's voyages with his own educated speculation. None of Cook's actual cartography is evident. What is present is a series of wishful inland seas and deep water river connections associated with the legends of Admiral de Fonte, which were almost certainly fictional, and Juan de Fuca, whose voyages were, in all likelihood, partial fictions and based upon reports stolen from Sir Francis Drake's voyages.

Cartographer

Robert de Vaugondy (1723-1786) was a publisher, engraver, and cartographer active in Paris during the 18th century. This was a period that combined rapid exploration of the world's seas with deepening scientific knowledge. As such, there was considerable pressure and competition among cartographers, particularly in Paris, to produce the most up to date 'scientific' maps of the world. In the absence of real geographical data, cartographers turned instead to speculative or positivist cartography, where they used their own scientific theories combined with factual information from actual exploration, and wishful thinking on the part of their royal or commercial patrons to fill the blank spaces on the map. Robert de Vaugondy was one of the most influential geographical theorists active in Paris during that time.

His nemesis was the equally influential French cartographer Phillipe Buache (1700-1773).

MAPPEMONDE

ou

DESCRIPTION DU GLOBE TERRESTRE

dressée fur les mémoires
les plus nouveaux,
et assujettie aux observations
astronomiques,
Par le Sr Robert de Vaugondy Géog. ord. du Roi
et Censeur royal.

avec les Routes, et
Decouvertes du Celèbre Capitaine Cook
qui a fait plusieurs fois le tour du Monde, et autres Navigateurs qui l'ont accompagné et qui s'en sont séparés.

A PARIS
Chez Antoine Boudet Libraire
Imprimeur du ROI, Rue St Jacques.
1783

OCEAN SEPTENTRIONAL

MER DU NORD

MER DU SUD

MER DES INDES

TERRES ANTARCTIQUES

AMERIQUE MERIDION.

NOUVELLE HOLLANDE

Equateur

Tropique du Cancer

Tropique du Capricorne

Cercle Polaire antarctique

85

MAPPEMONDE
Premiers Géographes

à l'usage de l'instr. Par...
et de l'Académie des Science...

MER GLACIALE

Intérieur de ce Pays est Inconnu

Cercle Polaire

AMERIQUE SEPTENTRIONALE

LOUISIANE

MER DU NORD

GRANDE MER

Bermudas

appellée vulgairement

MER DU SUD ou MER PACIFIQUE

Tropique du Cancer

Equateur ou Ligne Equinoctiale

ISLES DU CAP VERD

Tropique du Cancer

AFRIQUE

Equateur

GUINÉE

CAFRERIE

les Marquises de Mendoça

Pays des Amazones

AMERIQUE MÉRIDIONALE

BRESIL

PEROU

PARAGUAY

Tropique du Capricorne

Tropique du Capricorne

ZELANDE

Cap de Bonne Esperance

OCÉAN OCCIDENTAL

Cercle Polaire

Pôle Antarctique

AVERTISSEMENT
On a ajouté à cette Mappemonde les Nouvelles Découvertes faites par le Capitaine Cook dans ses trois differens Voyages, ainsi que celles faites depuis 30 ans, par les plus célèbres Voyageurs, soit au Sud du Cap de Bonne Espérance, soit au Nord de la Grande Mer, appellée vulgairement la Mer du Sud. L'On a suivi aussi les Plans de Philippe Buache, approuvés par l'Académie des Sciences, ainsi que d'après les fondemens qui lui en ont été exposés et qui sont contenus dans les Mémoires de la même Académie.
Garantie Nationale. An 9.

A PARIS, Chez DEZAUCHE Géographe, Successeur des S.rs De Lisle et Phil. Buache. Rue des Noyers.

Les Flèches indiquent la direction des Rotiles.

86

Mappemonde

et Philippe Buache
Decouvertes par Dezauche en 1808

Tis is an 1808 pocket map of the world issued by Jean-Claude Dezauche. Although based upon the Guillaume de L'Isle and Jean-Nicolas Buache de la Neuville map of 1785, this map followed the significant explorations of Captain Cook, Jean Francois de Galaup comte de La Pérouse, and George Vancouver. The voyages of these successive titans of exploration lifted the veil on many previously unknown coastlines of the world, particularly the American Pacific Northwest, Australia, the Pacific, and the northeast parts of Asia. Nevertheless, despite a wealth of new information, many of the speculations of the previous century remained, some of which may have been based on fact, and others of which are purely fictitious. One such was the legend of Fousang, identified here near modern day Alaska or British Columbia.

Here we find identified "Fousang des Chinois." This referred to little known records of a Chinese attempt to settle the west coast of America in the second century BC. First mentioned by Buddhist missionary Hui Shen in Chinese records of the 5th century, and again in a 7th century text by Yao Silian, Fousang was a Chinese colony supposedly located some 8,000 km east of China. The prominent French historian Joseph de Guignes embraced this idea in a publication on the subject in 1761. Subsequently, cartographers began including it in maps of the region. Today this legend is known only among enthusiasts of early maps and Chinese historical scholars, but occasional anomalous archeological evidence for an early Chinese presence on the west coast of America does come to light. Even so, the legend of Fousang remains, by any estimation, pure speculation.

Cartographer

Jean-Claude Dezauche (1750-1824) was a French map publisher active in Paris during the first half of the 19th century. Dezauche was often criticized for republishing earlier maps by Phillipe Buache and Guillaume de L'Isle, whose copper plates he acquired from Jean-Nicolas Buache, in 1780. These original plates were nevertheless revised considerably and his maps were widely distributed in their day.

Cartography of Colonialism

As European kingdoms expanded into global empires through colonization, their maps began to reflect national cartographic visions. Colonialism was not a mere political expansion, rather it was a reaching-out of all aspects of society including political, religious, social, military, and economic elements. Nor was colonialism a simple conquest, instead, it moved forward on the underlying assumption of cultural superiority and the profound belief that the invading party was "improving" the circumstances of the invaded.

With regard to European colonialism, this sense of supremacy derived not from militaristic, but rather from cultural and spiritual dominance. At the time, Europeans were the beneficiary of a unique synthesis of ideas: the Greco-Roman philosophical ethic of rational thought and the Judeo-Christian belief in a constant progression toward heaven. The result was a potent ideological system that combined cultural and religious expansionism with rapid technological advancement.

Typically, the earliest cartographic expressions of this ideology appear in the form of religiously themed maps. It was believed that paradise could only be achieved once the world had converted fully to Christianity. Many maps emerged that addressed this theme by dividing the world into various groups to be systematically addressed by missionary efforts: Christians; other Abrahamic religions such as Judaism and Islam; pagans, generally defined as those who were aware of but did not follow Christianity; and heathens, those who had never been exposed to Biblical teachings. Such maps allowed missionaries to prioritize their evangelism. Other Abrahamic religions were not liked, but could be tolerated. Pagans were perceived as akin to problem children who strayed from the righteous path and were in need of more forceful admonition. Heathens, on the other hand, were, literally, believed to be starving for the word of God.

The other major expression of colonialism in cartography appeared through commerce. Following in the wake of conquistadores and missionaries, merchants established global trading empires, sending their ships and caravans to all corners of the world in search of goods and, ultimately, wealth. The stamp of commerce on cartography was not as clear-cut as that of religion, but its presence was undeniable. The paintings of Dutch master Vermeer, for example, often feature wall maps in the background, adorning the homes of the wealthy merchants who provided his commissions. These wall maps, as well as world-spanning nautical charts and other maps, were not merely decorative, nor were they used for day-to-day navigation or travel. Instead, they were intended for the merchant princes of Europe to peruse in their luxurious offices while planning trading missions to China, the Spice Islands, the New World, or the African coast.

Nationalistic pride also found its way into colonial era maps. Few nations of this era were more nationalistic, or better at building and maintaining global empires than the British.

The "British Empire" map became a common feature in English atlases and wall maps issued in the 18th and 19th centuries. Typically, such maps illustrated British colonies and possessions with red highlighting, red being the color of the monarchy.

The British were justly proud of their foreign territories, hence the expression, 'The Sun Never Sets on the British Empire.'

The British, through colonialism and trade, accomplished something unique in the history of the world, a global empire where the disparate and significant parts were geographically disconnected from one another. In addition, many British cartographers of the period, while certainly producing significant and unique work, were also not above coopting the best of foreign cartography, and, in true colonial fashion, making it distinctly "British."

Maps of the colonial era were powerful expressions of cultural, economic, and military dominance. They illustrated the world through the eyes of the global empires that created them, laying down both the present situation, as understood by the cartographer, and the expectation of greater conquests to follow. While it is right to criticize the evils of the colonial era, and there were indeed many, the cartographic triumphs of this period, often achieved at a high price, must also be acknowledged.

Designatio Orbis Christiani

Thisc 1607 map by Gerard Mercator was a beautiful example of the early thematic mapping. Illustrating the global distribution of religious ideologies, the map was centered on Africa and extended from Central America to Japan. Symbols were adopted to indicate religious groups, among them a crescent for Islam, a cross for Christianity, and an arrow for "idolatry."

Cartography advocating the propagation of Christianity throughout the world was a common theme in the 17th and 18th centuries. It was believed that, once a certain "critical mass" of the global population was converted to Christianity the long awaited "Judgement Day" would arrive and the faithful would be elevated to paradise. This map was meant to convey to Christian missionaries just how much work lay ahead of them. Like many of Mercator's maps, the present example was published posthumously by Mercator's heir, Jodocus Hondius.

Cartographers

• **Gerard Mercator** (1512-1594) is a seminal figure in the history of western cartography. He was the first to introduce the idea of the "Atlas." Charles V, Holy Roman Emperor, became Mercator's patron, and commissioned several large-scale maps and a globe. Accused of heresy in 1552, Mercator fled to Germany to begin a new life, eventually revising Ptolemy's Geographia, and naming the work for the King of Mauritania, Atlas. Mercator also introduced the Mercator Projection, a unique type of world map of great importance to navigators because, if they set a course by it, they would actually arrive at their anticipated destination, an impossibility with earlier maps that had difficulty accounting for the curvature of the earth.

• **Jodocus Hondius** (1563-1612) was a Dutch cartographer active in the 17th century. Hondius revised and updated Mercator's work and the new editions became known as the "Mercator/Hondius series." Hondius also played a key role in the development of Amsterdam as the center of cartography in 17th century Europe.

Groënland

Norwegia

RUSSIA

Tenduc

Hybernia

Arglia

Moscovia

TARTARIA

Cathaio

Germa

EU

nia

RO

Graeia

Armenia

ASIA

Japan

Gallia

Italia

PA

Nato

lia

INDIA extra

Hispa

nia

Soria

Persia

Corasan

Gangem seu

Barbaria

INDIA

Chinarum

intra Gan

Reg.

A

Ægyp

Arabia

gem

Biledulgerid

tus

F

sive

R

I

Goa

Lucoma

Tombutto

Gangara

AYAMAN

GUINEA

Dangali

C

Medra

A

Abissino

rū Reg.

ORIENTALIS

Sumatra

Gilolo

Aethio

Cōgo

picus

Benomo

OCEANUS

Oceanus

tapa imeū

Deum agnoscit

Idololatrus

punit, at Ch

ignorat

S.Laurentii

Iaua

| 60 | 10 | 20 | 30 | 40 | 50 | 60 | 70 | 80 | 90 | 100 | 110 | 120 | 130 | 140 | 150 | 160 | 170 |

Universum genus hu:
manum ubique ter:
rarum vel colit Deum

Verum { verè
{ falsò
{ falsò } ut

Christianismus
Mahumetismus
Iudaismus } Cujus nota est
in hac tabula

Idololatrū verò

Falsum ut qui statuunt
eūnde esse vel essentiā

Corpoream
ut qui

Incorpoream
ut qui Demonia

Astra
Animalia
Vegetabilia

bona
mala

adorant

Carte Generale de Toutes Les Costes du Monde

This impressive large format 1703 map by Pierre Mortier was a practical nautical chart on a Mercator Projection. Rhumb lines, consistent arching paths measured by magnetic north, radiate from Ile del Pico in the Azores. While navigators would use more specific charts for day-to-day sailing, a chart like this would have been used to plan global voyages on a grand scale. The pilot or navigator needed only to orient his ship according to one of these lines and he would arrive at the desired destination. While most of the lines appeared systematic, some seemed remarkably useful, such as the rhumb line running from the British Isles to the rich cod fisheries off Newfoundland. Note also how the map offered considerable detail along coastlines and even river systems, where many locations were identified, but, in true maritime form, it had very little inland detail.

There are several elements here of considerable cartographic interest. There was a very ephemeral mapping of the Great Lakes, where at least three of the lakes were recognizable: Ontario, Erie, and Huron. In the western part of America, the R. de Nort, probably the Colorado River, had its source in an inland lake. This was most likely pure speculation, but it may also have represented early indigenous reports of the Great Salt Lake. California appeared in its insular form on the Luke Fox model with a fork-like upper coastline identified by Nouvelle Albion in deference to English claims dating to the circumnavigation of Sir Francis Drake.

On the opposite side of the world, Korea had been reattached to the mainland and was no longer insular. Hokkaido was also beginning to take form. Further north a strange peninsula extended towards north America. This was often referred to as the Witsen Peninsula, after Dutchman Nicolaes Witsen who first mapped it based upon Russian sources. The peninsula derived from the explorations of Simon Ivanovič Dezhnev, a Cossack fur trader who organized a voyage around the Chuckchi Peninsula in 1648, becoming, in the process, the first to pass through the Bering Strait, some 100 years before Vitus Bering.

Cartographer

Pierre Mortier (1661-1711) was a cartographer, engraver, and print seller based in Amsterdam. Mortier's outstanding nautical atlas, Le Neptune Francois, was his best-known work. His son, Cornelius Mortier later partnered with Johannes Covens, his brother-in-law, to form the prolific firm of Covens and Mortier.

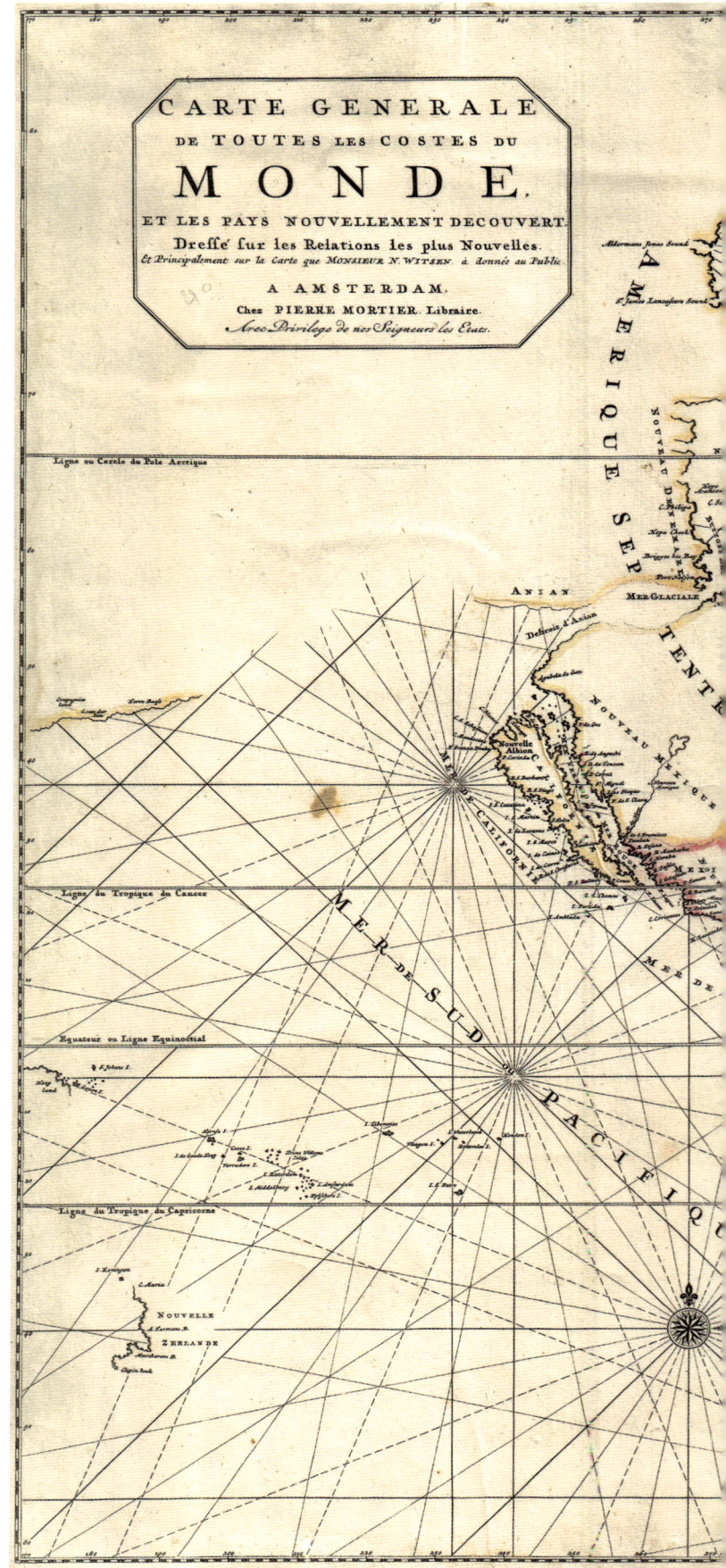

CARTE GENERALE DE TOUTES LES COSTES DU MONDE. ET LES PAYS NOUVELLEMENT DECOUVERT. Dressé sur les Relations les plus Nouvelles. Et Principalement sur la Carte que MONSIEUR N. WITSEN, à donnée au Public. A AMSTERDAM. Chez PIERRE MORTIER, Libraire. Avec Privilege de nos Seigneurs les Etats.

CARTE GENERALE
DES COSTES DE
L'AMERIQUE,
SUR L'OCEAN.
et les Pays Nouvellement decouvert.
Dressé sur les Relations les plus Nouvelles.
A AMSTERDAM.
Chez PIERRE MORTIER Libraire
Avec Privilege de nos Seigneurs les Cours

PARTIE ORIENTALE
DU MONDE.
Qui Contiennent
L'EUROPE,
L'ASIE, et
L'AFRIQUE.
A AMSTERDAM.
Chez PIERRE MORTIER Libraire.
Avec Privilege de nos Seigneurs les Cours

MER GLACIALE

MER DE TARTARIE

MER DE MOSCOVIE

GROENLANDE

NOUVEAU
GROENLANDE

ISLANDE

RUSSIE BLANCHE ou
MOSCOVIE

GRANDE TARTARIE

EUROPE

ASIE

OCEAN
ATLANTIQUE

NOUVELLE FRANCE

VIRGINIE
CAROLINE

ALLEMAGNE

SAVOYE

PERSE
EMPIRE DU
GRAND MOGOL

CHINA

MER DU NORT

MER DE MEXIQUE

Isles Lucayes

Isles Antilles

Isles Caribes

AFRIQUE
BULGERIS

LE SAARA ou LE FLE DESERT

PAYS DES NEGRES

ETHIOPIE

MER DE GUINEE

AMERIQUE
AMAZONES

MERIDIONALE

OCEAN MERIDIONAL ou ETHIOPIEN

OCEAN ORIENTAL ou MER DES INDES

NOUVELLE
HOLLANDE

Ligne du Tropique du Capricorne

MER MAGELLANIQUE

MER DU CHILI

CARTE GENERALE

DOMAINES, QUE LES
LA GRANDE-BRETAGNE
EN EUROPE EN AFRIQUE

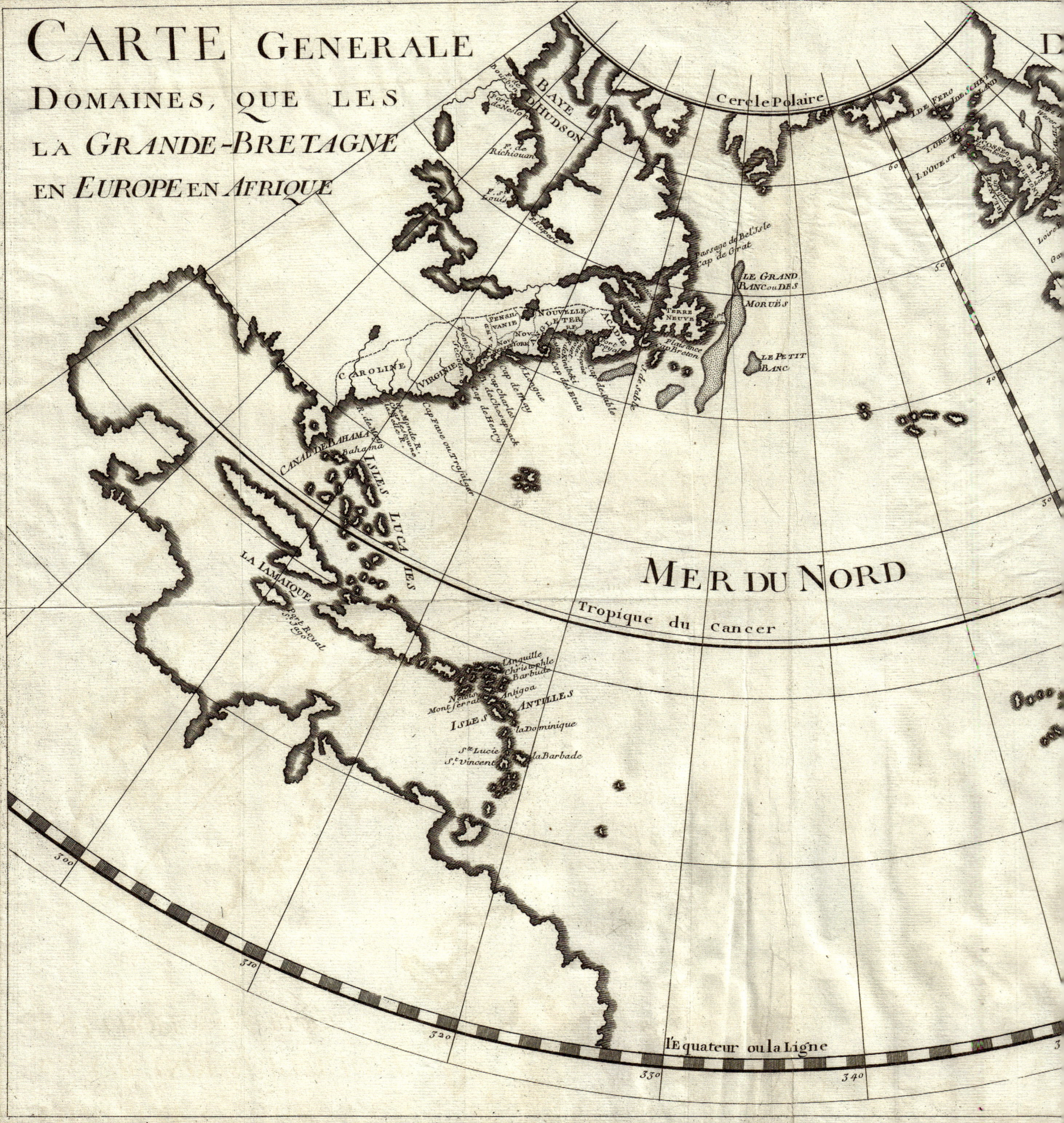

BAYE D'HUDSON

Cercle Polaire

CAROLINE

VIRGINIE

CANAL DE BAHAMA

ISLES LUCAYES

Bahama

LA IAMAIQUE

Port Royal

ISLES ANTILLES

Anguille
Christophle
Barbuda
Neiv's
Montserrat Antigoa
la Dominique
St.e Lucie la Barbade
St.e Vincent

NOUVELLE TER.

ACADIE

TERRE NEUVE

Plaisance

Cap Breton

LE GRAND BANC ou DES MORUËS

LE PETIT BANC

Passage de Bel'Isle
Cap de Grat

MER DU NORD

Tropique du Cancer

l'Equateur ou la Ligne

300

310

320

330

340

S ROYAUMES ETATS &

ROIS & LA COURONNE DE

ONT POSSÉDEZ OU POSSÉDENT

& EN *AMERIQUE*.

Tom. XII. pag. 1.

BARBARIE

GUINÉE

CÔTE D'OR

Premier Meridien

J. Ste Helene

*L'Angleterre posséde au
dela de la Ligne l'Isle de
Ste Helene situeé a 15. d. 55. m.
de Longitude sous les 17. d. de
Latitude sud.*

Carte Generale des Royaumes, Etats et Domaines

This map of the English dominions was in the form of a triangular section of the globe. It showed the British colonies in Europe, Africa, and the Americas in 1724. British claims in the New World were shown as well as British claims in France, the West Indies, Africa, and The Netherlands. From the Mediterranean to the Gulf of Mexico, and from the Polar Circle to the Equator, this map depicted the world as it was viewed by the British before the Seven Years' War.

This map was intimately connected to the rise of the House of Hanover in England during a period of extensive global expansion of British culture and sovereignty. George Ludwig, the German Duke of Brunswick-Luneburg, became George I of Great Britain when he assumed the thrones of Ireland and England in 1714. The 1701 Act of Settlement barred Catholics from ascending to the British throne. When Queen Anne died, more than 50 contenders were ahead of George I in the line of succession; nevertheless, he was the closest living Protestant and so assumed the mantle. The Hanovers were a German royal dynasty who held titles not only in England, but also in Germany, then under the Holy Roman Empire, and France. These intricate royal networks were on display here.

This map was included in a 1724 book entitled *L'Histoire d'Angleterre* by Paul de Rapin de Thoyras. Although originally printed in French, *L'Histoire d'Angleterre*, was even more successful in its English translation, which was prepared by Tindal.

Cartographer

Paul de Rapin de Thoyras (1661-1725) was a French historian. Rapin de Thoyras fled to the Netherlands following the revocation of the Edict of Nantes in 1685. There, his scholarship attracted the patronage of William of Orange. When, in 1688, William ascended the British throne as William III, Rapin de Thoyras followed him, settling in England as royal historian.

95

Essay d'une Carte Reduite

his elegant map and nautical chart on a Mercator Projection was published in 1778 by Jacques-Nicolas Bellin. Bright and calm, the world was presented here with the precision of an engineer, which of course is what Bellin was. The focus on usability at sea was likely to have made traversing the vast and volatile oceans a more manageable endeavor.

In North America, French hopes of connecting their colonies in Louisiana and Canada with the Pacific Ocean, and hence the rich markets of Asia, were still strong. The apocryphal River of the West (*Fl. de l'Ouest*), extending inland from the American west coast near Oregon, can be found in many maps of this era. Here it appeared to connect, through a variety of waterways, the west coast with the Great Lakes and thus the Mississippi Valley and, ultimately, the Atlantic.

Much of the American West was still shrouded in mystery. Drawing on limited information from the explorations of La Salle, de Soto, and de Coronado, lands west of the Mississippi were notably vague. Hopeful legends of the Seven Cities of Gold, founded by wealthy Spaniards fleeing the invasion of the 12th century Moors, were reflected here in the identification of Teguayo and Quivira in modern day California, Nevada, and Utah.

Australia (New Holland) was mapped with an uncertain southern border and Tasmania (Van Diemen's Land) was mistakenly connected to the mainland. Mapped twice, New Zealand was correct in its shape and location while New Guinea remained fully unexplored. Numerous Polynesian islands were noted, although most had yet to find their correct positions. The Aleutian Islands were identified here as *Archipel du Nord* and were beginning to take on recognizable form. The *Dépôt des Cartes et Plans de la Marine* updated and reissued many of Bellin's excellent maps long after his death – as in the present example.

Cartographer

Jacques-Nicolas Bellin (1703-1772) was the Hydrographer and Ingénieur Hydrographe for France's Dépôt des cartes et plans de la Marine *for more than 50 years. Bellin produced hundreds of maps, some of great importance, and composed nearly 1400 articles on geography for Diderot's historic Encyclopedie.*

MER GLACIALE

GROENLANDE

MER DU NORD

ISLANDE

LAPONIE OU

SPITZBERG

SAMOJEDES

JAKUTI

LES OSTIACS

LES TUNGUS

JUCAGRI

EUROPE

MOSCOVIE

SUEDE

POLOGNE

HONGRIE

UKRAINE

A S I E

S I B E R I E

T A R T A R I E

PAYS DES ELUTS

PAYS DES KALKAS

MONGOL

OCÉAN SEPTENTRIONAL

ISLES BRITANIQUES

ISLES ACORES

MER MEDITERRANÉE

TURQUIE EUROP.

TURQUIE ASIAT.

PERSE

BUKARIE

THIBET

TARTARIE CHINOISE

CHINE

LES ISLES DU JAPON

TERRE DE LA COMPAGNIE

TERRE DU JESO

OCÉAN OCCIDENTAL

Tropique du Cancer

ISLES DU CAP VERD

ISLES CANARIES

BARBARIE

SARA ou LE DESERT

AFRIQUE

NEGRETIE

GUINÉE

ABISSINIE

ÉTATS DU MOGOL

BENGALE

PRESQUISLE

I. de Ceylan

GOLFE DE BENGALE

Tropique du Cancer

ISLES MARIANES

MER DES INDES

Equateur

Ligne Equinocuale

OCÉAN MÉRIDIONAL

CONGO

MONOMOTAPA

CAFRERIE

Cap de Bonne Esperance

OCÉAN ORIENTAL

Tropique du Capricorne

NOUVELLE HOLLANDE

Terre d'Endract

Terre de Diemen

NOUVELLE GUINÉE

PARAGUAY

TUCUMAN

BUENOS AIRES

MÉRIDIONAL

NOUVELLE ZELANDE

Terre de Diemen

Antipodes de Paris

Cercle Polaire Antarctique

OUEST

NORD

EST

SUD

Heures du Matin — Midi XII à Paris — Heures du Soir

Échelle reduite de lieues Marines de France et d'Angleterre de 20 au Degré

Tome Ier. in 8°. après la Préface.

97

British Empire, Showing the Commercial Routes of the World

This handsome 1895 map by John Cassell presented commercial shipping routes and ocean currents throughout the world. This map could be viewed as a glorification of the extensive reach of the British Empire. Colored red, the areas under British rule included the British Isles, India, New Zealand, Australia, Belize, Cyprus, and parts of Africa, Borneo, and New Guinea.

The development of steamships had a profound impact on the world by altering the speed, cost, and risk of sailing. Steamship lines were shown in the inset maps along the bottom. The first inset map showed steamship lines in Central America and the West Indies. The second inset map showed steamship lines in Western Europe and the third showed steamship lines in the eastern Mediterranean.

Published by the London Times newspaper, the *Times Atlas of the World* became an iconic British production. The first edition was printed in 1895 and editions frequently included over a hundred maps. Many of the maps published in the *Times Atlas of the World* were derived from Cassell's 1893 *Universal Atlas* which was also printed in London. Ironically, as they were considered by some to be an expression of British superiority, Cassell's maps were themselves derived from a German publication.

Cartographer

John Cassell (1817-1865) was an English entrepreneur, coffee trader, and publisher active in London during the middle part of the 19th century. He was the son of a tavern owner and, curiously, he embraced the temperance movement, publishing the Teatotler Times. *This map was published well after Cassell's death, but maintained his imprint due a continued partnership with the firm of Petter & Galpin.*

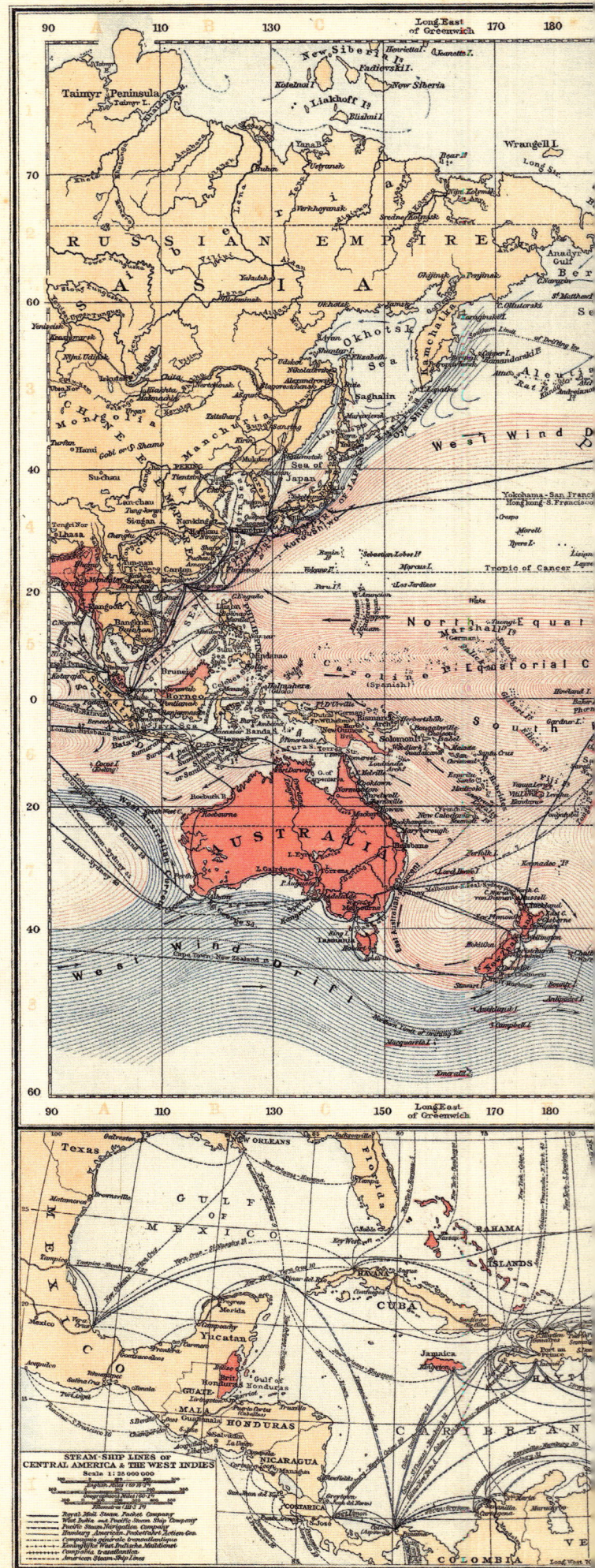

NORTH AMERICA

BRITISH NORTH AMERICA

Baffin Land

Greenland

Alaska (United States Territory)

UNITED STATES

MEXICO

PACIFIC OCEAN

North Equatorial Current

Equatorial Counter Current

Equatorial Current

Brazil

AFRICA

SAHARA

ATLANTIC OCEAN

Congo State

GUINEA

EUROPE

ASIA

RUSSIA

Barents Sea

Kara Sea

Arctic Circle

Spitzbergen

Iceland

INDIA

Tibet

CALCUTTA

BAY OF BENGAL

INDIAN OCEAN

Equatorial Current

Equatorial Counter Current

Tropic of Capricorn

Brazil Current

Cape Horn Current

Agulhas

West Wind Drift

West Wind Drift

West Wind Drift

Northern Limits of Drifting Ice

Tristan da Cunha

Kerguelen

Gulf Stream

Irminger Current

Equator

Scale of Miles on the respective Latitudes:

Geographical Miles (60 = 1° at the Equator)
Equatorial Scale 1 : 90.000.000.

Warm Currents   Cold Currents

British Empire

Overland Telegraph
I Anglo-American Telegr. Company (London)
II Direct United States Cable Comp.
III Cuba Submarine Telegr. Comp.
IV West Indies and Panama Tel. Comp.
V West Coast of America Tel. Comp.
VI Western and Brazilian Tel. Comp.
VII Brazilian Submarine Tel. Comp.
VIII Direct Spanish Tel. Comp.
IX Spanish Nat. Submar. Tel. Comp.
X India Rubber, Guttapercha, and Telegraph Works Comp. (London)
XI Eastern and South African Tel. Comp.

Submarine Telegraphs (Cables)
XII Eastern Telegraph Comp. (London)
XIII Indo-European Tel. Comp.
XIV Black Sea Telegraph Comp.
XV Eastern Extension, Australasian and China Telegr. Comp. (London)
XVI Vereinigte deutsche Kabelgesellsch. (Berlin)
XVII Grosse Nordische Telegr. Ges. (Copenhagen)
XVIII Compte Franc. Paris New York (Paris)
XIX Commercial Cable Comp. (New York)
XX Western Union Telegr. Comp.
XXI Markonis Telegr. Comp.
XXII Central & S.W. American Tel. Comp.

Steam-ship Lines with duration of passage in days
British Steam-ship Lines

Principal Railways
Equatorial limits of floating ice

STEAM-SHIP LINES FROM THE PORTS OF WESTERN EUROPE
Scale 1:25.000.000

ENGLAND
LONDON
FRANCE
PARIS
SPAIN
Madrid
MOROCCO
ALGERIA
Meridian of Greenwich

Royal Mail Steam Packet Comp.
West Indies and Pacific Steam Ship Comp.
White Star, Cunard Line
American Line
Anchor Line
North German Lloyd
South Steam Ship Co. & East Coast Line
Union Steam Ship Co.
Messageries Maritimes
British and African Steam Navigation Co.
African Steam Ship Comp.
New Zealand Shipping Comp.
Leyland & Bibb to Liverpool
Hamburg-South Amerikan. Ste. line
Norddeutscher Lloyd
Hamb. Südamerik. Dampfschifff. Ges.
Österr. Deutsche Afr.(Wörmann)
Austrian, Ungarischer Lloyd
Compagnie générale transatlantique
Hamburg to American
Navigazione Generale Italiana
Deutsch-Ostafrika
Empresa Insulana
Empreza Insulana de Navegação
Cia. Real Portugueza
Rodez-Loanda
For Stea to the East see adjoining map.

BOSNIA
SERVIA
BULGARIA
East Rumelia
TURKEY
GREECE
ASIA MINOR
CONSTANTINOPLE
Adrianople
Salonika
Sicily
Crete
Cyprus
TRIPOLI
BARCA
EGYPT
Cairo
IRAN

EASTERN STEAM-SHIP LINES
Scale 1:25.000.000

Peninsular and Oriental Steam Nav. Co.
Orient Line
British India Steam Nav. Co.
Norddeutscher Lloyd
Austria Dampfsch. Rhederei
Österreich. Ungarischer Lloyd
Fraissinet & Co.
Navigazione Generale Italiana and Florio Rubattino
Austro-Hungarian Lloyd
Spanish Ships
Hellenic Steam Ship Co.
Egyptian Mail Steam Ship Co.
Russian Steam Navigation Co.

The Oriental Perspective
The East Asian Global Vision

The East Asian cartographic tradition evolved in isolation, separate from the influence of contemporaneous European cartographic developments for several hundred years before the two very different cartographic styles began to influence one another. Cartographic art and science in the Far East developed in three centers, China, Japan, and Korea.

The earliest known cartographers in East Asia were Chinese. As with so many scientific and cultural developments, Chinese cartographers reached a very high state of advancement quite early in history. A Chinese legend of the Xia Dynasty (c. 2070-c. 1600 BC) describes how a River God presented the Great Yu, a descendant of the Yellow Emperor, with a map of China etched on stone. That map is long lost, but other stone maps of great antiquity survive, such as the Yu Ji Tu, or 'Map of the Tracks of Yu Gong,' which was found in the Stele Forest of Xi'an. The Yu Ji Tu Map, which focuses exclusively on China, dates to 1137. At that time, European maps were little more than basic T-O sketches in religious books, Yu Ji Tu, on the other hand, is a highly-sophisticated map laid out on a rectangular grid with a graduated scale and precise delineation of China's extensive river network.

Although the Yu Ji Tu is a highly advanced map by any historical cartographic standard, subsequent Chinese maps rarely exhibited the same level of scientific accuracy. Instead, most later Chinese maps, published in the 16th and 17th centuries, were developed using less scientific models. They were designed to showcase the glories of the Empire or for administrative use. Where European maps strove to achieve accuracy through mathematics, the Chinese built their maps on scales of religious and cultural significance. In those maps, places of importance, by whichever standard the map embraced, appeared larger, while less important places were shown to be smaller, regardless of whether one was geographically larger than the other.

Around 1600, there began to be cultural interactions between Chinese and Europeans in the form of trade and missionary activities. Probably the most cartographically significant of these was the 1602 publication of the Kunyu Wanguo Quantu (坤輿萬國全圖, "A Map of the Myriad Countries of the World"), better known as the Matteo Ricci Map, for its namesake Jesuit missionary. This map synthesized Eastern and Western cartographic styles and provided Chinese cartographers with the most up to date European cartography, including introducing the Chinese to the discovery of America. The publication of the Matteo Ricci Map had a lasting influence on Chinese cartography but it did not negate earlier, purely Chinese, cartographic traditions. These continued to flourish until the 19th century, when Chinese mapmaking underwent a period of decline. Probably, the most significant effect the Matteo Ricci Map had on Chinese cartography was the subsequent mapping of the New World on many Chinese charts. Knowledge of the Matteo Ricci Map also filtered out to neighboring countries, influencing Korean and Japanese mapmaking.

The Japanese were actively producing maps as early as the 6th or 7th century AD. Early Japanese cartography is intimately associated with Chinese geomancy, Buddhist spiritual practices, and the tradition of landscape painting. Consequently, Japanese maps are quite beautiful with rich calligraphic elements, vibrant balanced color, and pictorially rendered topography. At the same time, they are difficult to understand from a western perspective. Unlike western maps, which had a fixed orientation, Japanese maps were made to be laid out on the floor where viewers could walk around the map and study it from a variety of angles. Text, topography, and other elements were often set in several different orientations, with the main point of focus being the center of the map.

The most significant figure in Japanese cartography was Inō Tadataka (伊能忠敬, 1745-1818). Inō mastered geography, mathematics, and western astronomical sciences under the astronomer Takahashi Yoshitoki. He conceived a vast astronomical survey of Japan and spent several years lobbying the Shogunate for rights to perform the survey. He was finally granted permission to begin the work in 1800 as long has he did so with his own funds, he was 55. Inō began the project in earnest and it consumed the remaining 17 years of his life. His magnum opus, the Ino-Zu, a great map of the coastline of Japan, is a masterpiece of unprecedented cartographic genius. Many of Inō's map are accurate to 1/1000 of a degree, a near impossible achievement given the tools he used. In fact, when the British Royal Navy arrived in 1863, they found it impossible to improve upon Inō's map, so they just copied it. Sadly, the Ino-Zu, along with most of Inō's other work, was destroyed by a fire at the royal palace in 1912. Thankfully, a near complete copy was recently discovered at the Library of Congress in Washington D.C.

In terms of World Maps, Japanese cartography lagged behind due to the Sakoku (鎖国) or 'Closed Country' policy. Most Japanese world maps predating the arrival of the American Commodore Perry in 1853 were based upon a version of the Matteo Ricci Map that leaked into Japan from China during the 17th century. After the arrival of Perry's 'Black Ships' and the forced opening of Japan that followed, Japanese cartographers were quick to update their maps with the most current western cartographic data. Along with new cartographic knowledge, the American and European merchants that followed in Perry's wake introduced lithography and other modern printing techniques. In the span if a single momentous year, Japanese perspective on global cartography transitioned from the 16th century to the 19th century.

In Korea things moved a little more slowly. Where Japanese maps were influenced by the Buddhist cosmographical vision, Korean maps were Confucian and thus more retrogressive in style. While earlier Korean maps do exist, the rise of Korean cartography generally coincided with the rise of the Confucian Joseon Kingdom (1392-1897). Korean maps, even world maps, need to be understood within the Confucian context, which focused on legitimizing and centralizing political power. The first great Korean world map was the Gangnido map, a map commissioned by Joseon ministers in 1402. The Gangnido was derived from Chinese and Japanese sources but had been revised to give Joseon Korea a central place on the world stage. China, the dominant political and cultural power in East Asia, was front and center. Korea, just to the right, was nearly as large as China, a clear case of carto-advocacy for Korea's power and position in the world. In true East Asian fashion, lesser nations, places the Joseon either sought to belittle or cared little about, were reduced and distant. An excellent example was Japan, Korea's ancient nemesis, which appeared significantly reduced just to the south. Similarly, Europe, Africa, and other distant lands were also reduced. America, still undiscovered, made no appearance on the Gangnido map.

The high point of Korean cartography was most likely the 1861 publication of the Daedong Yeojido (Map of the Great East). Composed of 22 folding segments, the Daedong Yeojido was a massive construction that meticulously mapped every detail of Korea. It was issued by Kim Jeong-Ho (1804-1866) and was the first large scale map of Korea to incorporate Sino-Jesuit scientific mapmaking techniques imported from China. Kim traveled throughout Korea for more than 30 years, with his family, making detailed surveys based upon astronomical observations. When he completed the project, a legend tells that he was arrested and jailed for too accurately portraying reality. That may or may not be true, as little is known of Kim's life, but today he is a nationally recognized hero throughout Korea.

Other East Asian nations, such as the empires of Southeast Asia, also had cartographic traditions, but these were largely derivative and lacked the sophistication of Korean, Japanese, and Chinese cartography.

Complete Map of the Nine Border Towns of the Great Ming

This impressive large format 1663 (Kangxi 2) map encompassed the known world. Unlike western maps, Chinese maps were not universally based on a mathematical system, but rather on a scale of importance. In this case, the map's focus was Ming China. It was easy to orient oneself on this map by identifying the Great Wall of China running along the top of the map. The most densely annotated regions were the provinces of China.

Late Ming China operated on a Tribute system, so that even distant lands which sent missions to China were considered part of the system and thus subjects of the Ming Emperor. This map was not merely a map of China, but rather a map of the world. North America appeared as an island in the upper right quadrant. It's form, particularly the St. Lawrence river, Baja California, and the Gulf of Mexico, was, with some imagination, recognizable. South America appeared at the bottom right. It was attached to an unnamed *Terra Australis*, but both the Amazon and the Rio de la Plata were evident. Africa was rendered as a peninsula. Although the form was hard to distinguish, the presence of the Nile with a two-lake source, on the Ptolemaic model, was easy to recognize. Europe was in the upper left. The Mediterranean Sea, the Black Sea, and the Caspian Sea were all apparent, as were the general forms of Italy, the Greek peninsula, and Anatolia. England was an island off the coast.

Largely unfamiliar with western terminology, Chinese cartographers resorted to floral descriptive terminology for foreign peoples and places. South America was "the Land of Giants," probably a reference to Magellan's tales of giants in Patagonia. Other colorful terms included the "Land of the Hairy People" and the "Land of Women."

Cartographer

Wang Junfu (1650-1680) was a Chinese publisher based in Suzhou.

大明九邊萬國人跡路程全圖

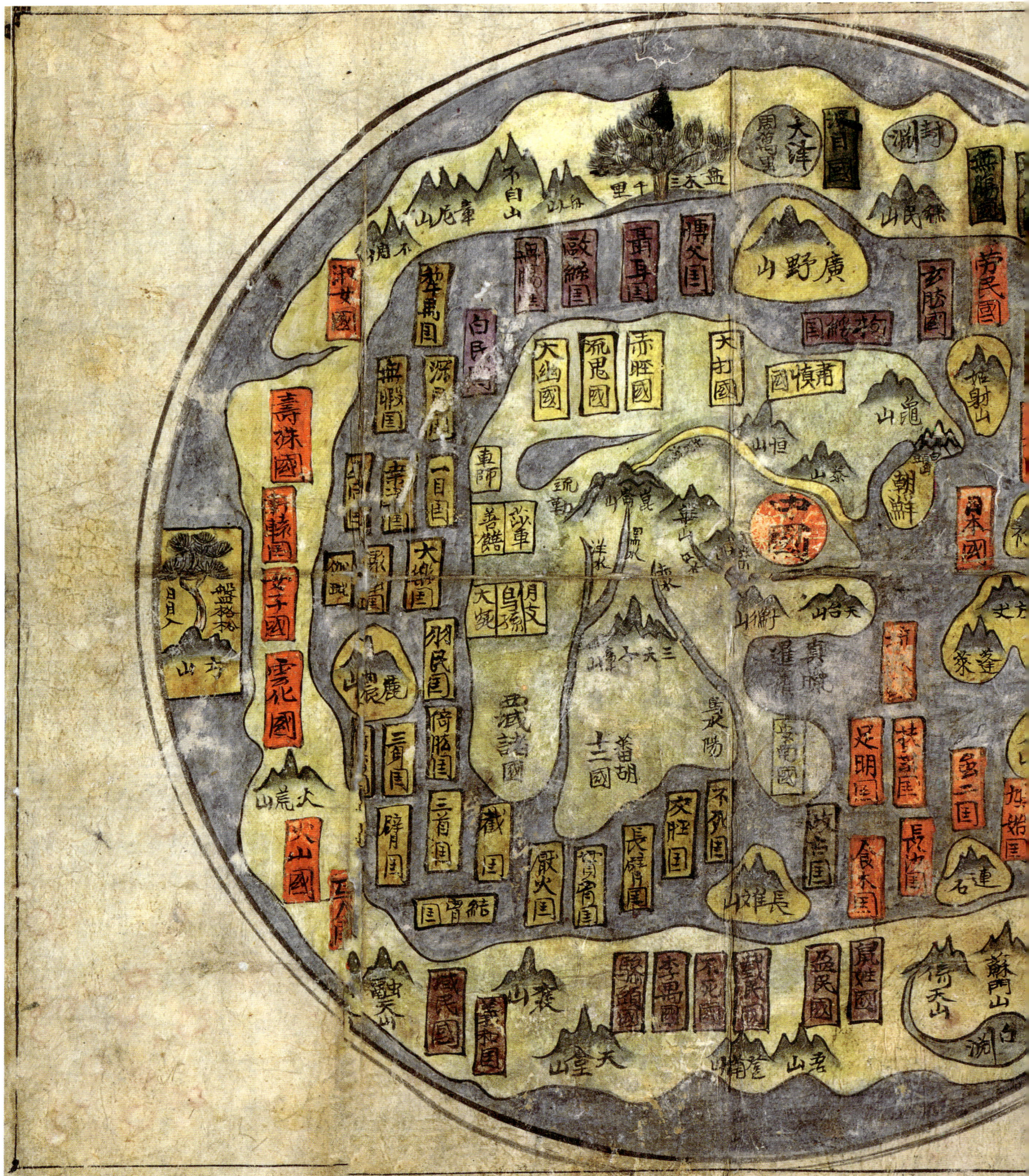

天下圖 (Cheonhado — Map of All Under Heaven)

大澤　周饒國
封　淵
無腸國
勞民國
傅父國　廣野山
雨師國　啟縷國
細柳國　玄股國
奇肱國
白民國
無啟國　深目國
大綱國　流鬼國　赤脛國　天毒國　肅慎國
拒射山　貫匈
朝鮮
中國
日本國
壽麻國　一目國
車師　菩薩
崑崙山　華山　恒山　岱山
月支國　鳥喙國　大宛
三危山
羽民國　荷股國
巫咸諸國
臂國　三首國
藏國　結胸國
貫胸國　不死國
交脛國　長臂國　長股國
厭火國
壽狩國　軒轅國　芝子國　雲化國
盤桃山　扶木
大荒山　火山國
巫女國
足明國　決胸民
長右山　食木
天帝山　昊山　騰根山
蘇門山　儋天山

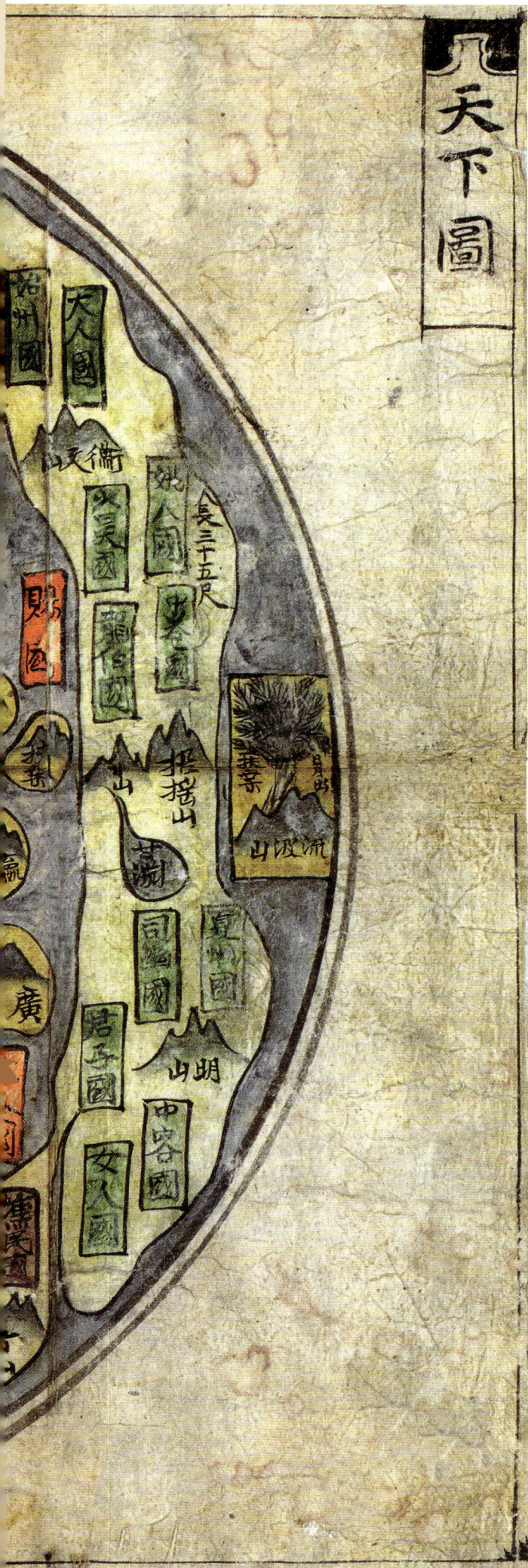

Map of all Under Heaven

This unusual Korean world map was drawn in manuscript during the middle part of the 18th century. The map was a fine example the Cheonha-do (World Map) convention popular in Korea during the Joseon period (1392-1897). There were many versions of this map, some of which were printed in woodblock while others were copied in manuscript, as with this example.

From the earliest examples of the 16th century, to later examples dating to the late 19th century, there was little variation in the general design and layout. Although distinctly Korean, this map was based upon the teachings of the Warring States Period (475-221 BC) Chinese diviner, Zou Yan. Zou Yan's teachings appeared to have been codified into map form in Korea during the 16th century.

The map presupposes a flat earth with an inner sea (Pihai, or "Little Sea") and an outer sea (YangHai, "Greater Sea"). The large red dot at the center was Beijing and the central part of the map was occupied by China. The four great rivers of China were apparent: The Yellow River (Colored Yellow), the Yangtze River (running just south of Beijing), the Pearl River (central continent, bottom right) and the Lancang River (bottom left). Korea was a yellow region just to the east of Beijing and Japan appeared just offshore. The surrounding sea was bounded by a ring of land representing the rest of the world, although most of the place names were fictional. To the right and left of the outer ring continent were the sacred trees, Busang and Bangyeoksong, believed, according to the ancient shamanistic system of Korea, to be the sites of the sun's rising and setting, respectively.

Cartographer

The cartographer is unknown.

南瞻部洲萬國掌菓之圖

106

Outline Map of All Countries of the Universe

This is one of the most important, beautiful, and influential maps ever printed in Japan. It was the model for all subsequent Japanese Buddhist world maps well into the 19th century. Printed by woodblock in 1710, this was the first Japanese printed map to depict the world, including Europe and America, from a Buddhist cosmographical perspective. This map was scaled not by distance but by religious importance. India, the birthplace of the Buddha, was the central locale on this map.

Believed to be the center of the universe, Lake Anavatapta, a whirlpool-like quadruple helix, was the legendary site where the Buddha was conceived by Queen Maya. From Lake Anavatapta, radiated a four-headed beast (the heads of a horse, a lion, an elephant, and an ox) representing the sacred rivers of the region: the Indus, the Ganges, the Brahmaputra, and the Sutlej. This map represented a significant step forward in the Japanese attempt to combine religious and contemporary geographic knowledge.

On the side of the map, a series of islands was intended to represent Europe including Umukari (Hungary), Oranda, Baratan, Komo (Holland or the country of the red hair), Arubaniya (Albania?), Itarya (Italy), Suransa (France) and Inkeresu (England). India was recognizable in its peninsular form. Japan appeared as a series of Islands in the upper right. China and Korea appeared to the west of Japan. Southeast Asia was the island cluster to the east of India. Africa appeared as a small island identified as the 'Land of Western Women.'

Cartographers

- **Zuda Rokashi Hotan** (fl. 1654-1728), founder of Kyoto's Kegonji Temple, was a prominent Buddhist scholar-priest active in Japan during the late 17th and early 18th centuries.

- **Bundaiken Uhei** (fl. 1680-1720), a Japanese publisher and bookseller, active in Kyoto during the early part of the 18th century.

All-Under-Heaven Complete Map of the Everlasting Unified Qing Empire

"All-Under-Heaven Complete Map of the Everlasting Unified Qing Empire" was the translated title of this seminal 1806 map by Qianren Huang: *Da Qing Wannian Yitong Tianxia Quantu*. This grand map was extremely rare and was often referred to by the key terms in the title, "unified under heaven" (Tianxia Quantu), with the implication that the Qing Empire was heaven. Like many Chinese maps of the world, this one was not scaled by distance but rather by degree of importance to the Qing.

A nomadic people, the Manchu Qing did not operate under a paradigm limited by geographic boundaries and that was reflected in the cartography here. Their territory extended as far as their influence. Thus, a map of Qing China was a map of the world. European countries could be found in the upper left hand corner. Portugal (Land of the Great Western Sea), The Netherlands, the Mediterranean (Little Western Sea), Arabia (Homeland of Islam), Africa (Land of the Black Ghosts) and even the Atlantic Ocean (Great Western Sea) were identified.

There were notations about various regions and peoples, with particular attention paid to how grateful they were to endure extensive hardships to pay tribute to the culturally superior Qing.

A key to the map was included on the right side. Different symbols represented different government entities and thus different types of tribute. For example, local magistrates were identified by a symbol that looks like a simple house with a triangular roof whereas a provincial capital was identified by a rectangle atop a square.

This map appeared in several editions, all attributed to Qianren Huang. The earliest was a manuscript dating to 1800, although since Qianren had died nearly 30 years earlier, it is likely that a now lost earlier version existed. The present example was issued in 1806 and was the earliest known printed version.

An important edition of 1811 in either red, green, or blue negative, was exceptionally striking.

Cartographer

Qianren Huang (1694-1771) was a Chinese cartographer active 18th century during the reign of the Qianlong Emperor. Little is known of his life, but his grandfather was Xi (1610-1695), father of Huang Baijia (1643-1709).

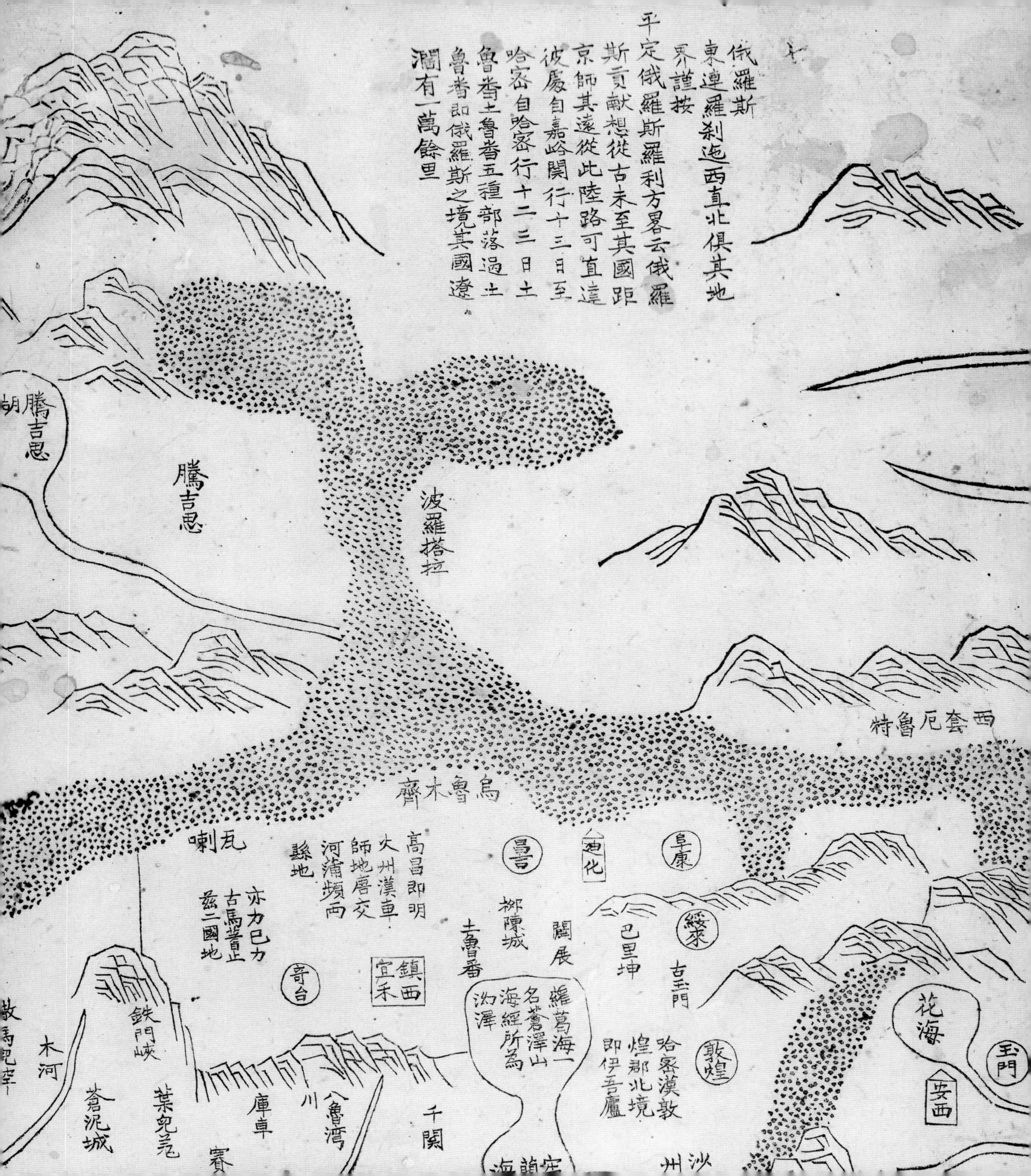

俄羅斯東連羅剎迤西直北俱其地界謹按平定俄羅斯羅利方暑云俄羅斯貢獻想從古未至其國距京師其遠從此陸路可直達彼慶自嘉峪關行十三日至哈密自哈密行十二日土魯番即俄羅斯之境其國遼闊有一萬餘里

騰吉思

胡

騰吉思

波羅搭拉

特魯厄套西

烏魯木齊

瓦喇

喇

高昌即明

火州漢車

師地唐交

河浦頻兩

縣地

昌吉

西化

阜康

綏來

敦煌

安西

玉門

花海

木河

蒼泥城

葉兒羌

鐵門峽

庫車賓

八魯灣川

亦力巴力古馬耆止茲二國地

奇台

鎮西宜禾

土魯番

闢展

椰陳城

巴里坤

哈密漢敦煌郡北境即伊吾廬

古玉門

敦煌

羅葛海一名蒼澤山海經所為沟澤

千閻海

敦馬兒

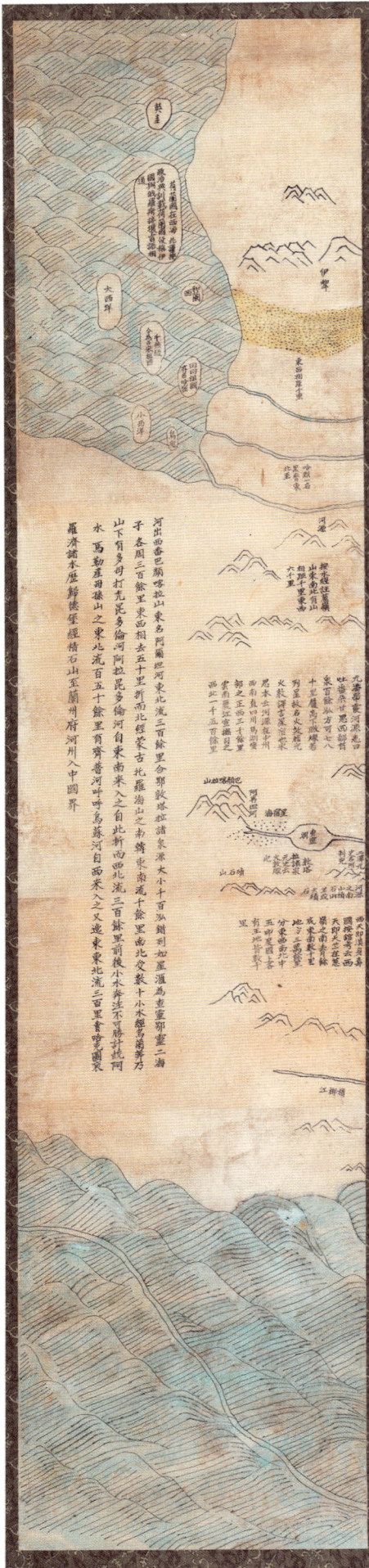

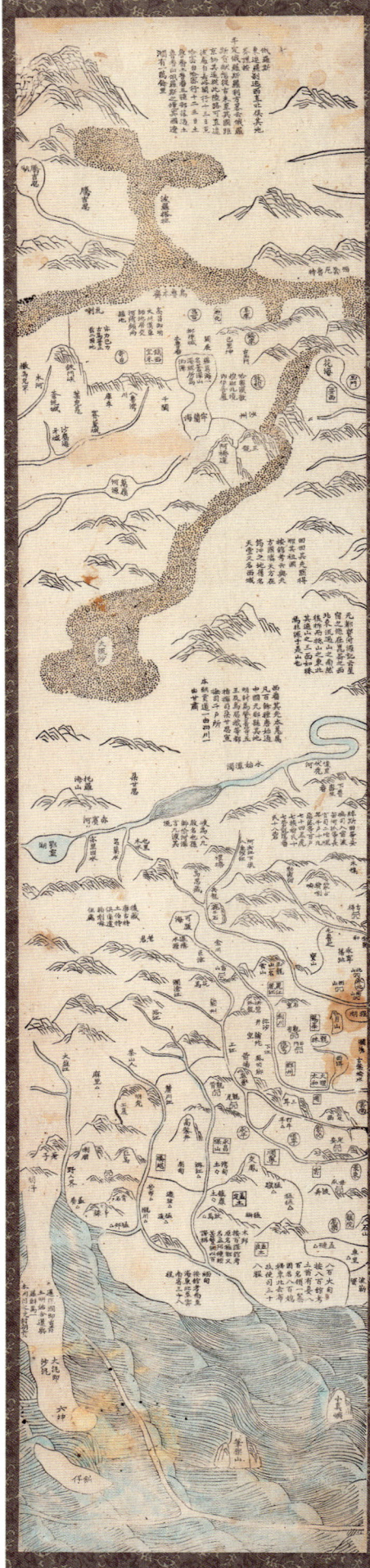

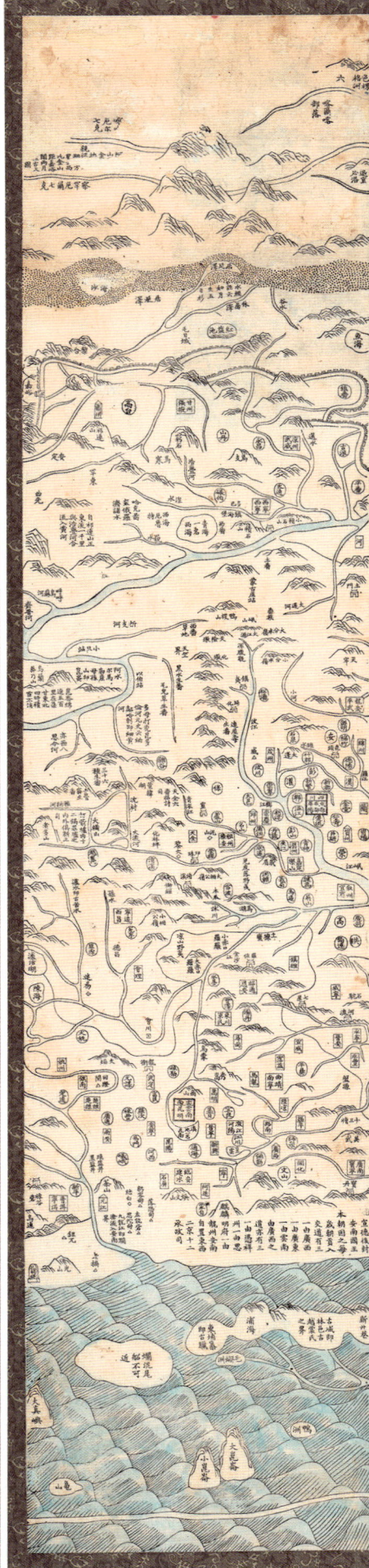

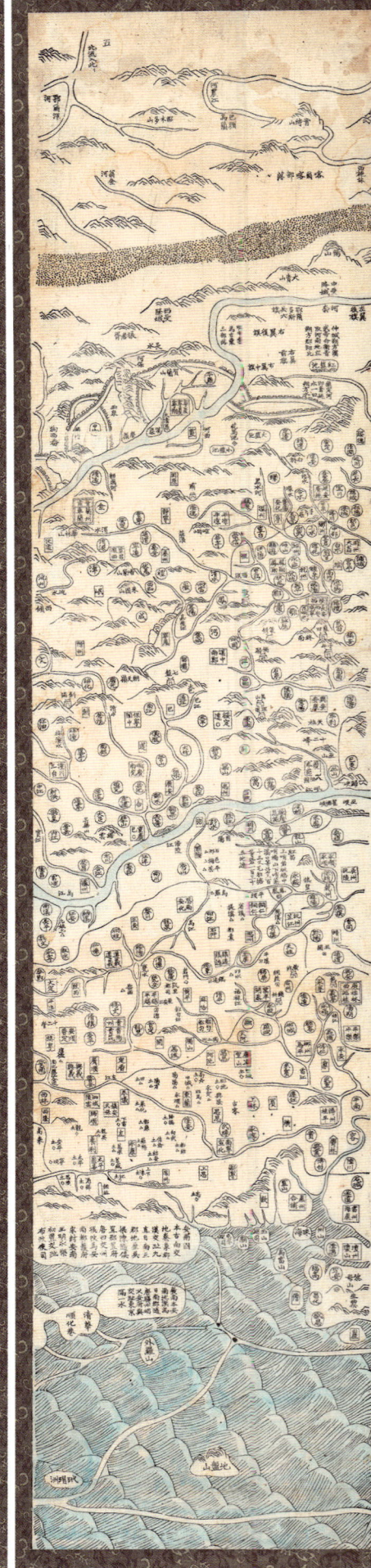

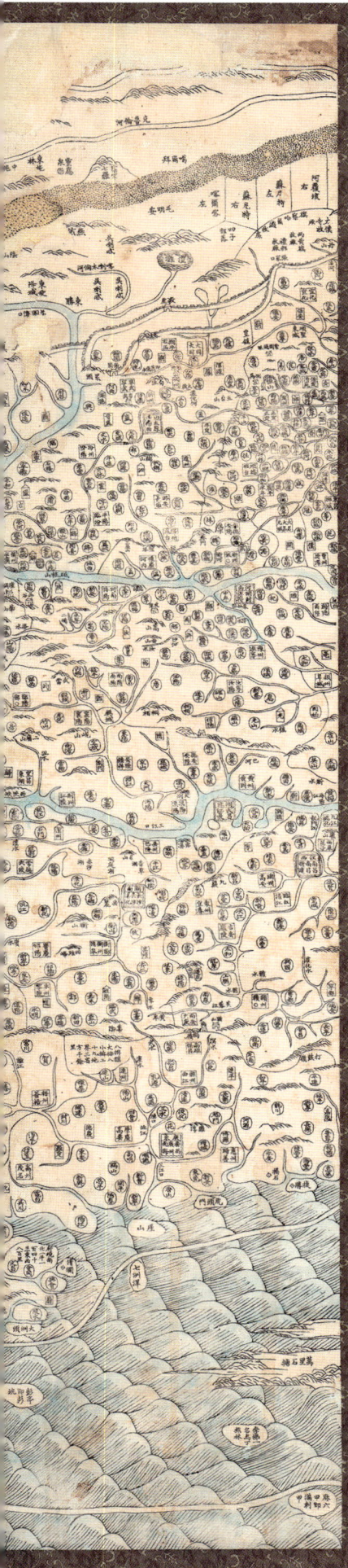

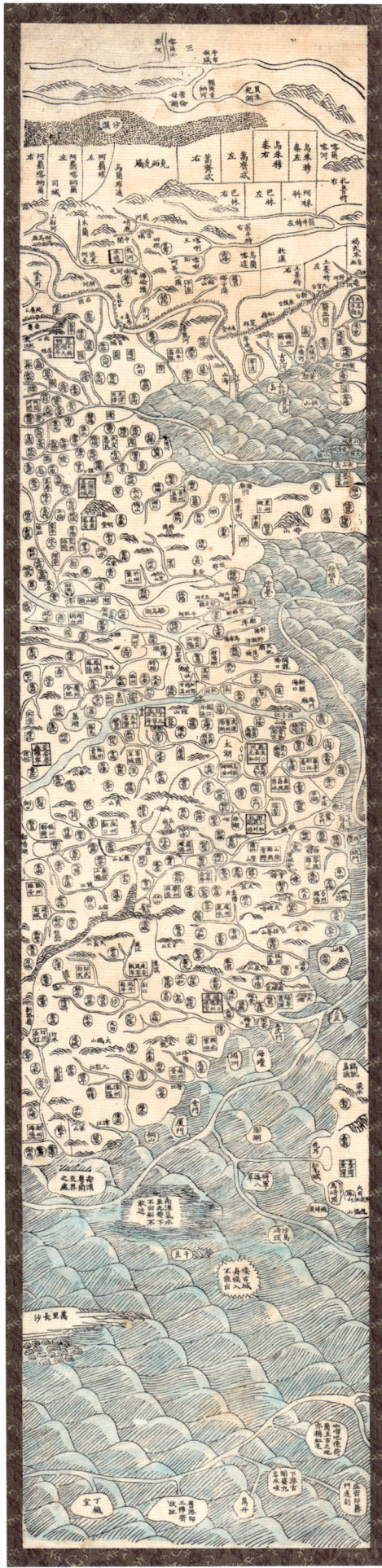

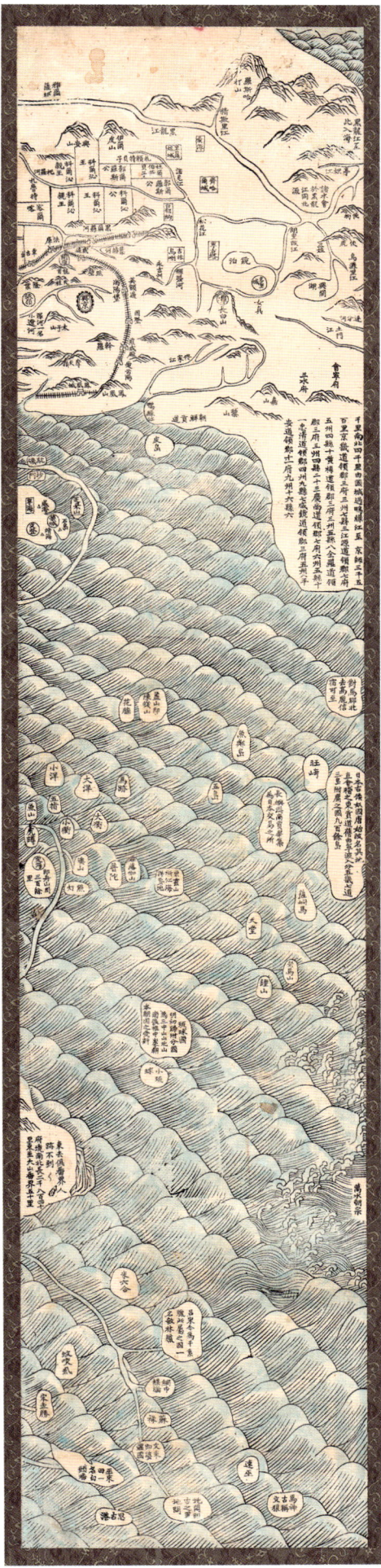

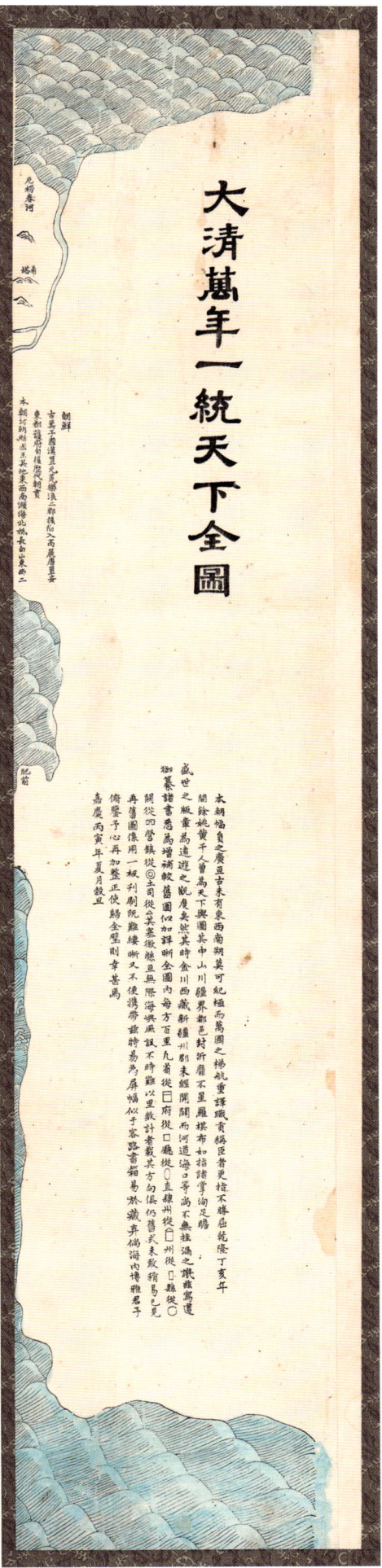

大清萬年一統天下全圖

Map of the World

Beautifully engraved in traditional Japanese woodblock style, this 1840 map titled *Oranda Chikyu Zenzu* by Ryukei Tajima illustrated the entire world on double hemisphere projection. The engraving and detail work followed the conventions of Japanese Edo era cartography: title cartouches identified each region, rivers were depicted as open waterways, and mountains were distinctively rendered in low profile.

This map can be understood as an expression of Japanese Tokugawa 220-year-old policy of seclusion. Despite being a 19th century map, the cartography here reflected European maps of the late 17th century. It was most likely copied from maps brought to China by Jesuit missionaries and traded to Japanese merchants via the Ryukyu Kingdom (Okinawa). Outdated cartographic elements included Australia conjoined with New Guinea to the north and to mythical continent of *Terra Australis* to the south. In addition, California was depicted as an island.

Cartographer

Ryukei Tajima (fl. c. 1830-1860) was a Japanese mapmaker and printer active in Tokyo during middle part of the 19th century.

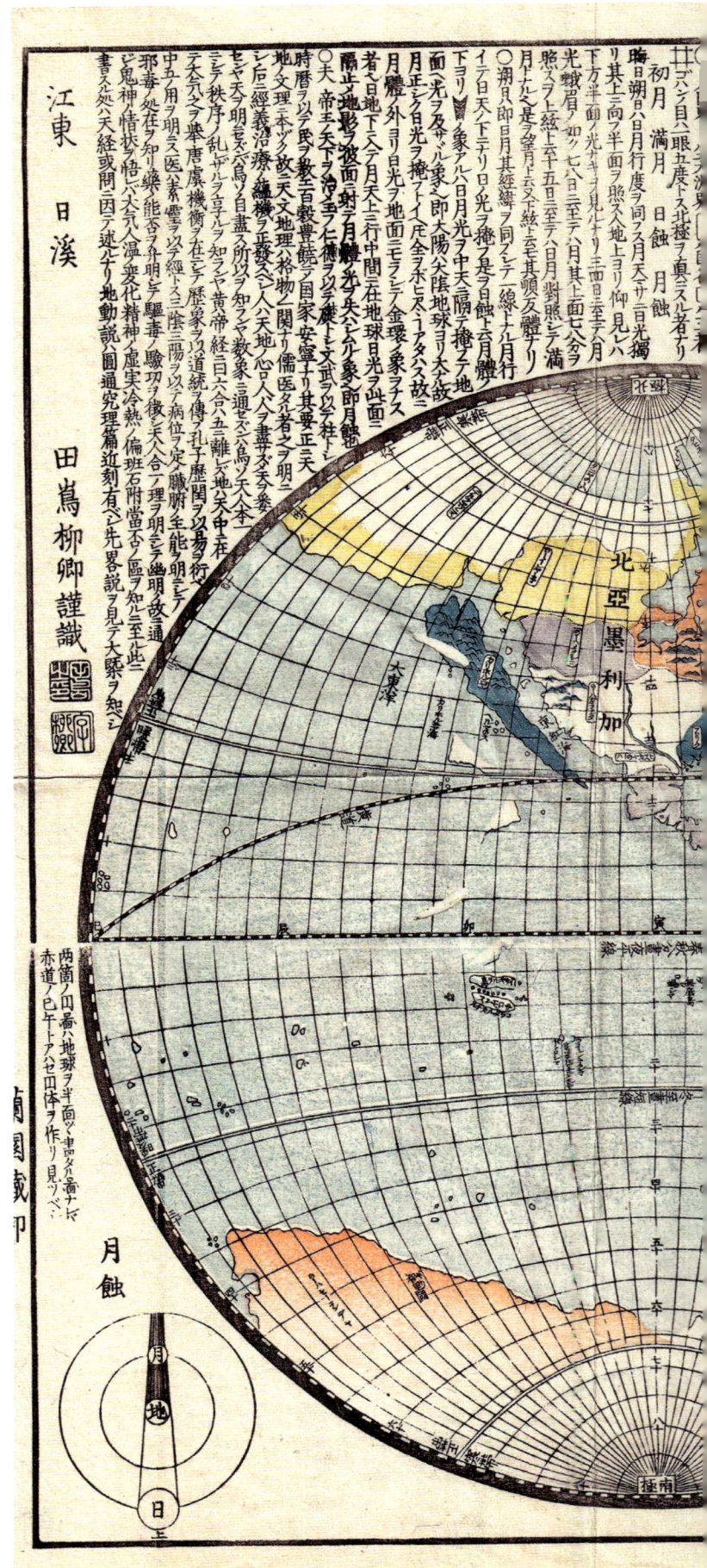

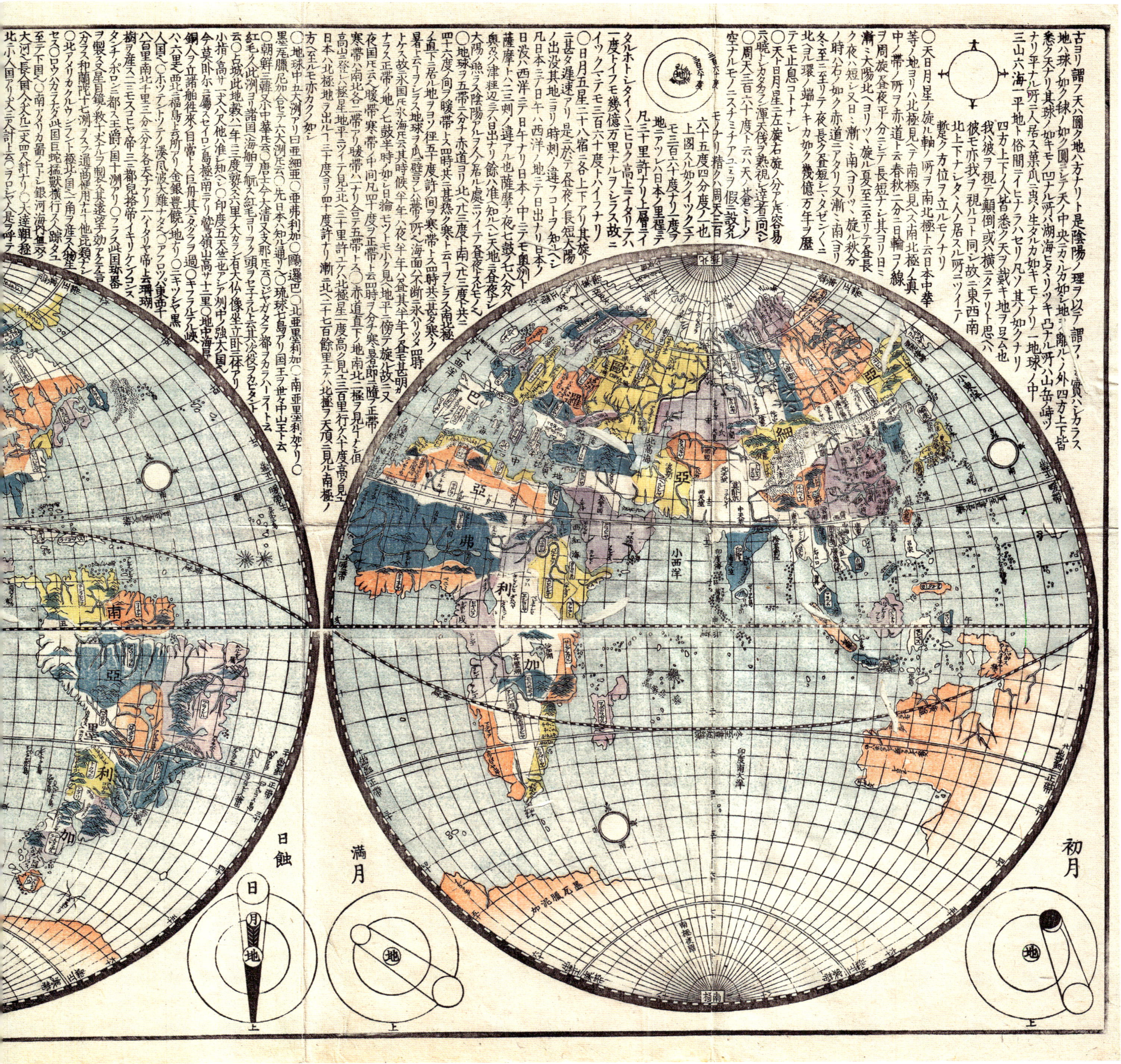

初月

満月

日蝕

地

上

南極

北極

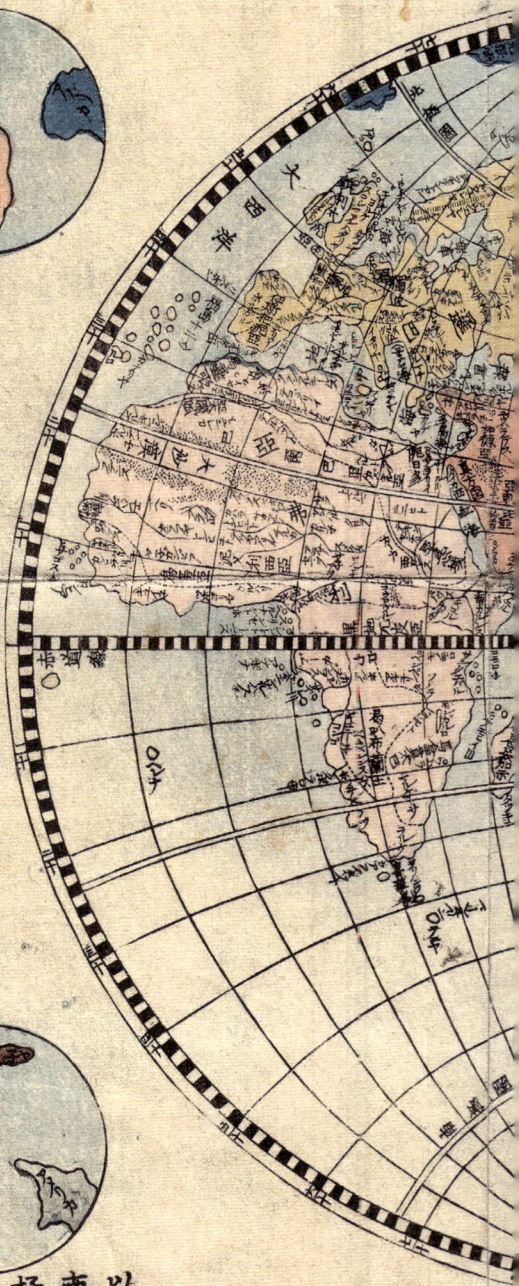

Newly Made Map of the Earth

Shinsei Yochi Zenzu or "Newly Made Map of the Earth" was the title of this important Japanese map from 1848. One of the first modern maps to appear in Japan, this map by Shinchō Kurihara and Heibē Chōjiya was based upon a French map of 1835 and incorporated most of the contemporary European cartographic knowledge of the time. Although predating Perry's 1853 opening of Japan, this map was, relative to Japanese maps issued just a few years earlier, under the seclusionist "Closed Country" or Sakoku system, considerably advanced. For example, New Zealand appeared properly as two islands, California was attached to the North American mainland, and Tasmania and Australia were accurately mapped as separate entities.

This map also exhibited several stylistic advances. Katakana, a phonetic Japanese adaptation of foreign words, replaced most of the traditional Chinese characters previously used during the Edo era to identify the names of places and geographic elements. Another change from Edo era Japanese maps was the removal of the traditional cartouche used to separate place names from geographical elements. In addition, Kurihara and Chōjiya incorporated stippling, or small dots, an advanced European map illustration technique, to indicate both shallow seas, as in the Grand Banks, and deserts, as in the Sahara.

Cartographer

Shinchō Kurihara and Heibēi Chōjiya were Japanese printers and mapmakers active in Tokyo during the 19th century.

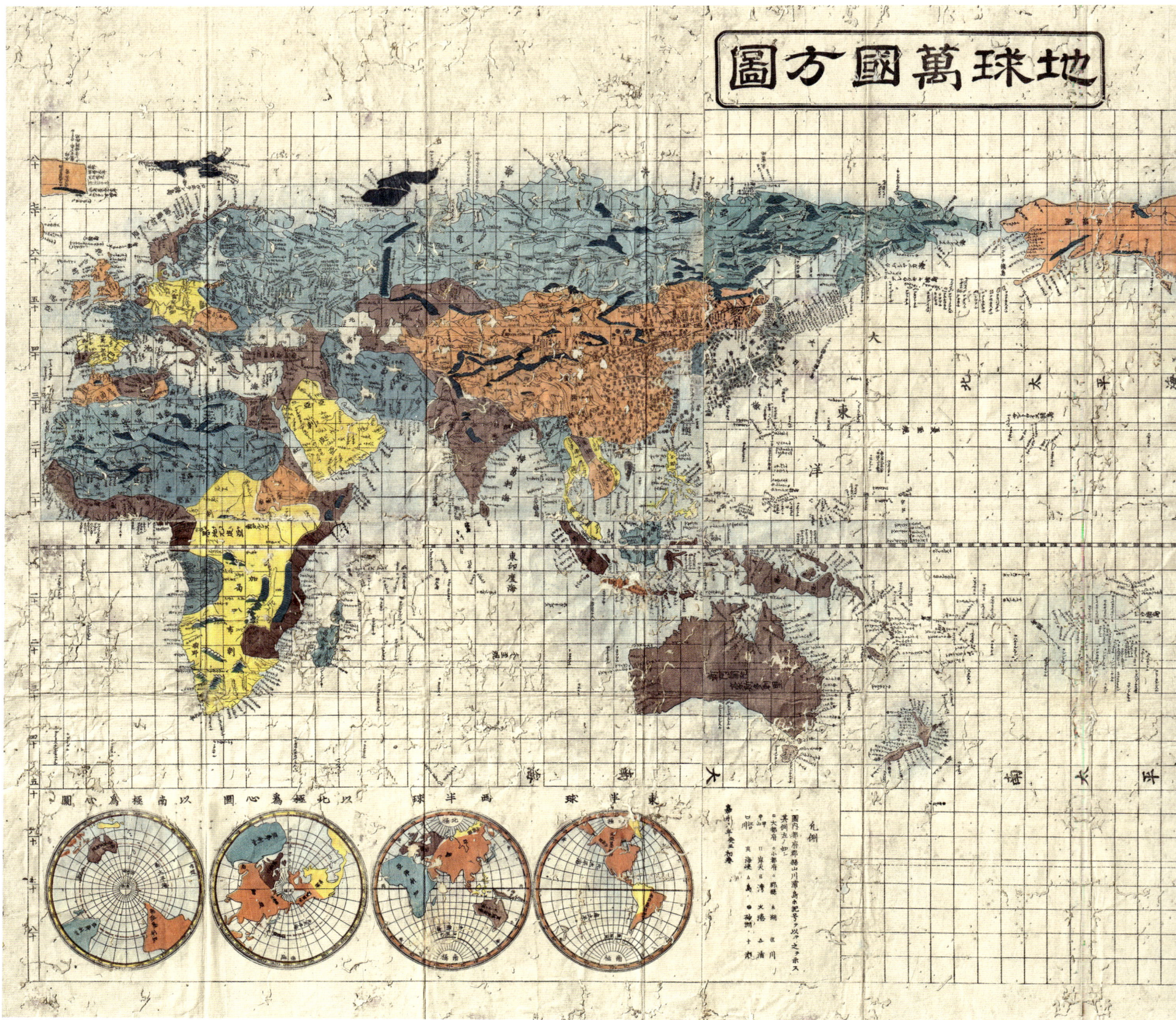

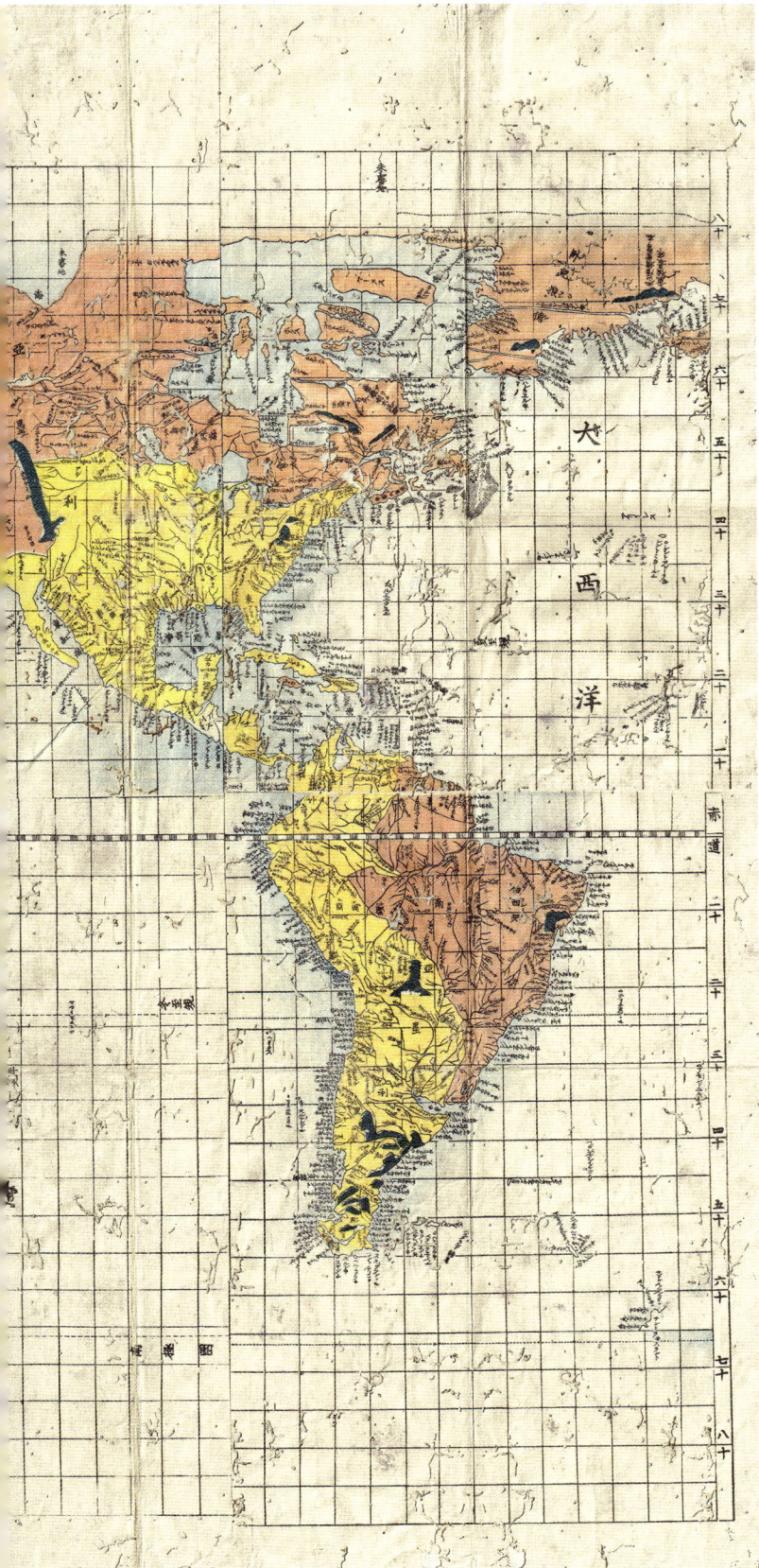

Square Map of all the Countries on the Globe

Issued by Suido Nakajima in 1853 (Kaei 6) this map called *Shintei – Chikyu Bankoku Hozu* represented a major advance in East Asian cartography. The American Commodore Matthew Perry sailed into Edo Harbor (Tokyo) with his "black ships" just before this map was issued. Through a show of force, Perry forced the Tokugawa Shogunate to open Japan to global trade by signing the Treaty of Kanagawa. Despite the aggressive approach by Perry, the exchange went both ways, and Japan benefited significantly, in subsequent decades, from exposure to foreign ideas and technologies.

One such example was this map. Although printed using traditional Japanese techniques, Nakajima's map was, in essence, a European map. It was presented on a Mercator Projection. The sophisticated cartography, reflecting the most up to date European geographical knowledge, suggested that this map was copied directly from a European prototype, which may account for the uncommonly rigid grid structure. Although we must presume the source map to have been left over from Perry's visit, the political deportment of the Pacific Northwest suggests that Nakajima copied from a British model. Note how the map honors British claims to Washington and Oregon, an oddity that would have been reversed were this based upon an American issued map.

Cartographer

Suido Nakajima (fl. c. 1850-1860) was a Japanese printer and mapmaker active during the late Tokugawa Period.

Map of the World

An amalgam of styles, this 1862 map, *Bankoku Kokai Zu*, on a Mercator Projection was issued jointly by the Japanese publisher Kango Takeda and the Dutch arms dealer, Edward Schnell. Despite being opened to western trade 9 years earlier by the 1853 arrival of the American fleet under Commodore Perry, Japan was initially reluctant to adopt western cartographic knowledge. Schnell must have brought John Purdy's 1845 English map with him to Yokohama and, recognizing an opportunity for profit, partnered with Kango Takeda to translate it into Japanese.

In recognition of global interest in Japanese trade, the Schnell-Kango map was issued with two side panels. Typically, these were both mounted to the right of the map proper, but, originally, they may have been intended to appear to either side of the map proper. The largest side panel featured illustrations of flags from various nations including most European countries, the United States, and other Asian powers. Schnell's imprint appeared in manuscript in the lower right.

Cartographer

Edward Schnell (1834-1890) was a Dutch arms dealer active in Japan. A former military man, he traveled with his brother Henry Schnell to Yokohama, Japan in search of riches in 1860, shortly after the signing Treaty of Kanagawa. He became a prominent figure in Japanese society, even taking a Japanese name, Hiramatsu Buhei, and wife, Kawai Tsugonusuke.

Home Education Round-the-World Sugoroku

This delightful Japanese pictorial map was printed by the *Osaka Mainichi Shimbun* (Osaka Daily News) in 1926. The map was a game board for a Japanese round-the-world snakes-and-ladders style game known as *sugoroku*. Navigating various paths and pitfalls, players could visit Moscow, Paris, New York, Australia, Africa, China, the Mediterranean, Jerusalem, the Alps, and even the Panama Canal, among other destinations.

The geography here may initially be difficult to visualize. The map was oriented to the west with North America at the top. The statue of Liberty helped to isolate New York. Japan was at the center, where Mount Fuji was recognizable. The British Isles appeared at the bottom of the map. It extended south as far as North Africa and the Amazon, limiting the scope of the map to the Northern Hemisphere.

Following a winding path, this playfully-illustrated game board included the Americas, Southeast Asia, India, Europe, and a variety of landmarks and mountain ranges. Planes and ships, dancers and skiers, windmills and whales, were all charmingly illustrated in a cartoonish manner. The players started in Japan and traveled to the finish line in London. The rise of visually rich game boards, made possible with advancements in printing technologies, helped to popularize this game during the Japanese Meiji and Edo periods.

Cartographer

*The **Osaka Mainichi Shimbun** (1876-present) was an Osaka-based daily newspaper active in the late 19th and early 20th centuries. The* Osaka Mainichi Shimbun *(*大阪毎日新聞, *Osaka Daily News) was founded in 1876 as* Osaka Nippo. *In 1888 it was renamed* Osaka Mainichi Shimbun. *In 1911, it merged with the* Tokyo Nichi Nichi Shimbun *(*東京日日新聞*) to become the* Mainichi Shimbun *(*毎日新聞, *Daily News).*

大阪毎日新聞附録

世界一周すごろく

家庭
音楽

北氷洋　グリーンランド

大西洋

北アメリカ

カナダ

アラスカ

北アメリカ

ツケクベ　ニューヨーク　ワントン　セントルイス　シカゴ　オタラワ　ロサンゼルス　サンフランシスコ　シャトル　バンクーバー

メキシコ

パナマ

太平洋

オーストラリア　メルボルン　オセアニア

ハワイ　ホノルル

**日本から
ロンドン**
ウラジオ 1 ホノルル
大連 2 サンフランシスコ
上海 3 シヤトル
香港 4 バンクーバー
メルボルン 5 メルボルン
（ふり出し）

東京　大阪

シベリヤ

アジヤ

ハルビン　ウラジオストック　大連　北京　上海　漢口　香港　玄界

バイカル湖

印度洋

コンボ　マドラス　ボンベイ　インド

スエズ

ヨーロツパ

ロシヤ　モスコウ　レニングラード

フィンランド　エストニヤ　リガ　リスアニヤ　ポーランド　ワルソー

ドイツ　ベルリン　ハンブルグ

スエーデン　ストツクホルム　オスロ　ノールウエー　デンマーク　コペンハーゲン

ハーグ　オランダ　ベルギー　ブラッセル　パリ　フランス　ボルドー　リヨン

イギリス　ロンドン　アイルランド

チエッコスロバキヤ　ウイン　ハンガリー　ブダペスト　プラーグ　ルーマニヤ　ブカレスト　ユーゴースラビヤ　ブルガリヤ　ソフイヤ　ベルグラード　ギリシヤ　アテネ

イタリヤ　ローマ　ベルン　スイス　ゼネバ

ルボン　スペイン　マドリド　ジブラルタル　ポルトガル　リスボン

地中海

アフリカ　スエズ　サマエル　エジプト　カイロ

**ロンドンから
日本へ**
ニューヨーク 1 ジブラルタル
パナマ 2 ヘーグ
ワシントン 3 パリ
ニューオルレアンス 4 ハンブルグ
ケベック 5 ブラッセル

北海

大西洋

くろごす月

グリーンランド

氷山

あざらし

カナダ

ナイヤガラ港布

横氏の征服した
カナヂヤン・ロッキー

白熊

アラスカ

北氷洋

ニューヨークの摩天閣

自由の神像

ワシントン記念塔

米國は世界一の自動車國

ツケツクベ

ニューヨーク

ワシントン

ナイヤガラ

シカゴ

セントルイス

米國の國技ベースボール

ロッキー山脈

合衆國

バンクーバー

シヤトル

サンフランシスコ

ゼルス

北アメリカ

ハワイ

ルル

(ロンドンへ)5
(ロンドンへ)1
(ロンドンへ)3
5(日本へ)
(日本へ)
(日本へ)
4(日本へ)
3(日本へ)
3(ヘマナパ)

**日本から
ロンドンへ**

[ヨーロッパまはり]
[アメリカまはり]

ウラヂオ **1** ホノルル
大 連 **2** サン,フランシスコ
上 海 **3** シヤトル
香 港 **4** バンクーバー
メルボルン **5** メルボルン

（ふり出し）

東京

大阪

ウラヂオストック

朝鮮人の長煙管

日本

世界一
家庭
教音

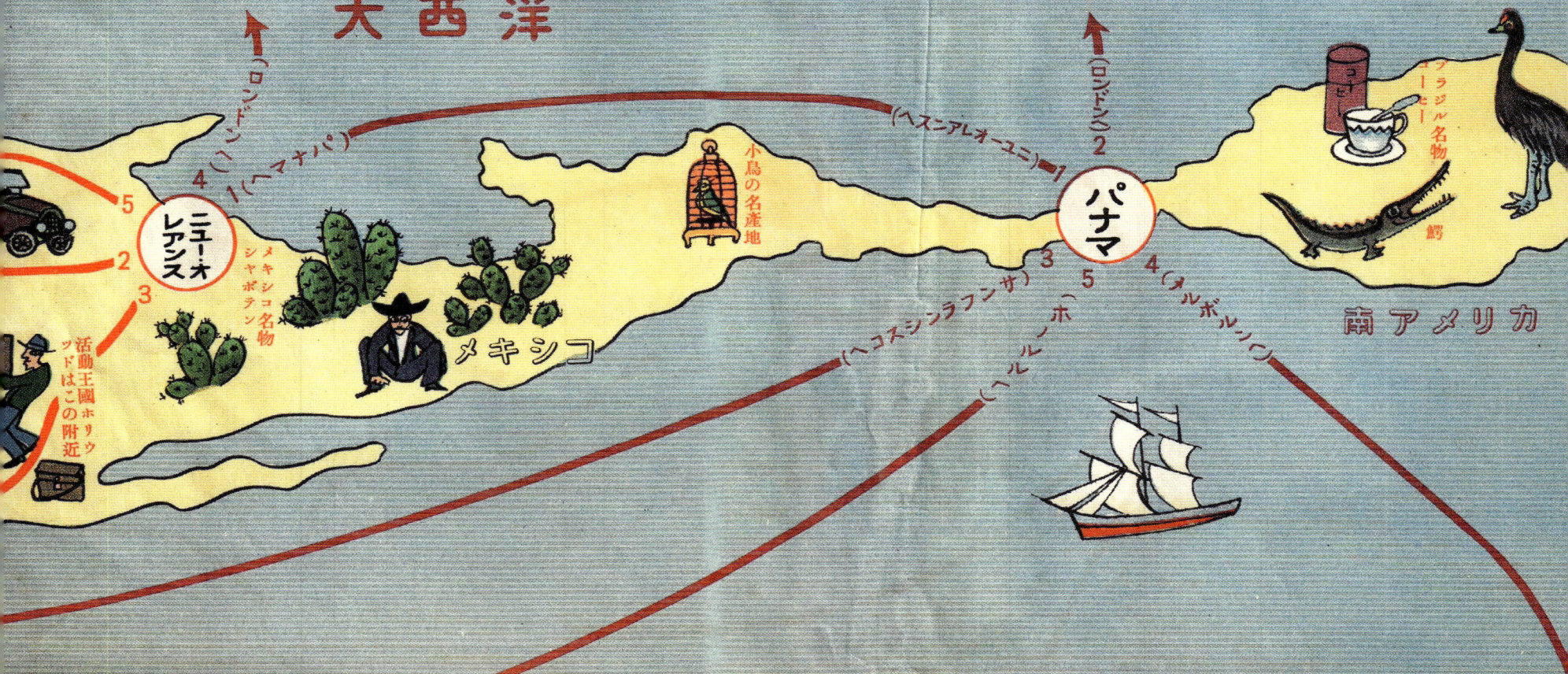

大西洋

ニューオレンス
5
2
3
4
1（ヘナハパ）
（ロンドンへ）

活動王國ホリウッドはこの附近

メキシコ名物シャボテン

メキシコ

小鳥の名産地

（ヘニユーオレアンスへ）

パナマ

3
5
4（ホルボルへ）
（サンフランシスコへ）
（ホノルへ）

ブラジル名物コーヒー

鰐

南アメリカ

（ヘマナパ）

（ヘンルボルメ）

カロリン、マーシャルは日本の委任領

オセアニア

（ホノルルへ）
（日本へ）
5　3

メルボルン
1（シンガポールへ）
2（ホンコンへ）
4（パナマへ）

カンガルー

オーストラリヤ

太平洋

南洋の食人種

島田啓三畫　佐藤保太郎監修　東京高等師範學校教諭

少年倶樂部　第二十二巻　第十二號　附錄

MADE IN JAPAN

世界パノラマ大地圖

Pictorial Map of the World

A fascinating and amusing Japanese manga map from 1933 by Keizo Shimada. Centered on the Japanese Empire, which was shown in red, this map included most of the world. Cultural and regional highlights including the Eiffel Tower and the Leaning Tower of Pisa were graphically illustrated. Further illustrations ranged from bull fighting in Spain to giant diamonds in Africa and underwater explorers near Australia. The variety of vignettes used illustrated landmarks, peoples, plants, and animals and was breathtaking. Considered by some as "kawaii," a Japanese term meaning 'too cute', many of the images were also representative of outmoded stereotypes, some of which might be considered racist by modern standards.

More menacingly, many of the illustrations foreshadow the tensions soon to come in World War II. Japanese war ships plied the western Pacific while the American fleet gathered on the Californian coast. Korea and Taiwan, which by 1933 had already been annexed, were included as part of the Japanese Empire.

Cartographer

Keizo Shimada (1900-1973) was born in Tokyo and became famous for his World War II comics, "The Adventures of Dankichi." The stories revolved around the adventures of a little boy, Dankichi, and his mouse. After being shipwrecked in the South Pacific, Dankichi after various ordeals became the leader of the indigenous local tribe. Following World War II, Shimada was criticized for the parts of his work that seemed to condone Japanese aggression and promote fantasies of easy wealth.

Scientifica: Maps and Science

Scientifically themed maps began to appear as early as the 16th century and continue to be produced today. Initially, scientific thematic maps were drawn to express theories of geology, oceanography, weather, and geography. Later, they became expressions of amalgamated scientific discovery and tributes to the greatness of modern civilization. In most cases, the cartographer was using maps to express scientific ideas that were greater than the map that contained them, thus transforming the strictly geographical map into a tool for forwarding a scientific agenda.

One of the earliest scientific thematic world maps is Athanasius Kircher's (1602-1680) Tabula Geographico-Hydrographica.

This work is considered to have been the first published map to illustrate ocean currents. Impressively, many prevailing current patterns were correctly identified. Kircher's world map was merely the tip of the iceberg, as his great work, the Mundus Subterraneus, featured many more specific maps of different parts of the world. This great two-volume compendium advocated Kircher's cosmographical theories using text, maps, and diagrams. As might be expected of a Renaissance polymath, Kircher's "Science" is in fact a combination of true observation-based science, speculation, myth, and Biblical positivism. Parts of the Mundus Subterraneus correctly described the formation of different types of rocks, the process of erosion, and current patterns, but other parts illustrated such wonders as the lost continent of Atlantis, the homeland of giants, and more.

While some of Kircher's ideas may seem absurd today, in the 17th century he was at the forefront of scientific innovation and was considered one of history's greatest geniuses. Kircher's use of thematic mapping to express his science was revolutionary and was subsequently embraced by many other cartographers. Peter Simon Pallas (1741-1811) for example, following Kircher, drew maps to illustrate his own geophysical theories, which revolved around undersea mountain ranges and proto-tectonic volcanic activity. Like Kircher, Pallas speculated where fact was unavailable, such as mapping fictional undersea volcanoes in the Atlantic and in unexplored parts of South American and Africa. Despite some of his ideas seeming illogical by modern standards, Pallas did stumble upon important scientific truths, such as the mechanism by which granite emerges from the Earth and the volcanic origins of some mountains.

Still other cartographers followed. The Bohemian oceanographer August von Jilek, for example, prepared an impressive map to illustrate his Lehrbuch der Oceanographie, an encyclopedic textbook compiling all known oceanographic theory. While Jilek cannot be considered a revolutionary oceanographer, his cartography work stands out for its bold and comprehensive expression of a wide range of cartographic theories.

While individual scientists like Kircher, Pallas, and Jilek made specific maps to elaborate upon their own ideas, or the ideas they embraced, other cartographers attempted to express the sum of all geological, scientific, and astronomical knowledge through their maps. Many of those, by cartographers such as Samuel Dunn, Laurie and Whittle, Baur and Bromme, and others, took the form of enormous wall maps dense with sub-maps, astronomical diagrams, mathematical charts, weather maps, and extensive annotations. From the modern simpler aesthetic perspective, these maps can appear busy and hard to understand. Nevertheless, from about 1790 they became increasingly popular and a perfect expression of scientific optimism. Serious scholars would have found such maps too simplistic to suit their needs, but the armchair scientist, interested in comparing different ideas and theories, would have found them invaluable tools.

Other scientifically themed maps were not intended to express or prove a new idea as much as to reaffirm or influence the establishment of convention. One example is the unusual and circular 1860 Henry James map of the world. James produced his map to argue for the Greenwich Meridian as the baseline for zero longitude, or the Prime Meridian. Today most maps follow James's model and use the Royal Observatory at Greenwich, London, as the Prime Meridian, but for most of cartographic history the Prime Meridian shifted according to the needs and nationality of the cartographer. Ptolemy used the Canary Islands, which he called the Fortunate Islands. Mercator used the Azores. French cartographers used Paris. Americans used Washington D.C. And of course, the English used Greenwich. With the invention of the Marine Chronometer by John Harrison, the English had the first tool that could guarantee an accurate measurement of time, and hence Longitude, at sea. With this momentous innovation, the influence of British mapmakers on cartographic models swelled and in the 1884 International Meridian Conference, Greenwich was adopted as the global Prime Meridian for most subsequent cartography. Today, a laser is used to identify the Greenwich Prime Meridian with perfect accuracy.

Around this time, another type of map or chart began to emerge. European scientists, navigators, and explorers were setting off on one expedition after another to reveal the mysteries of the Earth. With them, they carried ever more sophisticated equipment, including marine chronometers, theodolites, telescopes, and other measuring tools, all of which they put to extensive use measuring

the Earth. This was not purely academic and often had a practical purpose. Accurate measurements lead to more accurate mapping, better sea charts, and faster, safer, more lucrative trade.

Massive quantities of data were collected and it fell to scholars and academics to compile it. Much of this information found its way onto traditional maps, but other information called for another type of map, the comparative chart. With measurements taken of the heights of the world's greatest mountains and the lengths of the world's greatest rivers, it was only natural to set them against each other at the same scale to better understand the data globally. Individual comparative charts of the world's great mountain ranges began to appear around 1800. At the same time, comparative river length charts also began to appear. It was not until William Darton and W. R. Gardner published their 1823 New and Improved View of the Comparative Heights, of the Principal Mountains and Lengths of the Principal Rivers in the World *that the separate comparative mountains and rivers charts were compiled into a single easy to read diagram. This work gave birth to a new style of map, embraced by countless other cartographers in Europe and America. Some made modifications that separated the mountains and rivers into their respective continents, but the basic model remained consistent well into the latter part of the 19th century.*

Today, thematic scientific maps are part of nearly all geo-science research. Modern technology can produce new maps on the fly to illustrate conflicting ideas and theories, not just in the sciences, but also in political and economic arenas. While maps can be used to support and validate scientific discoveries and other facts, they can also be used to present alternative sciences, religious ideology, and political trends, as we shall discover in subsequent chapters.

Tabula Geographico-Hydrographica

An example of early thematic mapping, this extraordinary 1665 map by Athanasius Kircher was the first to illustrate global ocean currents. Kircher prepared this map to explain his revolutionary hydro-geographic theories concerning the movement of the tides and the currents. Inspired by two weeks of earthquakes in Calabria in 1638, and the volcanic eruption of Vesuvius in 1637, Kircher postulated a subterranean ocean that created currents, earthquakes, and tides by entering and exiting through an extensive network of tunnels and abysses.

Kircher was known around the world for his brilliant, often prescient, scholarly work. For example, Africa on this map was illustrated with far greater accuracy than on maps drawn hundreds of years later. Here, the Nile lacked the conventional Ptolemaic dual-lake model and instead followed an equally speculative but more accurate course. The Niger, even more remarkably, was drawn with some approximation of accuracy, predating the 19th century explorations of Mungo Park by several hundred years. Australia was depicted near New Guinea with a recognizable Bay of Carpentaria, but was connected in its southern extent to the apocryphal Aristotelian southern continent, *Terra Australis*.

Cartographer

Athanasius Kircher (c. 1602-1680) was a German polymath and Renaissance man active in the 17th century. He was one of the most well-respected and famous men of his time. Considered a true Renaissance man, Kircher was a master of science, physics, geography, and mathematics, as well as several languages. He had the distinction of being one of the first scholars to fully support himself through his work as a professor of Mathematics and Oriental languages in Italy. He was best known for inventing the Magic Lantern, an early stepping-stone towards modern cinema.

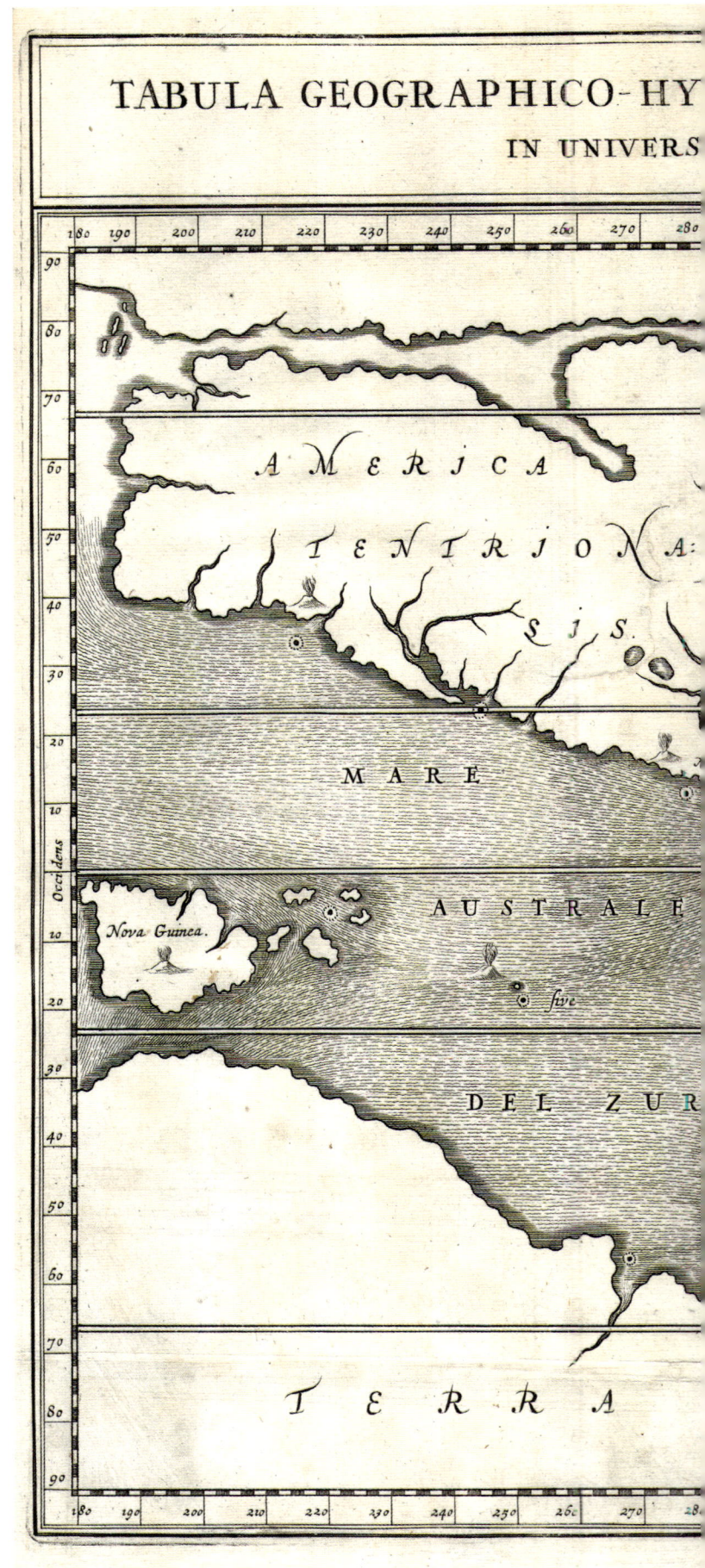

...OGRAPHICA MOTUS OCEANI, CURRENTES, ABYSSOS, MONTES IGNIVOMOS

...ORBE INDICANS, ⊙ NOTAT HÆC FIG. ABYSSOS 🌋 MONTES VULCANIOS.

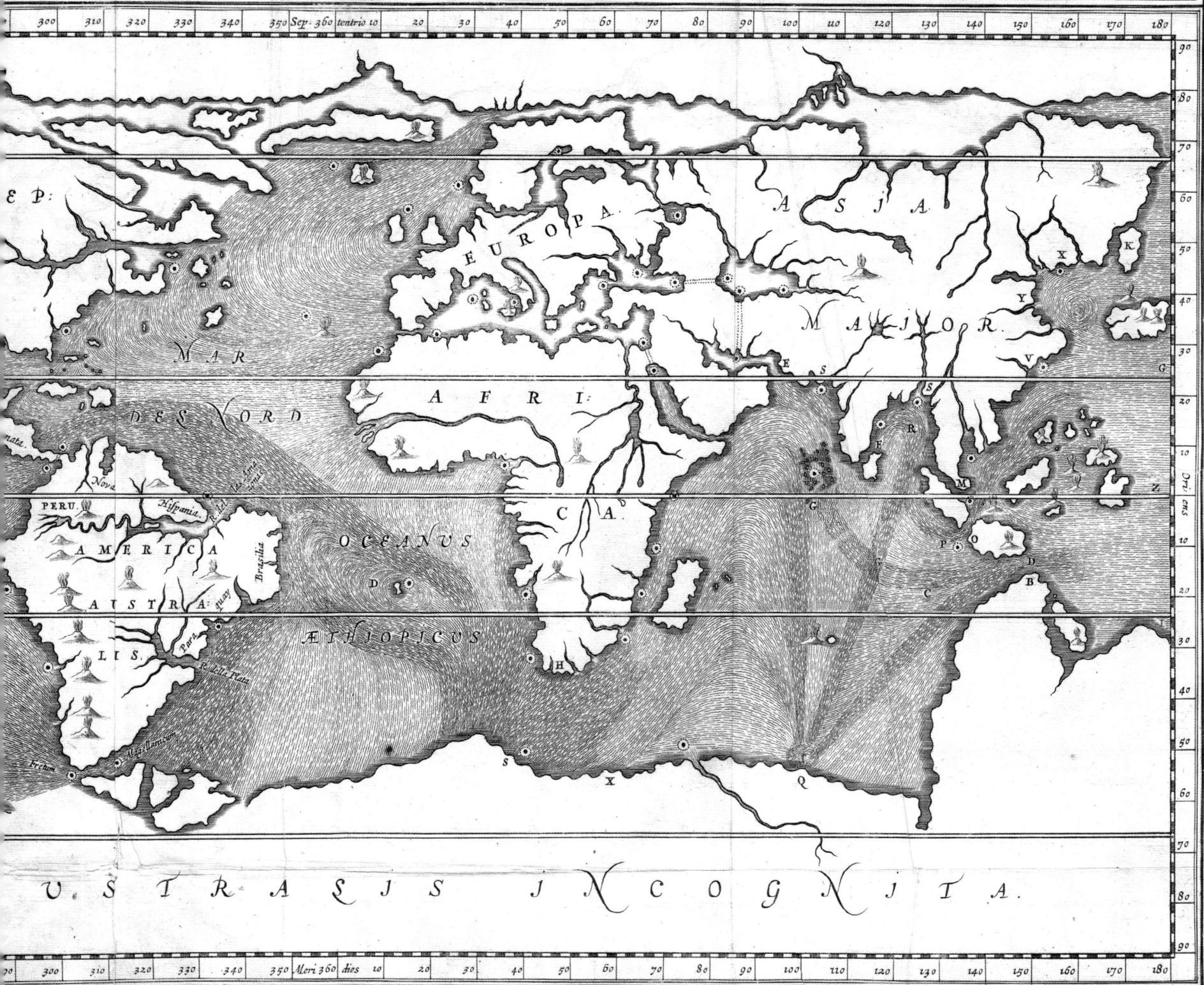

| 300 | 310 | 320 | 330 | 340 | 350 | Sep: 360 tentrio 10 | 20 | 30 | 40 | 50 | 60 | 70 | 80 | 90 | 100 | 110 | 120 | 130 | 140 | 150 | 160 | 170 | 180 |

90
80
70
60

...EP:

EUROPA

ASIA

MAJOR

MAR

AFRI:

DES NORD

50
40
30
20
10

Nova

PERU. Hispania

AMERICA

Brasilia

OCEANUS

C A

Ori: ens

10

AUSTRA:

Pará

D

20

LIS.

Rio de la Plata

ÆTHIOPICVS

30

H

40

Fretum Magellanicum

S

50

X

Q

60

70

...USTRALIS INCOGNITA.

80
90

| 300 | 310 | 320 | 330 | 340 | 350 | Meri 360 | dies 10 | 20 | 30 | 40 | 50 | 60 | 70 | 80 | 90 | 100 | 110 | 120 | 130 | 140 | 150 | 160 | 170 | 180 |

Mappe-Monde Physique d'après les Vues du Prof. Pallas

This map represented the speculative, geographical theories of Peter Simon Pallas. Engraved by Ambroise Tardieu for Edme Mentelle's *Atlas Universel*, this highly unusual map addressed aspects of submarine topography that, in the late 18th century, were entirely unknown. Nevertheless, Pallas, a German polymath, argued correctly that great mountain ranges lay beneath oceanic waters. Pallas postulated, again correctly, that these mountain ranges were created by a series of volcanic explosions and other proto-tectonic activity. On his map, asterisks were used to identify the multiple locations of these theorized geological events.

Consistent with cartographic conventions of the time, many speculative elements were included in this map. Near South America, two landmasses were shown south of Tierra del Fuego (Land of Fire). Tasmania, labeled here as Van Diemen's Land, was drawn attached to Australia's mainland. Perhaps derived from the mythical journals of Admiral de Fonte, there appeared to be a group of navigable channels located in Canada and in western North America, the apocryphal *Mer de l'Ouest* was present.

Cartographer

Edme Mentelle (1730-1816), was a French professor of Geology and Geography, and a tutor to the young Napoleon Bonaparte. Mentelle was a founding member of the Institut National des Sciences et des Arts *and published several works of importance within the field of geography.*

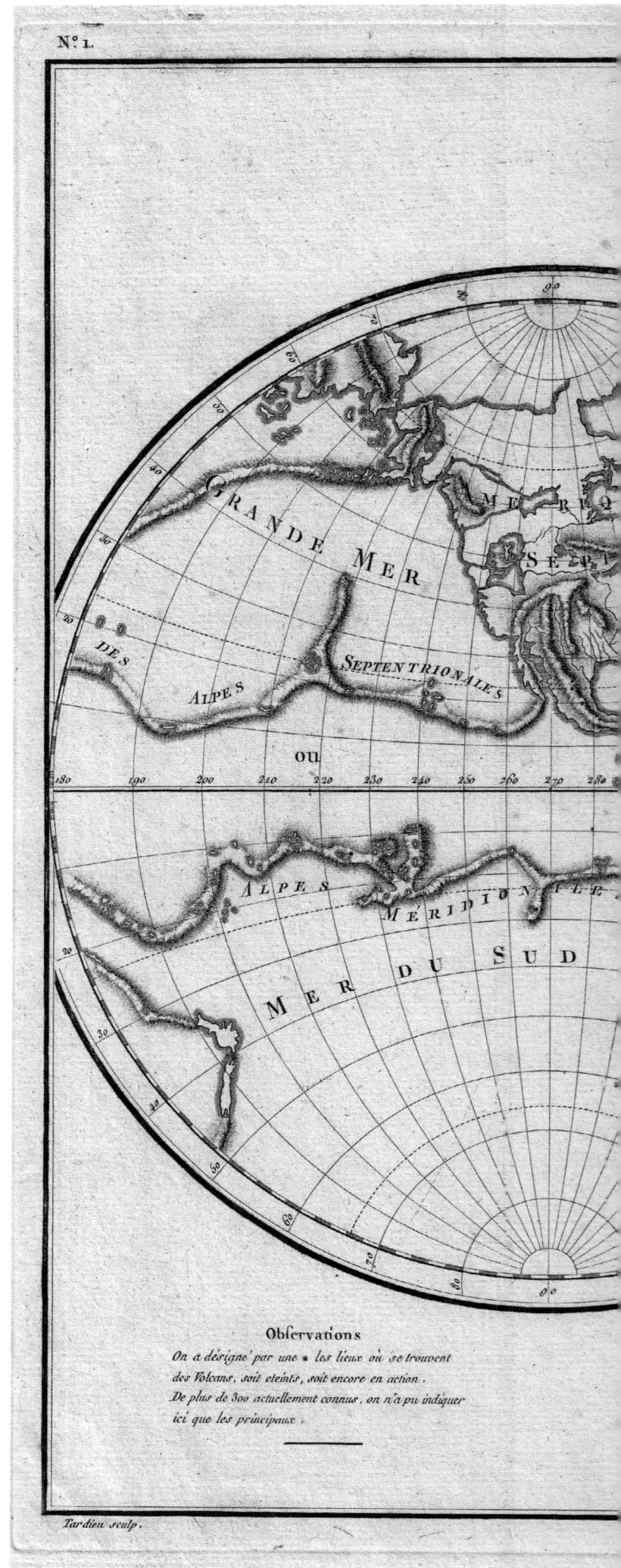

Observations

On a désigné par une * les lieux où se trouvent des Volcans, soit éteints, soit encore en action. De plus de 300 actuellement connus, on n'a pu indiquer ici que les principaux.

Tardieu sculp.

MAPPE-MONDE PHYSIQUE

D'APRÈS LES VUES DU PROF.R PALLAS
Rédigées par André Mongez
Journal de Physique,
Mai 1779.

OCÉAN ATLANTIQUE

EUROPE

ASIE

AFRIQUE

SUITE

AMÉRIQUE MÉRIDIONALE

SUITE DES ALPES

M.r MÉRIDIONALE

MER DES INDES

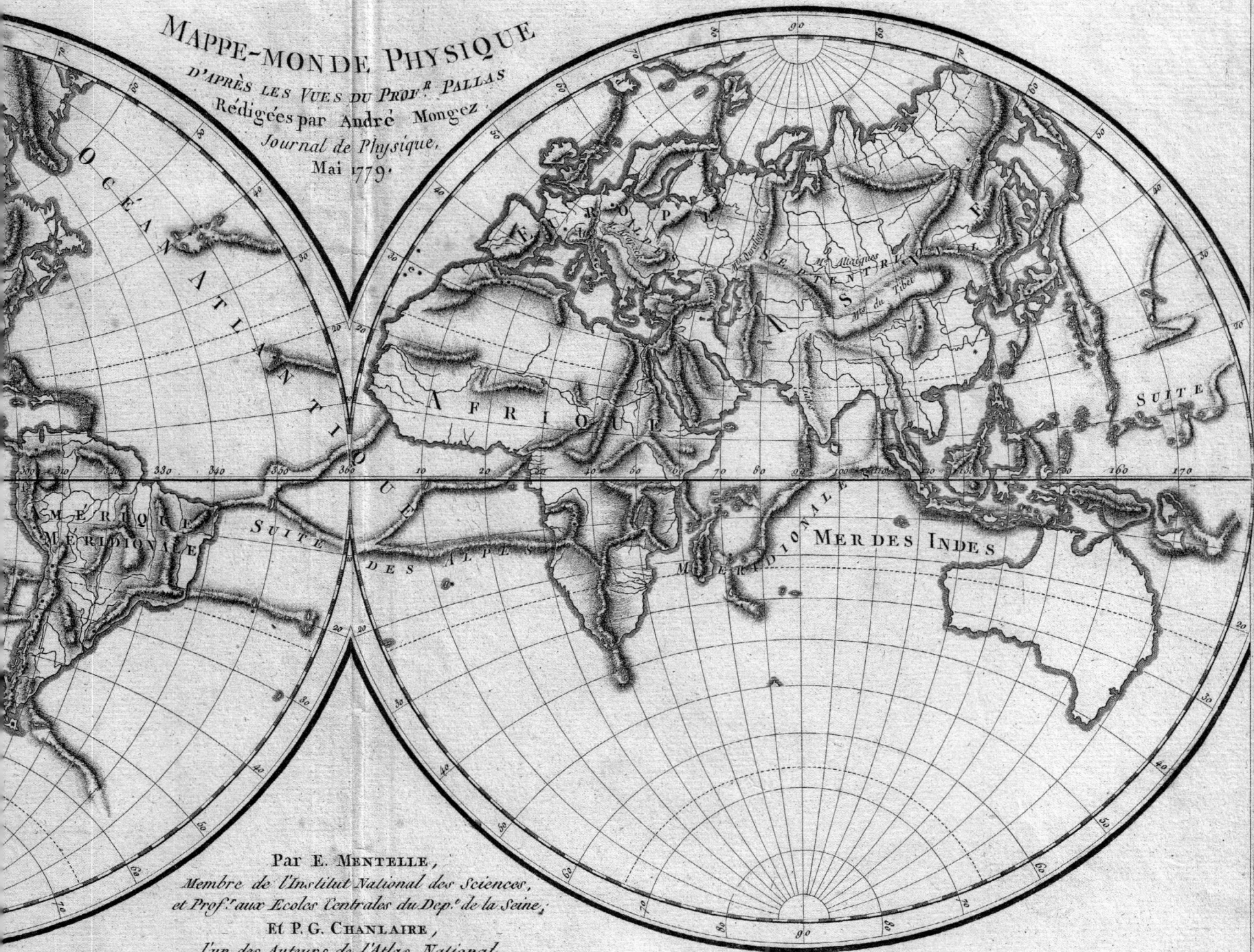

Par E. MENTELLE,
Membre de l'Institut National des Sciences,
et Prof.r aux Écoles Centrales du Dep.t de la Seine;
Et P. G. CHANLAIRE,
l'un des Auteurs de l'Atlas National.
An VI.

A PARIS CHEZ LES AUTEURS,
P.G. Chanlaire, | Et E. Mentelle,
Rue Geoffroy-Langevin N.° 328. | *Cour du Louvre, N.° 7.*

Hauteurs en Toises
a M.t S. Gothard 2750
b M.t Maudit 2447
c M.t Vesuve Volcan
d M.t Hecla Volcan   au dessus du
e Pic de Tenerife 1904   niveau de la Mer
f Cimboraco Volcan ... 3220
g M.t Etna Volcan

CARTE GENERALE DE LA TERRE

Appliquée a l'Astronomie pour l'etude de la Géographie Terrestre et Celeste, Dressée par le St. Flecheux, d'après les Nouvelles Observations.

COUPE SUPERIEURE DE L'EQUATEUR

CAPRICORNE. MER DU SUD

CERCLE POLAIRE MERIDIONAL

POLE MERIDIONAL

Rapports des Latitudes Meridionales.   Rapports des Latitudes Meridionales.

OCÉAN

TROPIQUE DU

AFRIQUE

TROPIQUE DU CANCER

MER DU NORD

EQUATEUR

POLE SEPTENTRIONAL

Rapports des Latitudes Septentrionales.   Rapports des Latitudes Septentrionales.

AMÉRIQUE

PARTIE SEPTENTRION

TROPIQUE DU CANCER

DE LA GRANDE MER DU SUD

COUPE INFERIEURE DE L'EQUATEUR

A Paris, Chez l'Auteur, Rue du Sentier, près le Boulevard, à l'Hotel de Mde la Présidente de Moslay.

Side panels

LEVER DU SOLEIL

LEVER DU SOLEIL
Quart de Cercle par le St Flecheux.

OBSERVATIONS.

COUCHER DU SOLEIL

COUCHER DU SOLEIL

APPLICATION A L'ASTRONOMIE.

TABLE DES CLIMATS

Lieu du Soleil et de la Terre dans l'Ecliptique.

Carte Generale de la Terre Appliquée a l'Astronomie

This complicated and unusual work is the only map issued by the French astronomer M. Flecheux. The projection of the map is odd. The main map, a hemisphere centered on the Atlantic is, to our modern perspective, upside down, with south at the top of the document. Half hemispheres appear at the top and the bottom of the page, both oriented to the north, and in concert, encapsulate the remainder of the sphere. The geography is derived from Guillaume de L'Isle and is sophisticated by the reckoning of 18th century France. The apocryphal Sea of the West (*Mer d'Ouest*) appears in North America and some of the great lakes of Africa's Rift Valley are beginning to appear – particularly an embryonic rendering of Lake Malawi.

Nonetheless, while this map's geography is interesting, the true focus Flecheaux's astronomical message. Following Flecheaux's tables, the map identifies the position of the Sun at sunrise in 10 day increments throughout the year. He also uses this map to advertise two of his own unique constructions, the 1784 *Loxocosme*, a unique device for determining the annual and diurnal movements of the Earth; and the *Quart de Cercle*, an angle surveying tool adapted for astronomical purposes.

This map was engraved by Jean Picquet, a map engraver active in Paris in the second half of the 20th century.

Cartographer

M. Flecheux (1738-1793) was a French astronomer active in Paris during the second half of the 18th century. Little is known of Flecheux's life, but he was active in French scientific circles and published several astronomical devices, including a planisphere, a loxocosme, planetary tables, and at least one map.

de faire quelques applications de l'Astronomie
à la Géographie

tt A l'instant que N° passe
au Meridien de 180 deg.
de Longitude.

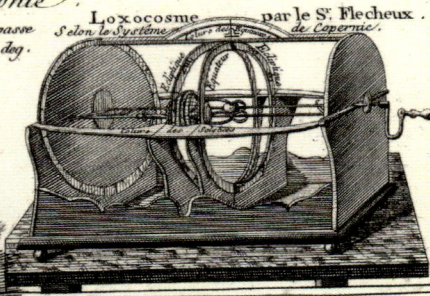

Loxocosme par le S.r Flecheux
Selon le Systeme de Copernic.

Rapports des Latitudes Meridionales.

LEVER DU SOLEIL

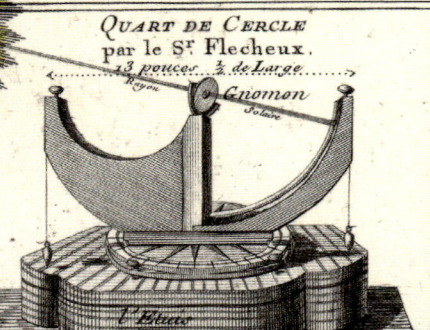

20. Decemb. SOLSTICE D'HYVER	
1.er Janvier.	10. Decemb.
10. Janvier.	1.er Decemb.
20. Janvier.	29. Novemb.
1.er Fevrier.	1.er Novemb.
10. Fevrier.	29. Octobre.
20. Fevrier.	1.er Octobre.
1.er Mars.	10. Octob.
10. Mars.	1.er Octobre.
20. Mars.	22. Septemb.
EQUINOXE DU PRINTEMS.	EQUINOXE D'AUTOMNE.
1.er Avril	10. Septemb.
10. Avril	1.er Septemb.
20. Avril	20. Aoust.
1.er May.	10. Aoust.
10. May.	1.er Aoust.
20. May.	20. Juillet.
1.er Juin	10. Juillet.
10. Juin	1.er Juillet.
20. Juin, SOLSTICE D'ETE.	

LEVER DU SOLEIL

Quart de Cercle
par le S.r Flecheux
13 pouces ½ de Large
Gnomon

SAGITTAIRE. SCORPION. BALANCE. LA VIERGE. LION. CANCER.
VERSEAU. POISSONS. BELIER. TAUREAU. GEMEAUX.

Declinaison Septentrionale du Soleil
Declinaison Meridionale du Soleil

ORIENT

CERCLE POLAIRE

Mer gelee
Glaces fixes

Route

Isle decouverte par M. Kerguelin
en 1772. ou M.r de
Bougneu descendit le
13 Fevrier 1772. et M.r Ronevet
le 6 Janvier 1774.

PIED DU CENTAURE
AU PIED DE LA CROIX
JAMBE DU CENTAURE

Cap de Bonne Esperance
TROPIQUE

CAFRERIE
CONGO
R.me de Macoco
ANGOLA

AFRIQUE
ABISSINIE
NUBIE
ARABIE
PERSE

NIGRITIE
DESERT DE BARBARIE ou SARA
BARBARIE
ETATS DU ROI DU MAROC

MEDITERRANÉE
EUROPE
GRECE
TURQUIE
M. NOIRE
RUSSIE

Les Isles MALDIVES

Isle de France
I. Rodrigues
I. St. Brandes

Canal de Mozambique
Madagascar

POLE

Rapports des Latitudes Meridionales.

18	64	49	21	1/2
19	65	21	21	1/2
20	65	47	22	
21	66	6	22	1/2
22	66	20	23	
23	66	28	23	1/2
24	66	31	24	
25	67	30	1 Mois	
26	69	30	2	
27	73	20	3	
28	78	20	4	
29	84	10	5	
30	90 au Pole	6		

COUCHER DU SOLEIL

CAPRICORNE — SOLSTICE D'HYVER	
20 Decembre	10 Decemb.
1er Janvier	1er Decemb.
10 Janvier	20 Novemb.
20 Janvier	10 Novemb.
1er Fevrier	1er Novembre
10 Fevrier	20 Octob.
20 Fevrier	10 Octob.
1er Mars	1er Octobre
10 Mars	
20 Mars — EQUINOXE DU PRINTEMS	22 Sept — EQUINOXE D'AUTOMNE
1er Avril	10 Sept.
10 Avril	1er Septembre
20 Avril	20 Aoust
1er May	10 Aoust
10 May	1er Aoust
20 May	20 Juillet
1er Juin	10 Juillet
10 Juin	1er Juillet
21 Juin SOLSTICE D'ETE	

COUCHER DU SOLEIL

APPLICATION A L'ASTRONOMIE.

On compte dans le Ciel environ 15 Etoiles de la 1ere grandeur, nous les avons placées sur cette Carte avec quelques unes de la 2e grandeur.

L'Ecliptique, l'Equateur Celeste et les Etoiles fixes, etant dans le fait des objets considérés immobiles, n'ayant d'autre mouvement, que celui que la rotation de la Terre paroit leur donner, en consequence cette

Map labels

MERIDIONAL · OCEAN · Vaisseau sur les Rames · Glaces · I. George · I.s Falkland ou Maloüines · Detroit de Magellan · Route du Capitaine · CAPRICORNE · CHILI · PARAGUAY · BRESIL · PEROU · Rio de la Plata · I. Fernandez · SIRIUS · EQUATEUR · PROCYON · REGULUS · TERRE FERME · NOUVELLE GRENADE · NOUVELLE ESPAGNE · Embouchure de la R. des Amazones · TROPIQUE DU CANCER · MER DU NORD · Açores · Golfe du Mexique · CANADA · ESQUIMAUX · LABRADOR · AMERIQUE SEPTENTRIONALE · Baye d'Hudson · Baye de Baffin · GROENLAND · MER GLACIALE · SEPTENTRIONAL · OCCIDENT · Declinaison Septentrionale du Soleil · Partie de l'Afrique

Zodiac signs: ♐ SAGITTAIRE · ♏ SCORPION · ♎ LA BALANCE · ♍ LA VIERGE · ♌ LION · ♋ ANCRE(?) · ♑ CAPRICORNE · ♒ VERSEAU · ♓ POISSONS · ♈ BELIER · ♉ TAUREAU · ♊ GEMEAUX

A General Map of the World, or Terraqueous Globe

This stunning and monumentally proportioned 1794 wall map of the world was issued by the Englishman Samuel Dunn. Dunn was a professor of mathematics, navigation, and astronomy and those interests were reflected in this informationally dense map. In addition to the map proper, which was presented on a double hemisphere projection, secondary maps illustrated the Solar System, the Moon, the northern and southern celestial hemispheres, and the world on an alternative Mercator Projection. Further charts and diagrams described the seasons, distance scales, astronomical calculations, and mathematical navigational systems.

Issued just before the turn of the century, Dunn's work could be understood in the terms of nascent scientific idealism that would reach its peak in the coming Victorian Era. From the late 18th century, scientists ranged over the globe collecting data in the form of specimens, astronomical observations, and other scientific measurements. It was believed that through the sheer accumulation of information and observation, the secrets of the natural world would be unveiled. This map was a product of that ideology. This map was published by the firm of Laurie and Whittle in the last year of Dunn's life.

Cartographer

Samuel Dunn (1723-1794) was a British publisher of scientific texts, maps, and charts. He was an instructor of navigation, mathematics, and astronomy, and also a Commissioner for the Discovery of the Longitude at Sea.

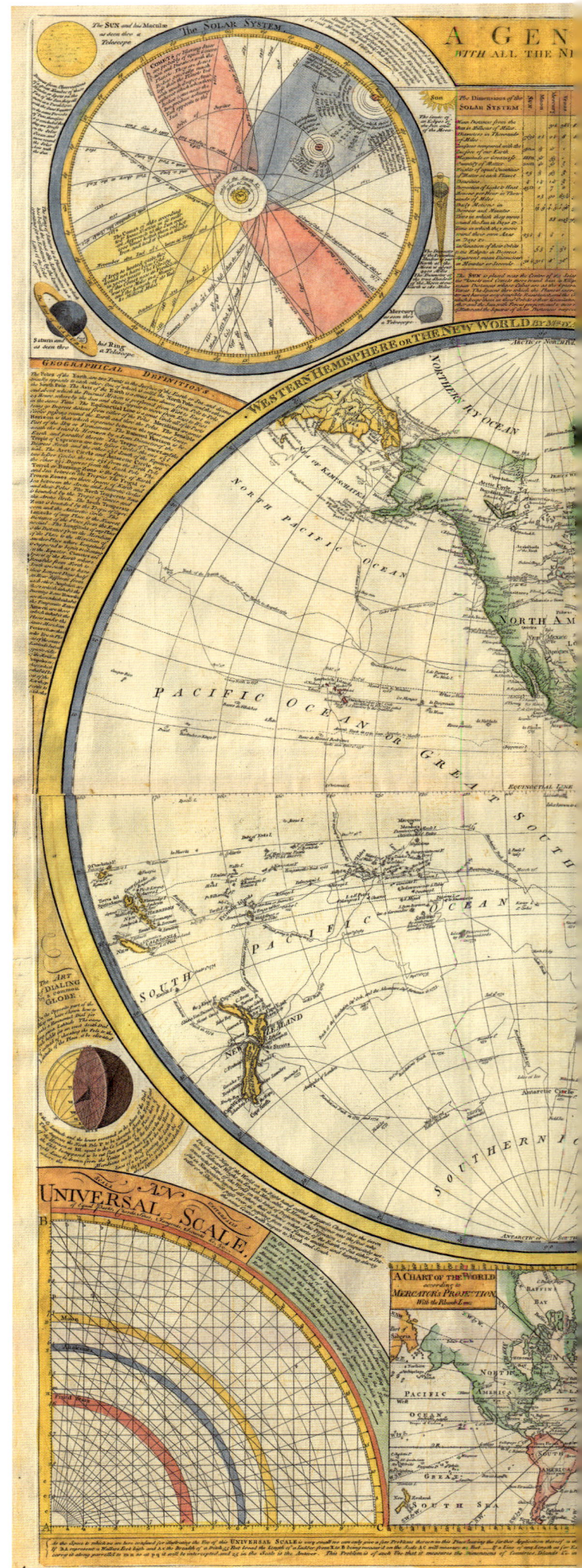

...AL MAP OF THE WORLD, OR TERRAQUEOUS GLOBE.
...VERIES and MARGINAL DELINEATIONS, CONTAINING THE MOST INTERESTING PARTICULARS IN THE SOLAR, STARRY AND MUNDANE SYSTEM, By SAM. DUNN, Mathematician.

LONDON.
Published by LAURIE & WHITTLE, N°53, Fleet Street, 12ᵗʰ May. 1794.

The NORTHERN HEMISPHERE The SOUTHERN HEMISPHERE

A TABLE of the Place of the SUN in the Ecliptic Declination

An Astronomical

Latitude & Longitude

GEOGRAPHICAL DEFINITIONS

EASTERN HEMISPHERE OR THE OLD WORLD, With the New Discoveries and Several Additions.

NORTHERN ICY OCEAN

ATLANTIC

WESTERN OCEAN

ASIA

EUROPE

AFRICA

NEGRITIA

GUINEA

ARABIA

SOUTH AMERICA

ÆTHIOPIC OCEAN

INDIAN SEA

INDIAN OCEAN

NEW HOLLAND OR TERRA-AUSTRALIS

SOUTH PACIFIC OCEAN

SOUTHERN ICY OCEAN

The Art of DIALING on the GLOBE

SELENOGRAPHY or A MAP of the MOON

TERRA STERILITATIS

The VICISSITUDE of SEASONS Explained.

The ANALEMMA

Sun

The Sun en-lightning the Earth and forming a Co-nical Shadow. Also the Earth's Atmosphere forming a Penumbra.

Earth

The Length of the Earth's Shadow is from 215 to 217 times the Semi-diameter of the Earth.

Spring · Sun · Winter
Summer · Autumn

The Earth moving round the Sun in a Year

ASTRONOMICAL

The Poles of the World are two Points in the Heavens opposite to each other. The Axis of the World is a strait Line drawn from Pole to Pole. The Equator is a great Circle all of its Parts being equally distant from the two Poles and dividing the Heavens into two Parts called the Northern and Southern Hemispheres. The Ecliptic is a great Circle passing thro' the Equator in two opposite Points and inclined thereto by an Angle of 23½. The Ecliptic con-tains 12 Signs viz Aries Taurus Gemini Cancer Leo Virgo Libra Scorpio Sagittary Capricorn Aquarius Pisces. A Meridian is a Great Circle passing thro' the Equator and the Poles. The Colures are two Meridians one of which passes thro' the Point where the Ecliptic cuts the Equator is called the Equinoctial Colure the other at 90 of the Equator therefrom is called the Solstitial Colure. The Poles of the Ecliptic are two Points 90 from the Poles of the World.

DEFINITIONS

The Latitude of a Star is the nearest Distance of the Star from the Ecliptic The Longitude of a Star is counted upon the Ecliptic according to the Order of the Signs terminated where a great Circle from the Pole of the Ecliptic cuts the Ecliptic itself. The Tropic of Cancer is a lesser Circle at the Distance of 23½ from the Equator & 66½ from the North Pole of the World. And the Tropic of Capricorn is a Circle at the Distance of 23½ from the Equator and 66½ from the South Pole. The Circle is 23½ from the North Pole of the World. And the Antarctic Circle is 23½ from the South Pole of the World. The Zenith is the Point over our Head. The Nadir is the Point under our Feet. The Amplitude of a Star is the Number of Degrees from the East or West where it rises or sets. The Azimuth of the Sun or a Star is the Number of Degrees from the North or South to the Point directly under the Sun or Star. Circles of Altitude are parallel to each other from the Ze-nith to the Horizon Circles of Azimuth or Vertical Cir-cles are great Circles drawn from the Zenith to the Horizon. The Altitude of the Sun or a Star is the Number of Degrees it is above the Horizon. The De-clination of the Sun or a Star is the nearest Distance from the Sun or Star to the Equator. Right Ascension is that Point of the Equator which is on the Meridian with the Sun or a Star. Ascen-sional Difference is the Time from Six o'Clock when the Sun or a Star riseth. Parallax is the Difference between the true & apparent Place in the Heavens.

with the New Discoveries and Several Additions.

CAUSE OF THE TIDES

Old Greenland

The Law of the Solar System

The Fixed Stars are so called because they keep nearly the same Position and Distance among themselves The Number of those which have been already accurately observed is no more than 3000. Yet by the help of Telescopes 21 Stars have been seen in the Space which forms the Cloudy Star of Orions Sword 36 in that of the Cloudy Star of Pegasus, 78 in the Asterism of the Pleiades, and 2000 in the Constellation of Orion. From which it has been conjectured that the Number of Fixed Stars is no less than 10 million, beside those of the Via Lactea or Milky Way and such as cannot be discerned by the best Glasses and that Twice or Thrice that Number would cover the Expanse of Heaven. The bright Star Sirius in the Constellation of the great Dog hath been estimated to be distant from us more than 2 Million of Million Miles And the Distance of a Star of lesser apparent magnitude hath been found to be more than 30 Million of Million Miles Wherefore it is concluded that every Fixed Star is a Sun having Planets & Comets moving round it like those which move round our Sun From all which it may be presumed that if the Universe doth not extend itself beyond the Powers of Number Weight and Measure it may be too far for human Reason to comprehend. Particles of Light are inconceivably small hard Bodies thrown off from the Sun Stars &c. which move at the Rate of 10 Million Miles in a Minute of Time & come from the Sun to our Earth in 8 Minutes & from the Fixed Stars in about 6 Years

Altho the Fixed Stars keep continually the same Positions and Distances among themselves, yet each of them hath a Motion and they all move forward according to the Order of the Signs at the rate of about 50 Seconds of a Degree in a Year in Longitude only whilst their Latitude or Distances from the Ecliptic continue the same. Or which is the same thing the Equinoctial Points move backward from the Stars at the same Rate By which apparent motion those Stars which about 2000 Years ago were at the Beginning of Aries are now at the Beginning of Taurus And in the space of 26000 Years every fixed Star will have mov'd thro all the twelve Signs of the Ecliptic, and consequently, no fixed Star that at any Time happens to be near the North or South Pole, will allways continue to be the North or South Pole Star. Another Motion of a few Seconds of a Degree in a Year the fixed Stars appear to have round their fixed Places in the Heavens by the progressive Motion of Light

A Representation of Part of the Universe

Moon

Moon

EXPLAINED

them together, were it not for the Centrifugal

Old Greenland found again in the preceding Century

Arctic C...

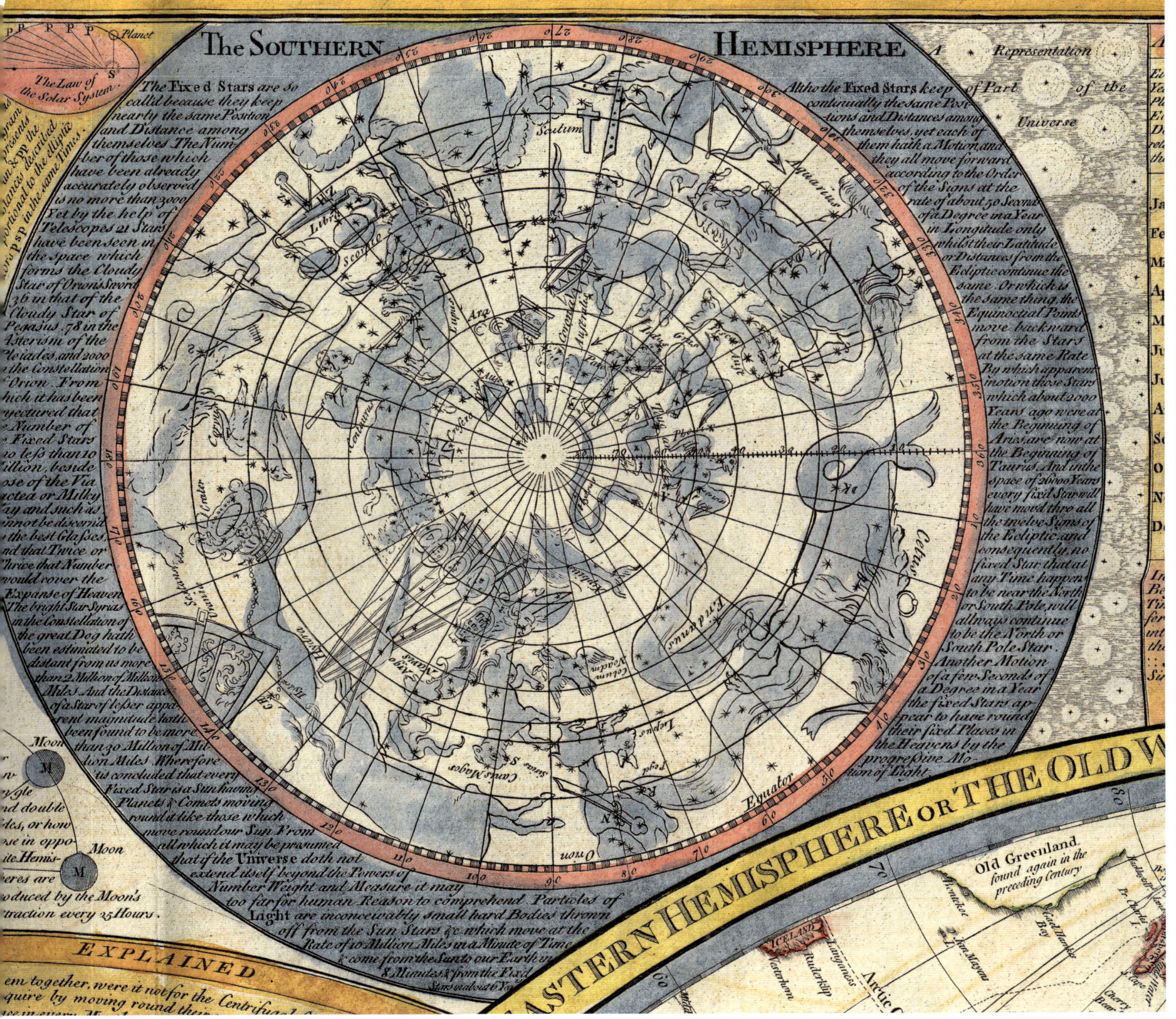

The map is very large and so rich in detail and it is surrounded by detailed scientific calculations and descriptions. Here, one can observe in detail the northern and southern hemisphere star charts, including studies of the Sun and solar projections on the Earth.

In these two images from the rich and detailed work of
Samuel Dunn one can read, in English, "The Vicissitude of
Seasons Explained," and the map of the Moon, according
to Father Riccioli, an Italian Jesuit priest and astronomer.

SOUTHERN

Albho the Moon be alway half Light, but once a Month it appears so to our Earth

The Axis of the Earth keeps alway in a same Parallel Position, & y Earth turns round the same every 24 Hours.

SELENOGRAPHY or A MAP OF THE MOON.
according to Father Riccioli.

REGIO HYPERBBOREA TERRA

It hath been long a disputed Question among Astronomers whether the Moon has an Atmosphere or without it, nor whether an inhabited. Conclusions Moon's Limb that she has raised on by others

The most material Arguments in Favour of a Lunar Atmosphere seem those of the noxious Loss or in the Occultal Observe Abroad or not Venus ed to have seen in probably

The above represents a full Moon as it appears thro a Telescope in which the light spots are generally taken to be Mountains the light streaks Ridges of Mountains, the broad white Places High Grounds the broad dark Places Seas, watry Plains or Forests, the dark spots within white ones Cavities or Pits with or without Water Astronomers have given Names to those Spots for knowing y Quantity of an Eclipse when y Earths Shadow hides part of y Moon

Altho the Moon always presents nearly the same Face toward Us, whilst she is moving round our Earth in the Space of 27 Days 8 Hours, and also turning round her own Axis in the same Time, Yet she has another Motion, whereby when she hath made a fourth Part of her Rotation round her Axis, and not described a fourth Part of her Orbit at the same Time, those Spots near the East Edge of the Moon do appear advanced on her Face, and the opposite Ones with-drawn The Contrary also happens in an opposite Part of her Orbit, This is Called the Moons Libration.

Moon. A F G, with the Analemma. A H I. with the Starry Hemispheres. a b. are Natural Sines qual Parts and you would have any other Number of Parts from such a Scale referd to the Sides, or the Degrees of Longitude as delineated in the Diameter, or any

of those Degrees cut in the Limb, to the Radius A B, and A a are their Cosines. In like manner count from B to m 55, and set the given Line from m to n, laying a Strait Slip of Paper Oblique short Distances, would otherwise require a Sector or Calculation to regulate the

View of the Comparative Heights, of the Principal Mountains and Lengths of the Principal Rivers in the World

An iconic example of 19th century scientific idealism, this chart compared the mountains and rivers of the world. Comparative charts of relative mountain heights had begun appearing on maps and in atlases in the early 19th century, following the influential 1809 South American mountain profiles issued by the Prussian naturalist Alexander von Humboldt. Around the same time, comparative river length charts also began to be issued. The convention initially involved separate charts, but design ingenuity quickly began synthesizing mountain and river diagrams into a single dynamic chart. Darton, with this chart, was the first mapmaker to issue a consolidated comparative mountains and rivers diagram.

Darton's consolidation involved setting the mountains of the world to the right, with the highest mountains appearing farthest to the right. The world's rivers filled the blank space on the left, with the longest river, in this case, the Amazon, farthest to the left. He also added reference points, such as a graphically illustrated sea level, comparative sailing ships, and buildings, and placed important cities at their correct elevations.

Darton identified the Amazon as the world's greatest river at 3600 miles – the Nile had yet to be fully explored. With Everest as yet unmeasured, nearby Dhaulagiri, was identified as the world's greatest peak. While much of the information Darton used was outdated by today's standards, his chart was revolutionary and influenced most subsequent comparative mountains and rivers charts, which copied his style.

Cartographer

William Darton (c.1800-c.1860) was an English Quaker bookseller, engraver, and publisher. After apprenticing with his father, who was also a printer, Darton opened his own shop, "Repertory of Genius," at 58 Holburn Hill, London.

New and Improved View of the Comparative Heights, of the PRINCIPAL MOUNTAINS and Lengths of the PRINCIPAL RIVERS in the WORLD.

The whole Judiciously arranged from the various Authorities Extant.

BY W. R. GARDNER.

NOTICES TO THE MOUNTAINS.

The Heights of the Mountains, &c. exhibited to View on this Print, are laid down from the most Esteemed Works relating to the subject.—The Mountains in Europe, Asia and Africa or those which constitute the Eastern Hemisphere, commencing at A, on the South West corner of the Print, and progressively according to B, near the North East corner, thus dividing the Eastern, from the Western Hemisphere or North and South America; the division of which is preserved by a lighter tint. The figure on the summit of each Mountain, refer to the Table of Reference, shewing the Region, Country, and the Altitudes, which are given in Feet above the Level of the Sea.

REFERENCE TO THE RIVERS, as Measured in the CENTRE of the STREAM.

	Region	Country	British Miles
Amazon	S.A.	Peru & Para	3,600
Missisippi	N.A.	U.d States	3,530
Hoan Ho	AS.	China	3,270
Yangtse Kiang	D.o	China	3,040
Nile	AF.	Egypt	2,680
La Plata	S.A.	Brazil	2,210
Volga	EU.	Russia	2,100
Euphrates	AS.	Turkey	2,025
Danube	EU.	Austria	1,790
Indus	AS.	Hindoostan	1,760
Ganges	D.o	Hindoostan	1,646
Orinoco	S.A.	Caraccas	1,585
S.t Lawrence	N.A.	Canada	1,210
Don	EU.	Russia	1,209
Dnieper	D.o	Russia	1,185
Senegal	AF.	Senegambia	1,130
Rhine	EU.	France	815
Gambia	AF.	Senegambia	809
Elbe	EU.	Prussia	698
Vistula	D.o	Prussia	660
Susquehanna	N.A.	U.d States	655
Oder	EU.	Prussia	648
Tagus	D.o	Spain	566
Loire	D.o	France	530
Rhone	D.o	France	492
Seine	D.o	France	430
Po	D.o	Italy	425
Ebro	D.o	Spain	380
Severn	D.o	England	225
Thames	D.o	England	218
Shannon	D.o	Ireland	210
Humber	D.o	England	200
Tay	D.o	Scotland	153
Forth	D.o	Scotland	120

NOTE.

The greatest Altitude attained by Man was 24,400 feet, they found the air intensely cold and piercing, and owing to the extreme tenuity, respiration was difficult. Blood oozed from the Eyes, Lips, and Gums. Some of the party fainted, and all of them felt extreme debility. (Vide Humboldt.) Authorities consulted, are Humboldt, Asiatic Researches, Coxe's Swiss.d Pallas.d Trav.d &c.

ABBREVIATIONS.
Swiss.d — Swisserland
Scot.d — Scotland
Engl.d — England
Suma. — Sumatra
Pyren.d — Pyrenees
Kamts. — Kamtschatka
Hung.d — Hungary
Bourb.I. — Bourbon I.
N.W.Coa. — N.t W.t Coast
Carac.d — Caraccas
Jama.d — Jamaica
S.t Vinc.t — S.t Vincent
EU. — Europe
AS. — Asia
AF. — Africa
N.A. — N.th America
S.A. — S.th America

ON THE CONSTRUCTION OF THE RIVERS.

Note. In order that the method resorted to in the construction of "The Comparative View of Rivers" may be clearly elucidated, it is necessary to observe, that they retain their true figure as laid down on the best Maps, with this exception, that the greater angles, for the sake of convenience are deduced on a perpendicular line drawn from the Source of each River to the Sea, as demonstrated on the annexed Diagrams.—The Letters in each intermediate space between the short horizontal lines marked thus // readily point out the true compass bearing of each angle or portion of the River therein contained &c.

Explanation of the Signs

Woods		Meadows	
Marshes		Sand	

REFERENCE TO THE MOUNTAINS IN THE EASTERN HEMISPHERE.

		Region	Country	Altitude			Region	Country	Altitude
1	Dhawalagiri	AS.	Bootan	26,462	45	d'Or (M.t)	EU.	France	6,190
2	Jamatron	D.o	D.o	25,400	46	Cantal	D.o	France	6,090
3	Dhaiban	D.o	D.o	24,740	47	Snœha	D.o	Sweden	6,050
4	Peak	D.o	D.o	24,625	48	Roettriük	D.o	D.o	6,000
5	Peak	D.o	D.o	24,250	49	Reculet (M.t)	D.o	Swiss.d	5,100
6	Peak	D.o	D.o	23,266	50	Dole (M.t)	D.o	France	6,410
7	Peak	D.o	D.o	23,053	51	Puy de Dome	D.o	D.o	6,226
8	Peak	D.o	D.o	22,768	52	Brenner (M.t)	D.o	Tyrol	6,210
9	M.t Blanc	EU.	Swiss.d	15,430	53	Hechla (M.t)	D.o	Iceland	5,010
10	M.t Rosa	D.o	D.o	15,527	54	Ida (M.t)	AS.	Turkey	4,960
11	Order Spitz	D.o	D.o	15,080	55	Tagoni	D.o	Russia	4,900
12	Cervin	D.o	D.o	14,750	56	Ballon	EU.	France	4,604
13	Loneria	D.o	D.o	14,450	57	Sna Fell	D.o	Ireland	4,560
14	Pelvoux	D.o	France	14,430	58	Ben Nevis	D.o	Scot.d	4,370
15	M.t Ophir	D.o	Suma.	13,888	59	Corea	AS.	China	4,300
16	Gross Glückner	EU.	Swiss.d	13,800	60	Cairn Gorm	EU.	Scot.d	4,060
17	Jungfrau Horn	D.o	D.o	13,720	61	Ben Lawyers	D.o	D.o	4,015
18	Eriet Horn	D.o	D.o	13,800	62	Vesuvius (Volc.)	D.o	Italy	3,935
19	Sochonda	AS.	China	13,600	63	Ben Wevis	D.o	Scot.d	3,720
20	Finaelite Peak	EU.	Gurayel	13,370	64	Snowden	D.o	Wales	3,568
21	Malehneen	D.o	Spain	11,804	65	Table Mountain	AF.	Africa	3,580
22	Scheck Horn	D.o	Swiss.d	11,490	66	Ben Lomond	EU.	Scot.d	3,250
23	Venkatta Peak	D.o	Spain	11,440	67	Sca Fell	D.o	Engl.d	3,160
24	M.t Perdu	D.o	Pyren.d	11,265	68	Skiddaw	D.o	D.o	3,020
25	La Viguemal	D.o	D.o	11,010	69	Tagoni	D.o	Wales	2,934
26	Etna Volcano	D.o	Sicily	10,940	70	Orsa Fell	D.o	Engl.d	2,901
27	Furca	D.o	Alps	10,580	71	Mangerton	D.o	Ireland	2,700
28	Bnitatoi	AS.	Tartary	10,555	72	Cheviot Hills	D.o	Engl.d	2,658
29	Hoch-Horn	EU.	Tyrol	10,680	73	Plynlimmon	D.o	Wales	4,463
30	Awatscha (Volc.)	AS.	Kamts.	9,600	74	Whernside	D.o	Engl.d	2,384
31	Grimsel	EU.	Swiss.d	8,960	75	Ingleboro'	D.o	D.o	2,361
32	S.t Gothard	D.o	D.o	8,820	76	Saronè	D.o	Italy	2,270
33	Lomnitz Peak	D.o	Hung.d	8,640	77	Carmel (M.t)	AS.	Syria	2,100
34	Velino (M.t)	D.o	Italy	8,300	78	Sna Fell	EU.	I.o.Man	2,004
35	Sneehutton	D.o	Norway	8,195	79	Black Comb	D.o	Engl.d	1,919
36	S.t Bernard	D.o	Swiss.d	8,040	80	Griffle	D.o	Scot.d	1,900
37	Puros del Bosco	D.o	D.o	7,695	81	Campsie Hills	D.o	Engl.d	1,500
38	Volcano	AF.	Bourb.I.	7,680	82	Malvern Hills	D.o	Engl.d	1,260
39	Montaigu	EU.	Pyren.d	7,320	83	Craig Pathick	D.o	Ireland	1,003
40	Turon Pass	D.o	Swiss.d	6,810	84	Brianc	D.o	Wales	900
41	Cnie	D.o	D.o	6,780	85	Holyhead	D.o	Wales	709
42	Simplon	D.o	D.o	6,174	86	Dover	D.o	Engl.d	469
43	Olympus	EU.	Greece	6,500	87	Shooter Hill	D.o	D.o	446
44	Cimone	D.o	Italy	6,400	88	Greenwich	D.o	D.o	284

REFERENCE TO THE MOUNTAINS IN THE WESTERN HEMISPHERE.

		Region	Country	Altitude			Region	Country	Altitude
1	Chimborazo	S.A.	Quito	21,460	15	Pambamarca	S.A.	Quito	13,500
2	Chica Cassala	D.o	Quito	20,480	16	Calbe	N.A.	Mexico	13,360
3	Cayambe	D.o	D.o	19,480	17	Ihibabaka	D.o	D.o	8,360
4	Antisana (Volc.)	D.o	D.o	19,155	18	Silla de Caraccas	D.o	Carac.d	8,640
5	Cotopaxi (Volc.)	D.o	D.o	18,670	19	Blue M.ten (Volc.)	N.A.	Jama.d	8,180
6	S.t Elias (M.t)	N.A.	N.W.Coa.	17,840	20	Stony M.ten	U.States	D.o	8,250
7	Puebla	D.o	Mexico	17,700	21	High Peak in D.o	D.o		
8	Hlinieea	D.o	Peru	17,390	22	La Souffrire	S.A.	S.t Vinc.t	3,810
9	Orizaba (Volc.)	N.A.	Mexico	17,370	23	Morne Garon	D.o	D.o	3,050
10	Cotocatche	S.A.	Peru	16,440	24	Junallo	D.o	Mexico	2,365
11	Pinchincha	D.o	Quito	15,000	25	Killingham Peak	U.States		2,464
12	Sierra de Nevada	N.A.	Mexico	15,000	26	Kataskill	D.o		3,490
13	Nevada de Toluca	D.o	D.o	15,168	27	Alleghany M.ten	D.o		3,000
14	Tunguragua (Volc.)	S.A.	Quito	14,950	28	Stony M.ten (low.part)	D.o		784

London: WILLIAM DARTON: 58 Holborn Hill 1o Mo. 23.d 1823.

W.R.Gardner Sculp.t 567 Strand.

Chart of the World Shewing the Tracks of the U.S. Exploring Expedition

The product of one of the largest, longest, and most successful voyages of discovery ever undertaken, this was the 1842 Charles Wilkes map of the world showing isotherms. The United States Exploring Expedition set sail in 1838 and, working primarily in the Pacific, where this map was centered, was a tour de force of global discovery and exploration unmatched since the voyages of Captain Cook.

This map not only illustrated the tracks of Wilkes' exploration, it also offered detailed records of global temperature measurements. Warmer areas were in red, while the cold polar seas appeared in blue. Perhaps the greatest achievement of the Wilkes Expedition was the first mapping of a significant part of the Antarctic Coast. Although other explorers, including Ross, had seen parts of Antarctica, Wilkes mapped great stretches of the icy barren coastline – much of which was illustrated here for the first time in a published form.

The parts of Antarctic now known as Wilkes Land were shown at the bottom of this chart directly south of Australia. The British and the French had launched concurrent expeditions in search of the seventh, and last, continent on Earth. An observer noted that the U.S. Expedition was "doomed to be frozen to death" as conditions were horrendous and the U.S. ships and crew were less well equipped and experienced than their French and British counterparts. Despite this, Wilkes and his fleet returned triumphant, vastly exceeding the achievements of their contemporaries.

Cartographer

Charles Wilkes (1798-1877) attended Columbia University before becoming an officer in the United States Navy. Wilkes led the United States Exploring Expedition on one of the greatest voyages of discovery ever undertaken. Nevertheless, his abrasive personality prevented him from being duly honored at that time. In fact, rather than being celebrated for his achievements, he was convicted by a court martial for the illegally extreme punishments he inflicted on his crew and for slaughtering 80 Fijians. Reportedly, Captain Ahab of Herman Melville's Moby Dick *was modeled after Wilkes.*

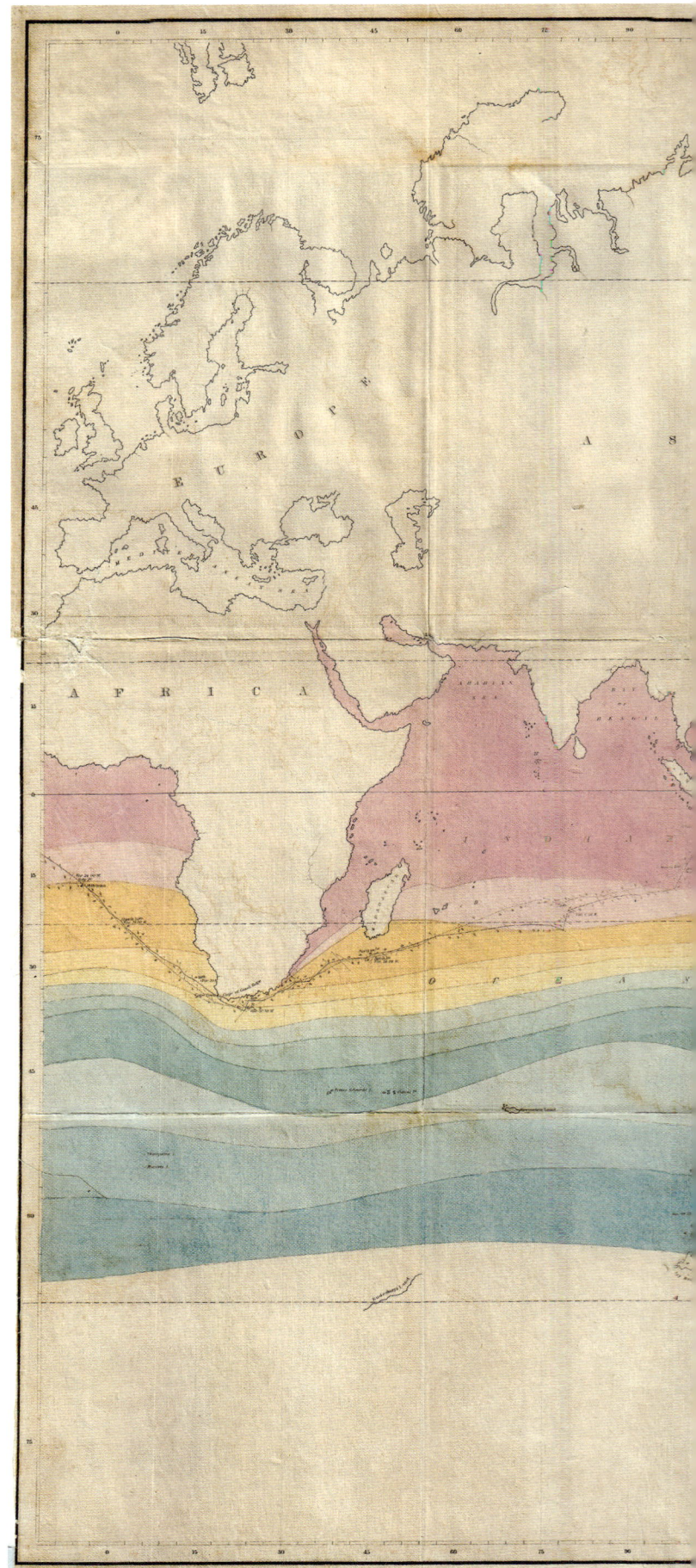

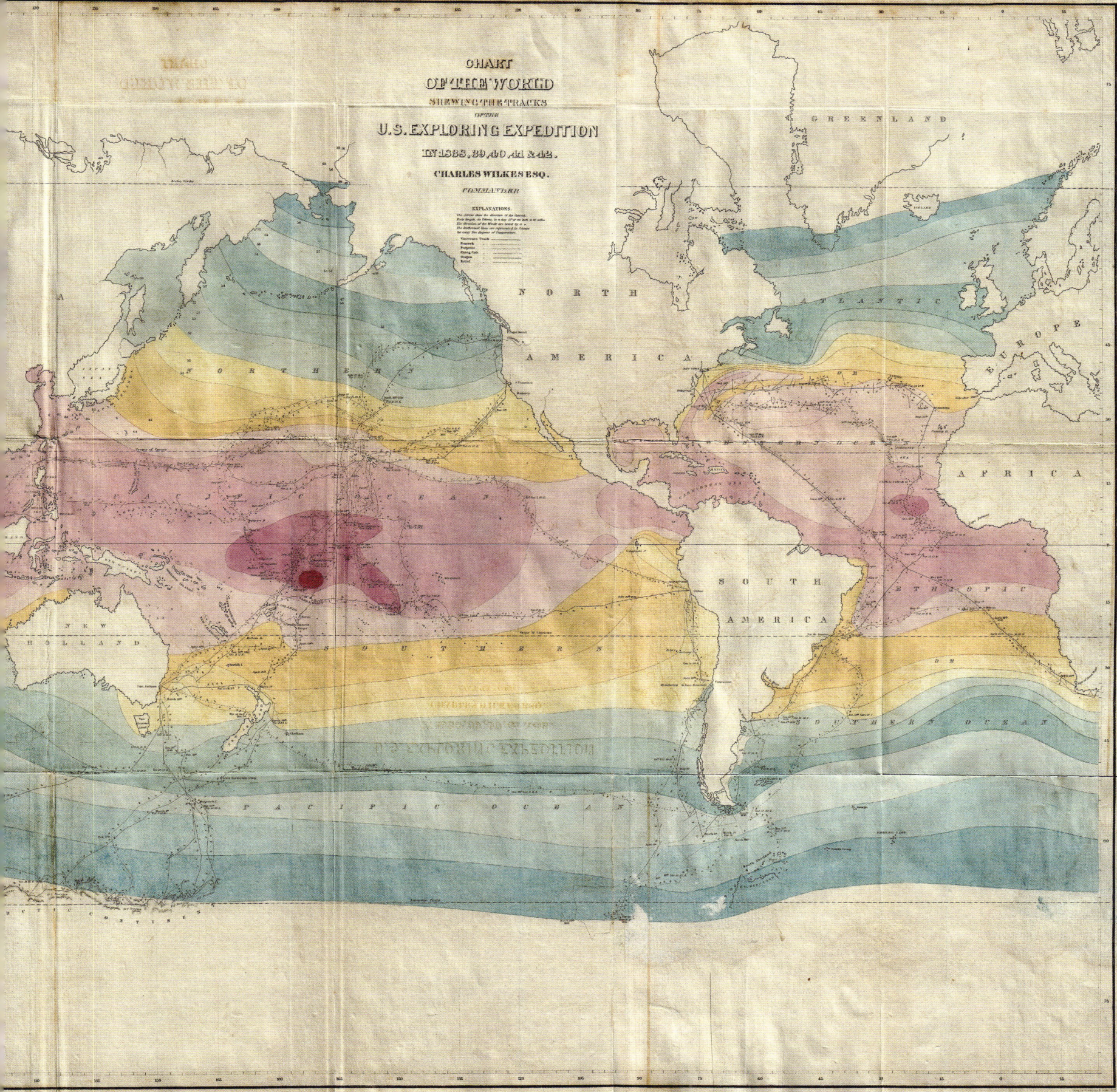

CHART
OF THE WORLD
SHEWING THE TRACKS
OF THE
U.S. EXPLORING EXPEDITION
IN 1838, 39, 40, 41 & 42.
CHARLES WILKES ESQ.
COMMANDER

EXPLANATIONS

145

GEOMETRICAL PROJECTION OF TWO THIRDS OF THE SPHERE (AFRICA CENTRAL) BY COLL. SIR H.JAMES.R.E.F.R.S.M.R.I.A. &c.

ESSE TENUS TERRARUM OCULIS PRÆTENDITUR ORBIS.

Geometrical Projection of Two Thirds of the Sphere

Intended to show the "habitable" parts of the earth, this rare map was drawn by Colonel Sir Henry James in 1860. The circular style was highly unusual and was probably intended to give the map a "globe-like" feel, as this stereographic projection, encompassing over 220 degrees of the Meridian, depicted nearly two-thirds of the Earth.

The wavy lines were drawn to illustrate degrees of longitude both east and west of the Greenwich Meridian. Working with the Ordinance Survey of the United Kingdom, Colonel James' intention had been to "map the world" based on the Greenwich Meridian. Influenced by the work of James and others, the Royal Observatory at Greenwich, England was, in 1884, chosen to be the location for the prime meridian by a group of 25 nations.

Centered at the bottom of the map, Antarctica was included as a white area where only those shores discovered and seen by navigators had been drawn using orange ink. The remainder of the southern continent was, when James drew this map, pure speculation.

Cartographer

Henry James (1803-1877), was a British Army officer. In 1857, he was appointed to lead the British Topographical and Statistical Depot at the War Office. There, working with assistant J. O'Farrell, he developed the unique geometrical projection presented here. Eventually, he was elevated to the rank of Major General and became the Director General of the Ordnance Survey, the British mapping agency. His great work, the 1868 Atlas Portfolio, was, unfortunately, not carried forward by his successors and was never completed.

Neueste Karte Der Erde

A wealth of information was included in this extraordinary 1870 Baur and Bromme German language map of the world. Designed to be educational, this map was intricate, complex, and remarkably large. By the end of the 19th century, much of the world had been explored and that exploration was documented here. Two weather charts, a wind chart, an isothermal chart, and a chart of magnetic variations were all included, as well as ocean currents, polar projections, and an inset of Panama.

The expeditions of many important explorers were illustrated, including the voyages of James Cook, Diego Álvarez, George Vancouver, Abel Tasman, John Biscoe, Charles Wilkes, William Bligh and several others. The Canadian Arctic, as depicted here, was surrounded by beautifully rendered glacial ice. The Antarctic remained largely unexplored, but some coastlines could be seen here near South America's Tierra del Fuego (Land of Fire) and south of Australia. The speculative Gillis Land could also be found in the Arctic and was presumably named after the Dutchman Cornelis Giles who was said to have discovered it in 1707.

Carl Baur and Traugott Bromme published this map using chromolithography, a multi-toned, lithographic, chemical process resulting from technological advances in printing science. This process was revolutionary in the cartographic field and offered, for the first time, an economical technique for mass-producing richly colored maps. The preset example was published after Bromme's death by his partner, Carl Friedrich Baur.

Cartographers

• **Traugott Bromme** (1802-1866) was born in Anger, Germany. As a young man, he left Germany and went to the United States. Bromme's early years were full of adventure. He worked as a surgeon on a Columbian war-schooner cruising the West Indies and, for a time, was imprisoned in Haiti. Some 20 years later, he returned to Germany, where he became a prominent publisher of books and maps.

• **Carl Friedrich Baur** (fl. c. 1850-1890) a German map publisher, was well known for producing one of the earliest commercial and industrial atlases of the 1800s.

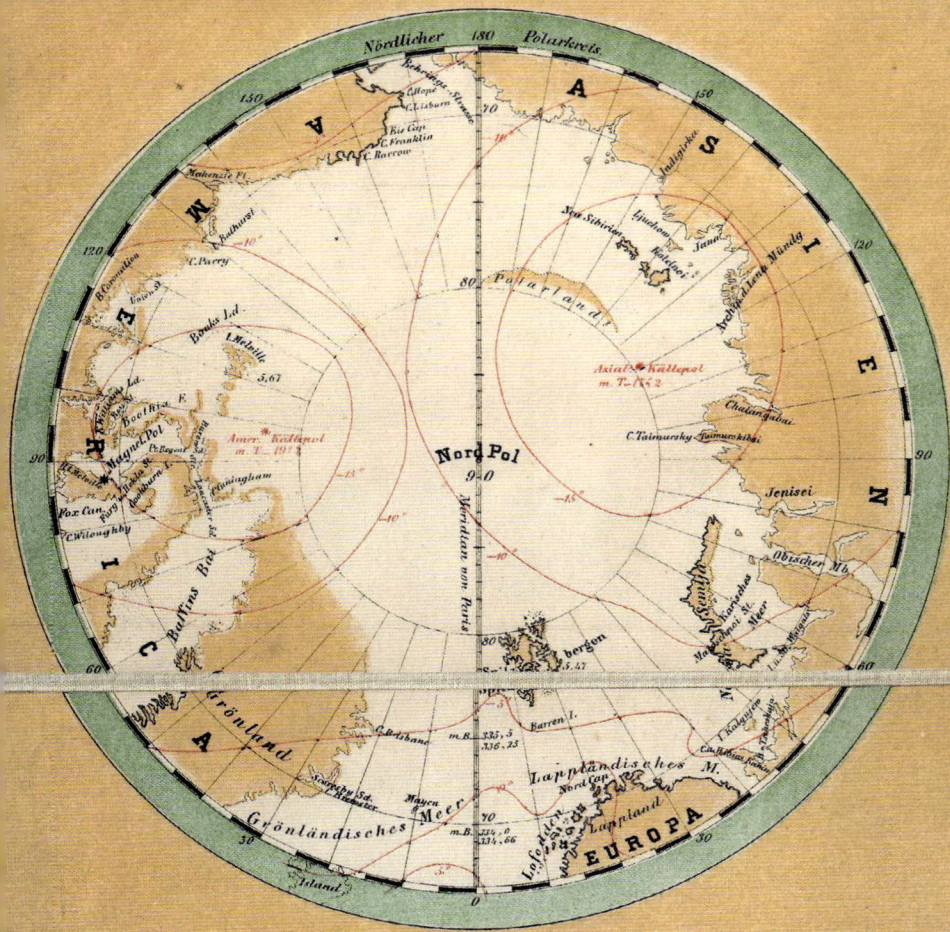

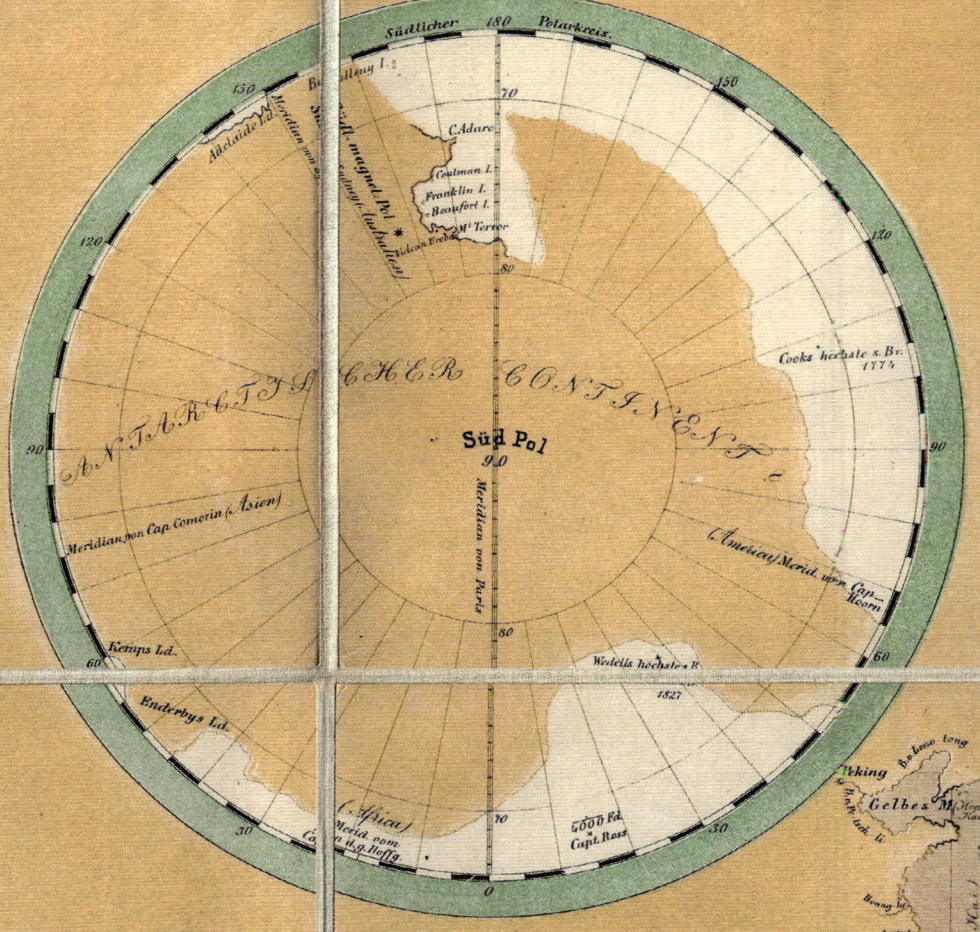

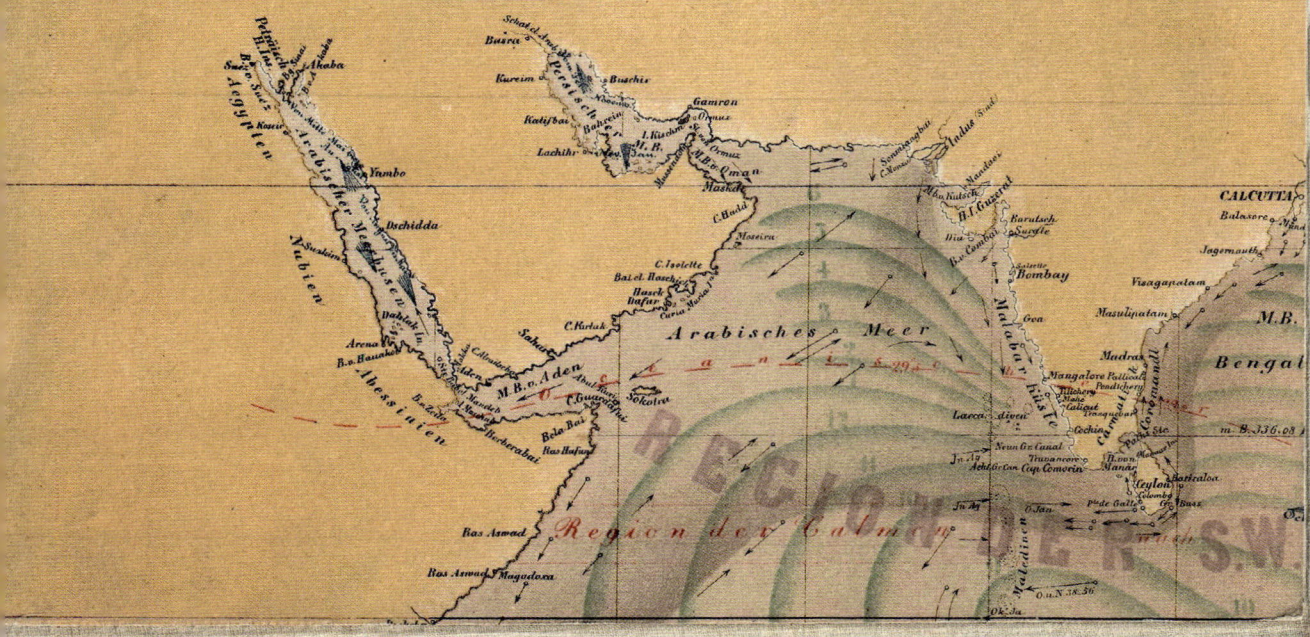

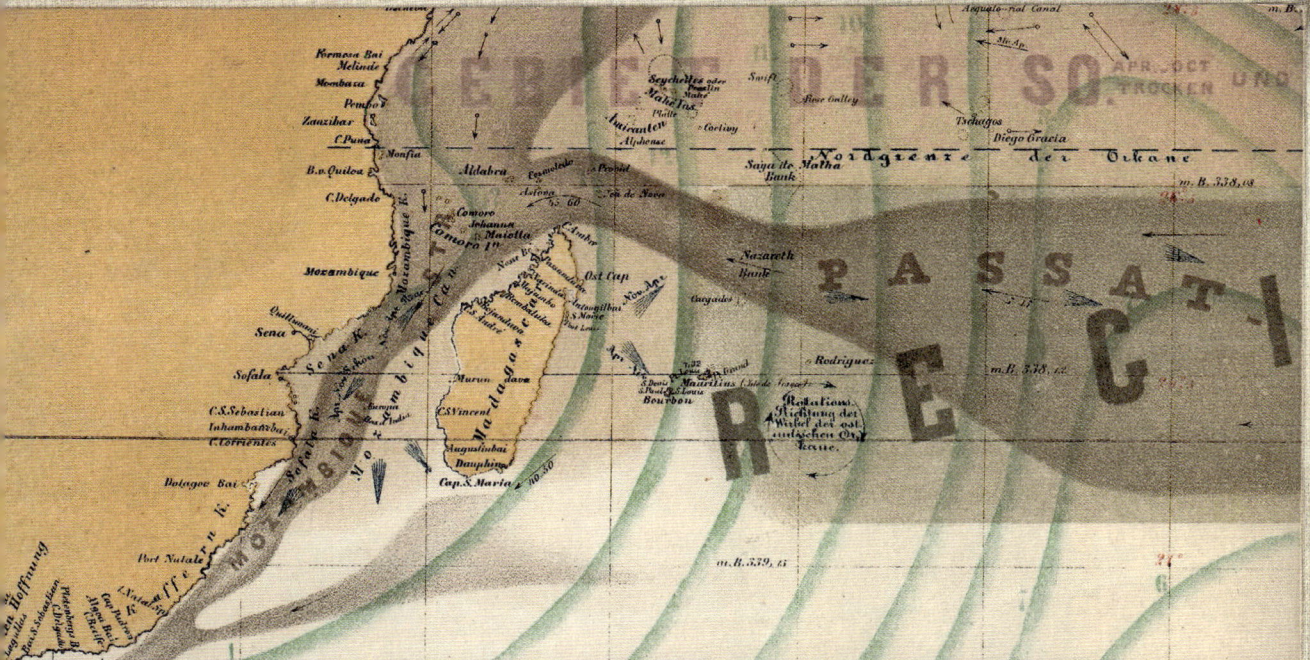

Zu Dr. Jileks Oceanografie

This rare 1880 chromolithograph map of the world was remarkable for its beauty and complexity. Created by Dr. August von Jilek, the map featured little inland detail but compensated with a lavish illustration of the world's oceans. The map showed currents, wind patterns, climatological, and geophysical phenomena, among them the Gulf Stream. Tables and diagrams, included throughout the map, added additional detail expounding upon the ideas expressed by Dr. Jilek.

While Jilek had no formal education as an oceanographer or climate scientist, he had a passion for the subject and, under the patronage of the powerful nobleman Archduke Ferdinand Maximillian, acquired a position teaching the subject at the Austrian Imperial Naval Academy. This map was intended to illustrate a textbook Jilek composed to fill that role, the *Lehrbuch der Oceanographie*. Jilek himself had limited oceanographic theories, but he was well educated and his map referenced the revolutionary work of Immanuel Kant, Eduard Brobrik, and Matthew Fontaine Maury.

Cartographer

August von Jilek (1819-1898) was a Czech physician, scientist, and bureaucrat active with the Austrian Imperial Navy in the second half of the 19th century. Jilek was the personal physician of Archduke Ferdinand Maximillian (1832-1867). While he had no formal education in Oceanography, he was passionate about the subject and, under Maximillian's patronage, flourished as a lecturer on the subject. Ferdinand Maximillian later became Emperor Maximillian I in Mexico, an ill-fated move that resulted in his execution just three years later.

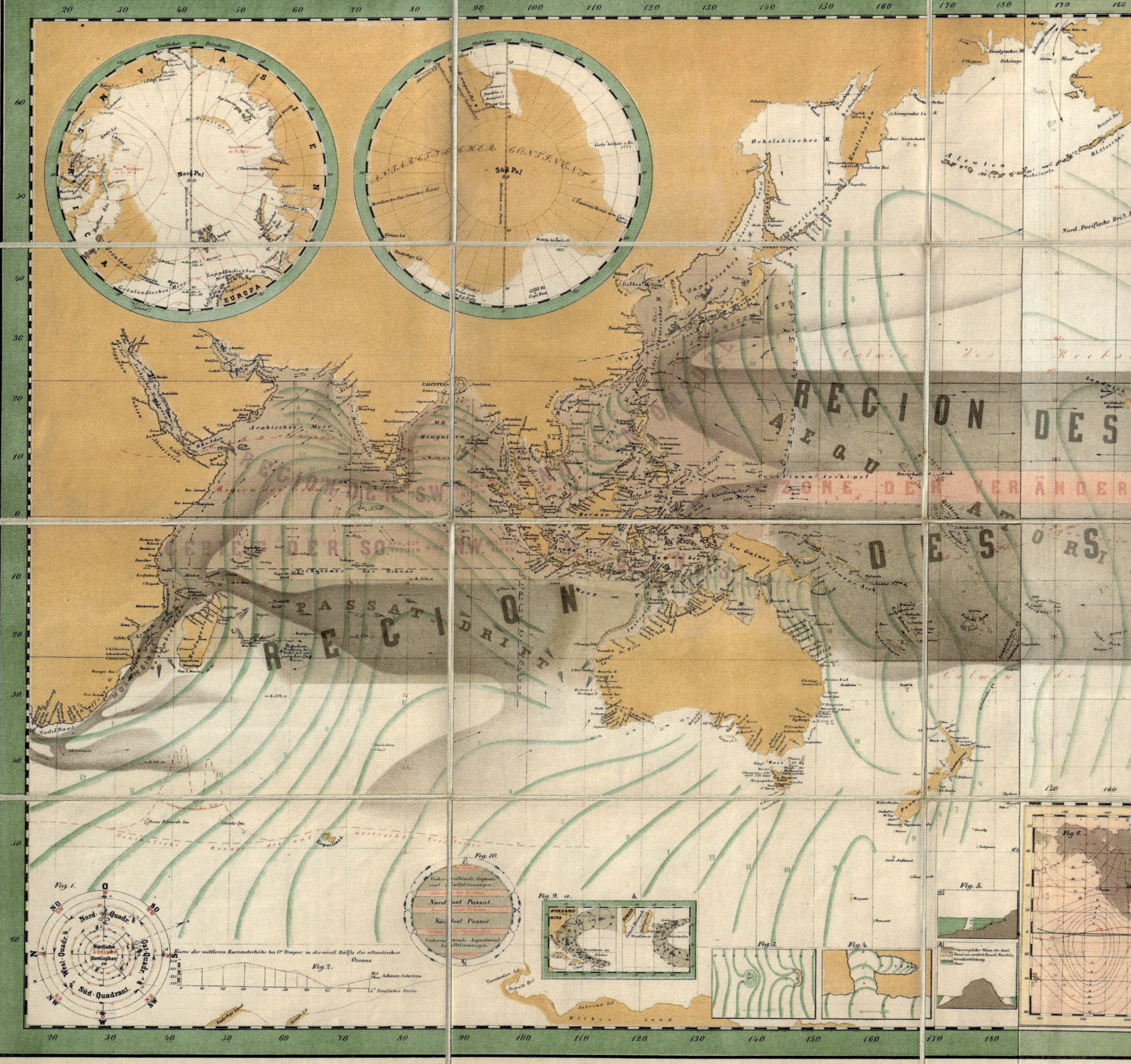

ASIEN

AMERICA

EUROPA

Nord-Pol

Grönländisches

ANTARCTISCHER CONTINENT

Süd-Pol

Ocholskisches M.

Aleuten

Nord-Pacifische Drift-Strö.

CALCUTTA

Arabisches Meer

Bengalen

REGION DES

ZONE DER VERÄNDERL

REGION DER SW

GEBIET DER SO UND NW.

PASSAT

REGION DER

Neu Guinea

Calmen

Region der Calmen

Fig. 1.

Nord-Quadr.

Nördliche Hemisphäre

West-Quadr.

Südliche Hemisphäre

Ost-Quadr.

Süd-Quadrant

Fig. 2.

Curve der mittleren Barometerhöhe bei 0° Temper. in der nördl. Hälfte des atlantischen Oceans

Fig. 10.

Nordost-Passat.

Südost-Passat.

Fig. 9.

NORDAME RIKA

Fig. 3.

Fig. 4.

Fig. 5.

Fig. 6.

Wilkes Land

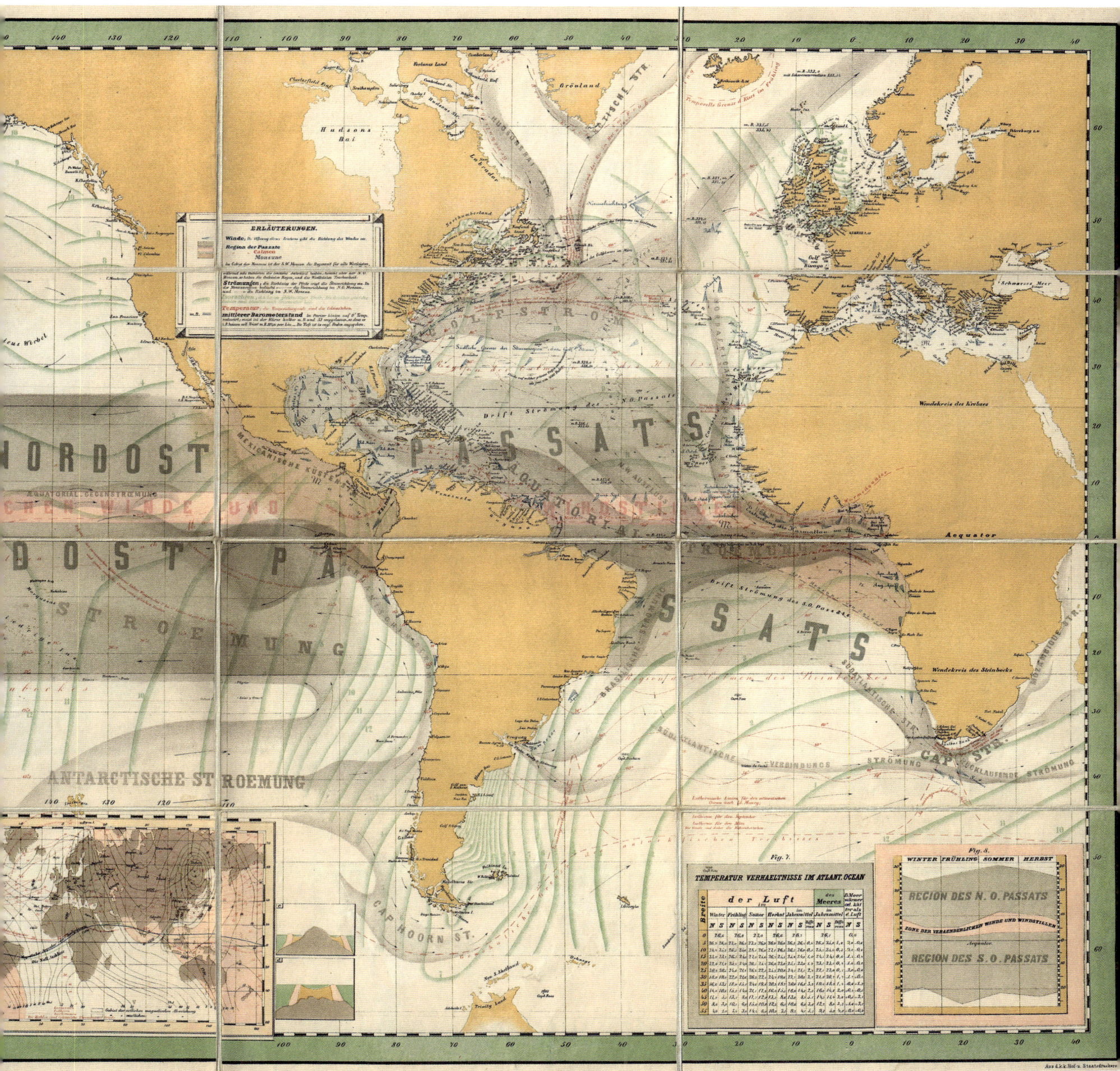

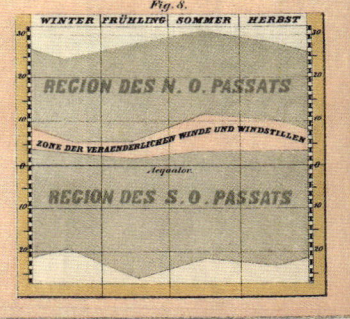

153

Whimsy and Persuasive Cartography

*I*first encountered persuasive cartography at a rare book fair in New York City. A library curator approached me and told me he wanted to buy maps that were "about something other than their geography." Such maps are the essence of this chapter.

As we have seen in previous chapters, cartographers rarely made maps without an agenda. Some were pursuing scientific truths, others were promoting religious values, and still others were appealing to political or nationalistic idealism. From the late 19th century into the middle of the 20th century, the employment of maps as persuasive tools reached new levels of sophistication. In a notable deviation from many earlier maps, the cartography itself became less important than the message being communicated. By making the cartography secondary to a powerful message, the importance of established cartographical conventions, such as geographical accuracy, advanced projections, and standardized proportions, was lessened. Many such maps therefore embraced wild geographical distortions to promote their points, often giving the maps a whimsical aspect.

While there are instances of persuasive cartography dating to some of the earliest printed maps, the sublimation of the geography to the map's non-cartographic message began to become increasingly common in Europe in the second half of the 19th century. The earliest such maps took the form of Serio-Comic maps, a style not invented by, but popularized by, Fred Rose in England. These maps, usually of Europe, replaced nation states with cartoonish personifications of those states. So, for example, England might have been represented by an elderly woman whose

form roughly corresponded to the shape of that country on a map. Such maps were both playful and deadly serious in their apt illustration of the complex political situations in late 19th and early 20th century Europe. Most importantly for our purposes though, are the underlying assumptions that allowed such maps to exist.

By the end of the 19th century, the study of geography, which earlier had been restricted to wealthy, typically male, merchants and noblemen, had democratized considerably. With the mid-19th century development of economical printing methods, such as lithography and wax process printing, maps and atlases were, for the first time, available to the general population. At the same time, globalization was on the rise. Military men, merchants, and tourists were traveling the world, and friends and family at home studied geography to better understand their travels.

As geographical knowledge waxed, the warping of that geographical knowledge, for persuasive or whimsical purposes, became practical. Maps like those of Fred Rose and other persuasive mapmakers depended on readers having a solid geographical background. It was essential that readers understood what the geography represented and looked like on a traditional map, before they could understand how the warping of geography transmitted the cartographer's message.

Most early persuasive cartography was not very subtle, but rather direct and clear in its communication. Cartographers often embraced bold color-coding to express their vision or message. The most basic type of persuasive map simply overlaid pertinent information on existing geography, as with Stanford's World War I propaganda map, What Germany Wants *or Reverend Arthur Tappan Pierson's* Map of the World's Religions. *These maps rely on established geography coupled with bold color-coding to send their message. In the case of the propaganda map, that message is, in essence "Beware! Germany is coming for you!" Pierson had a more complex message in his world religions map. He believed that the world could be fully evangelized to Christianity within his generation and his map was a battle plan.*

Another style of persuasive map embraces whimsical imagery and uses the map as an exceptionally effective background. The series of maps Lucian Boucher produced to promote Air France are perfect examples. His maps overlaid a recognizable map, with rich vignette imagery and bold colors to such a degree that the actual map receded into the background. His maps noted few actual geographical locations, and those that did appear were only present to promote Air France routes. The message was clear, "this is the world, and Air France can take you there in safety and comfort."

A 1925 sugoroku map issued by the Japanese daily newspaper, the Asahi Shimbun, *to promote the success of the historic biplane fights of the* Hatsukaze (First Wind) *and* Kochikaze (East Wind) *from Tokyo to Rome, used a similar technique. The map was there, at the center, and effectively promoted the global aspect of the voyage, but, despite its central casting, is little more than a background. Instead, the graphics dance around the frame, with the* Hatsukaze *and* Kochikaze *superimposed on the global image. Behind it all, the iconic Rising Sun of Japan is subtle but impactful, effectively conveying*

a message of Japanese nationalism and promoting Japanese technological achievements.

Other techniques used by persuasive cartographers warped the Earth itself to conform to their vision and message. Consider Orlando Ferguson's remarkable 1893 Square and Stationary Earth. *Ferguson transformed the familiar globe into an inverse toroid to conform to his flat Earth belief system. To the right of the main map, he mocked "Globe Theorists" who hold on for their lives to a globe hurtling through space at 65,000 miles per hour. He traveled extensively with this map, promoting it everywhere he went, as a Biblical alternative to questionable "science." Its message was effective enough that "Flat Earthers" still use Ferguson's map today, over 125 years later.*

More subtle takes on the technique of warping the globe to sell an idea were Harrison's Target Tokyo *and* Target Berlin. *These World War II propaganda posters, issued by the American government, relied on an intense global image with exaggerated photographic relief work to intensify the centralized graphic, Target Like, on Tokyo. Like many persuasive maps, its impact was immediate and visceral and did not require in depth study in order to understand it. What it did require was a basic understanding of geography. Harrison presented the world as a great target and Tokyo and Berlin, respectively, were the bull's eyes. These maps were issued at the end of the war and the message, "the enemy is in our sights" rang loud and clear.*

Today, persuasive cartography remains very much alive in the form of commercial advertising, political propaganda, and humorous cartography.

London
Pub.d Feb.y 26th 1805.
by H. Humphrey 27.
St. James's Street

J.s Gillray inv. & fec.t

or *State Epicures taking un Petit Souper.*
is too small to satisfy such insatiable appetites

— vide M.ᶜ W——m's. eccentricities, in ÿ Political Register.

295

The Plumb-pudding in danger : or State Epicures taking un Petit Souper

This is one of the few Gillray satirical political cartoons that feature geographical elements. The present map/cartoon was issued early in the Napoleonic Wars (1803-1815) when Napoleon's empire building seemed unstoppable in Europe. In this image, Napoleon Bonaparte sits down to a fine earthy dinner with William Pitt, the Prime Minister of England. Pitt championed British partnership with Austria, Russia, and Sweden to oppose Napoleon as the Third Coalition. Joining the coalition soon led to the October 1805 Battle of Trafalgar, in which Admiral Horatio Nelson soundly defeated French naval forces, thus assuring British dominance of the sea. Thus, as illustrated here, Napoleon carves of Europe for himself while Pitt, assured of his dominance at sea, reserves for England the greater part of the globe.

Gillray's influential career as a graphic satirist was doubtless influenced by what his elders considered to be a misspent youth. Showing little skill or interest in letter-engraving, a career in which he apprenticed, Gillray instead spent his time with the itinerant theater groups that toured through London. Such groups typically poked fun at the powerful and at political events as they unfolded, providing the British public with a critical take on news. Although not an actor himself, Gillray applied the same printable to his graphic art, in the process creating the modern political cartoon.

Cartographer

James Gillray (1757-1815) was a British satirist and graphic artist generally considered to be the "Father of the Political Cartoon." Gillray was born in London where extensive exposure to satirical street theater influenced his development of graphic political satire. He produced hundreds of engravings, some quite racy, and was supported fully by his artwork. Because of the profane and politically critical nature of his work, much of it was suppressed until the 1850s, when it again became popular.

Missionary Map of the World

Cartographers

George Woolworth (1827-1901) and **Charles B. Colton** (1832-1916) were the sons of the important American map publisher Joseph Hutchins Colton (1800-1893). J. H. Colton brought his sons into the map business in 1855, harnessing them to spearhead the publication of his first major atlas in 1855. After Colton's bankruptcy in 1858, most of the subsequent maps issued by the firm bore the imprint of G. W. and C. B. Colton. The two brothers continued to manage the Colton firm after their father's death in 1893 until 1898, when they sold the firm to the August R. Ohman Company.

P OF THE WORLD

PREACH THE GOSPEL TO EVERY CREATURE

ntral Stations

MISSIONARY

TIES.

TON & Co.
M ST
RK.

ASIA

CHINESE EMPIRE

EUROPE

SIBERIA

PERSIA

ARABIA

ARABIAN SEA

BAY OF BENGAL

PACIFIC OCEAN

INDIAN OCEAN

AUSTRALIA

SOUTHERN OCEAN

AFRICA
205.000.000.

North Africa and Senegambia(Egypt) 12.000.000
Northeast Africa 11.500.000
Egypt Abyssinia etc.
Equatorial region 41.000.000
Southern Africa 23.500.000
Guinea 26.000.000
Central Africa etc. 52.000.000
Liberia 500.000
Madagascar etc. 4.500.000
Other African islands 600.000

Stations occupied by
Foreign Miss.l Societies

RELIGIONS

Protestant 105.500.000
Roman Catholic 205.500.000
Greek Church 85.500.000
Mahometan 170.000.000
Jews 5.000.000
Pagans etc. 650.000.000
Depressed Jews 21.000.000

TABLES OF POPULATION

ASIA
EAST INDIA ISLANDS
831.000.000.

Asiatic Turkey 17.500.000
Arabia 12.500.000
Persia 15.000.000
Beloochistan 2.000.000
Afghanistan 4.000.000
Bootan & Geordzia 18.170.000
Japan 35.025.000
Chinese Empire 435.000.000
India 213.416.000

British Borneo 27.500.000
Burma 5.000.000
Siam 3.750.000
Anam 21.000.000
Other Indian sub... 2.500.000
Sumatra 3.250.000
Java 8.000.000
Borneo 2.900.000
Celebes 6.500.000
Philippine Is. 71.000.000
The Sunda Islands
and other islands 2.750.000

This sheer size of this map, extending almost 4 m across and 2 m high, is exceptionally striking. The map has further been printed on waxed linen cloth. It was thus intended to be durable, easy to transport, and large enough to command a room. One imagines missionary lectures in far off countries. When the Colton brothers issued this map, it was received with great fanfare in the American missionary community, as described by the *Missionary Herald* (December, 1845) "Mr. J. H. Colton, map publisher, New York, is preparing a large map of the world, which may be superior, in some important particulars, to any thing of the kind yet published. It is on the general plan of Campbell's map presenting to the eye a picture of the moral and religious condition of the world. With these advantages, it will combine geographical accuracy and completeness in a high degree. For monthly concerts, Sabbath schools, lectures on missions, and even for the instruction of common schools in geography, it will be found and important auxiliary. The whole cost of the who hemispheres, separately or together, will be about ten dollars." We are aware of at least three historical variants of this map. The first edition was presented by J. H. Colton in 1845. A second edition, as here, appeared in 1878. A reduced version at approximately 50% size, was published in 1892. The final variant, issued for the Seventh Day Adventists, was published by August R. Ohman, successor to the Colton firm.

Map of the Square and Stationary Earth

Truly a wonder, this bizarre 1893 map by Orlando Ferguson exemplified the inherent conflict that emerged between faith and science in the late 19th century – a conflict that continues today. Ferguson was a man of deep religious convictions who felt that well established scientific ideas about the nature of the Earth and its place in space contradicted his understanding of Biblical scripture. This map was his reconciliation.

The tiny image, at the right of the map, showing the Earth hurling comet-like through space while two hapless gentlemen hold on for dear life, illustrated Ferguson's understanding of the "Globe or Flying Earth Theory." Ferguson constructed his alternative map based almost entirely upon scripture. His Biblical starting point contradicted theories of planetary movement: "The world also shall be stable that it be not moved." (Chronicles 16:3). He then addressed the shape of the Earth by attesting that it must be square with four defined corners (Isaiah 11:12). Other Biblical quotes, generally used out of context, completed the map, which took the form of an inverse toroid with the Northern Hemisphere convex and the Southern Hemisphere concave.

Ferguson accompanied this map with an 1891 book, *The Latest Discoveries in Astronomy: The Globe Theory of the Earth Refuted*, which he boldly claimed "Knocks the Globe Theory Clean Out!" Although it may seem hard to believe, with mountains of factual evidence refuting it, modern day flat Earth theorists still quote Ferguson.

Cartographer

Orlando Ferguson (1846-1911) was a real estate developer and self-proclaimed "professor" based in Hot Springs, South Dakota. He lectured extensively on his 'Square and Stationary Earth' theory and was lampooned even in his own day by more scientifically minded parties.

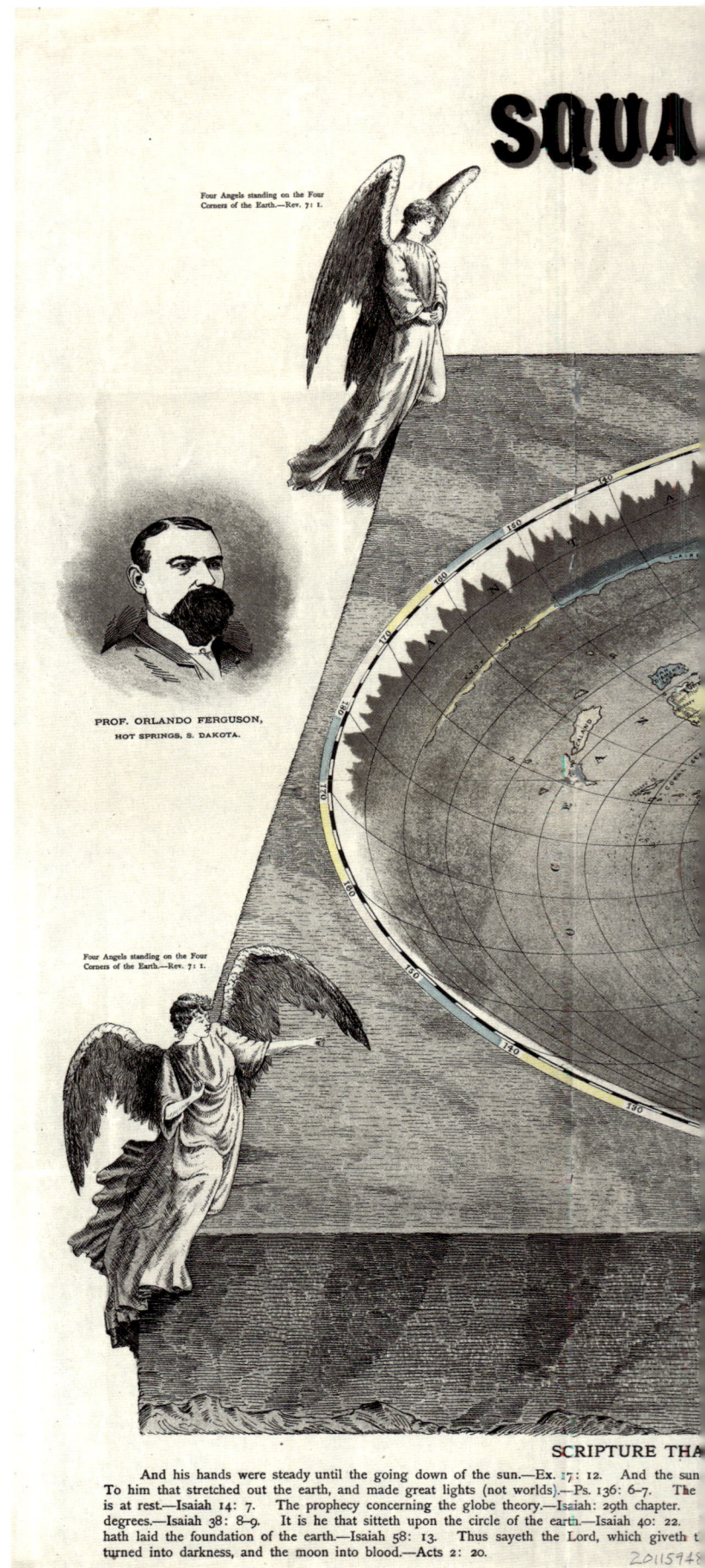

SQUA

Four Angels standing on the Four Corners of the Earth.—Rev. 7: 1.

PROF. ORLANDO FERGUSON,
HOT SPRINGS, S. DAKOTA.

Four Angels standing on the Four Corners of the Earth.—Rev. 7: 1.

SCRIPTURE THA

And his hands were steady until the going down of the sun.—Ex. 17: 12. And the sun To him that stretched out the earth, and made great lights (not worlds).—Ps. 136: 6-7. The is at rest.—Isaiah 14: 7. The prophecy concerning the globe theory.—Isaiah 29th chapter. degrees.—Isaiah 38: 8-9. It is he that sitteth upon the circle of the earth.—Isaiah 40: 22. hath laid the foundation of the earth.—Isaiah 58: 13. Thus sayeth the Lord, which giveth t turned into darkness, and the moon into blood.—Acts 2: 20.

MAP OF THE
E AND STATIONARY EARTH.

BY PROF. ORLANDO FERGUSON,
HOT SPRINGS, SOUTH DAKOTA.

r Hundred Passages in the Bible that Condemn the Globe Theory, or the Flying Earth, and None Sustain It.
This Map is the Bible Map of the World.

COPYRIGHT BY ORLANDO FERGUSON, 1893.

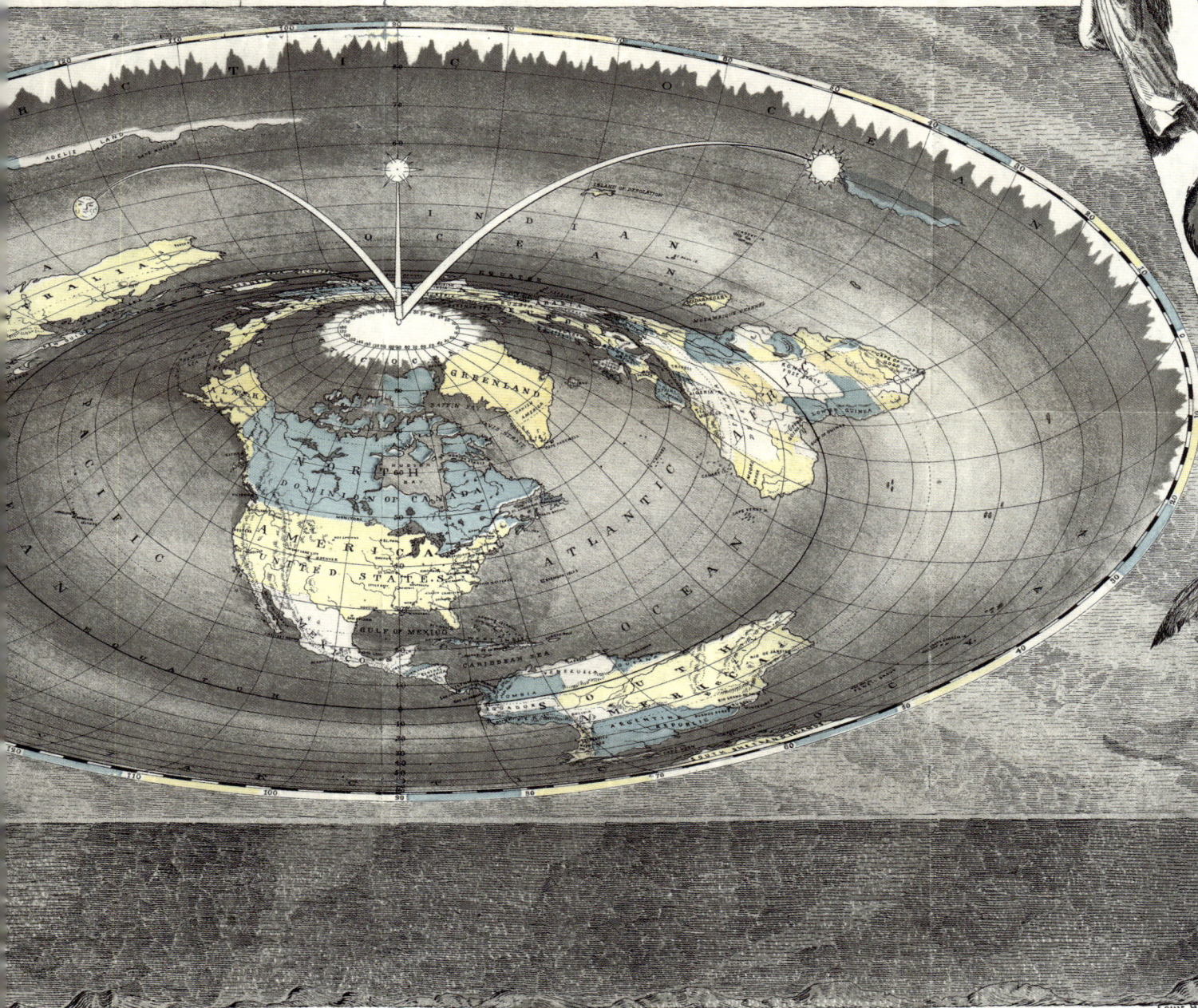

Four Angels standing on the Four Corners of the Earth.—Rev. 7: 1.

These men are flying on the globe at the rate of 65,000 miles per hour around the sun, and 1,042 miles per hour around the center of the earth (in their minds). Think of that speed!

Four Angels standing on the Four Corners of the Earth.—Rev. 7: 1.

Louis H. Everts & Co. Litho. Phila.

NDEMNS THE GLOBE THEORY.

till, and the moon stayed.—Joshua 10: 12–13.   The world also shall be stable that it be not moved.—Chron. 16: 30.
be darkened in his going forth.—Isaiah 13: 10.   The four corners of the earth.—Isaiah 11: 12.   The whole earth
the rebellious children, sayeth the Lord, that take counsel, but not of me.—Isaiah 30: 1.   So the sun returned ten
spread forth the earth.—Isaiah 52: 5.   That spreadeth abroad the earth by myself.—Isaiah 54: 24.   My hand also
or a light by day, and the moon and stars for a light by night (not worlds).—Jer. 31: 35–36.   The sun shall be

Send 25 Cents to the Author, Prof. Orlando Ferguson, for a book explaining this Square and Stationary Earth. It Knocks the Globe Theory Clean Out. It will Teach You How to Foretell Eclipses. It is Worth Its Weight in Gold.

Prevailing Religions of the World and Progress of Evangelization

This 1894 color-coded map was designed to express Christian evangelicalism around the world. It was created for the Protestant Reverend Arthur Tappan Pierson, to help advance his global missionary ambitions. The map was printed on waxed linen, an unusual choice that doubtless was intended to preserve the document while it was being carried to the far corners of the Earth by young missionaries.

Pierson associated each religious group with a color: red for Roman Catholics, yellow for Protestants, pink for Orthodox Christians, black for Jews, green for Muslims, grey for pagans, light grey for heathens. Yellow dots represented "mission stations and centers."

Definitions for "pagan" and "heathen" were not provided but it is likely that "heathen" was being used to refer to those who had been contacted, but had not yet converted to Christianity. "Pagan" most likely referred to peoples who had no experience or exposure whatsoever to Christian ideology.

The Protestant population was listed at 150 million individuals and 40 million church members. The Roman Catholic population was listed at 175-210 million. Orthodox Christianity ("Greek and Oriental") was listed at 84-99 million. The Muslim population ("Mohammedan") was listed at 160-200 million. The pagan population was listed at 200-250 million. The Jewish people were visually represented as a tiny segment on the color key and no number was provided. It was noted that as a "dispersed" population no location was indicated on the map. The heathen population was listed at 609-714 million – so Pierson had his work cut out.

Cartographer

Arthur Tappan Pierson (1837-1911) was an American Presbyterian pastor, scholar, and missionary active in the late 19th and early 20th centuries. Pierson believed the world could be fully evangelized to Christianity in his own lifetime and advocated passionately for increased missionary activity in all parts of the world. His own missionary work took him to Korea, England, Scotland, and throughout the United States where he worked to convert the First Nations population.

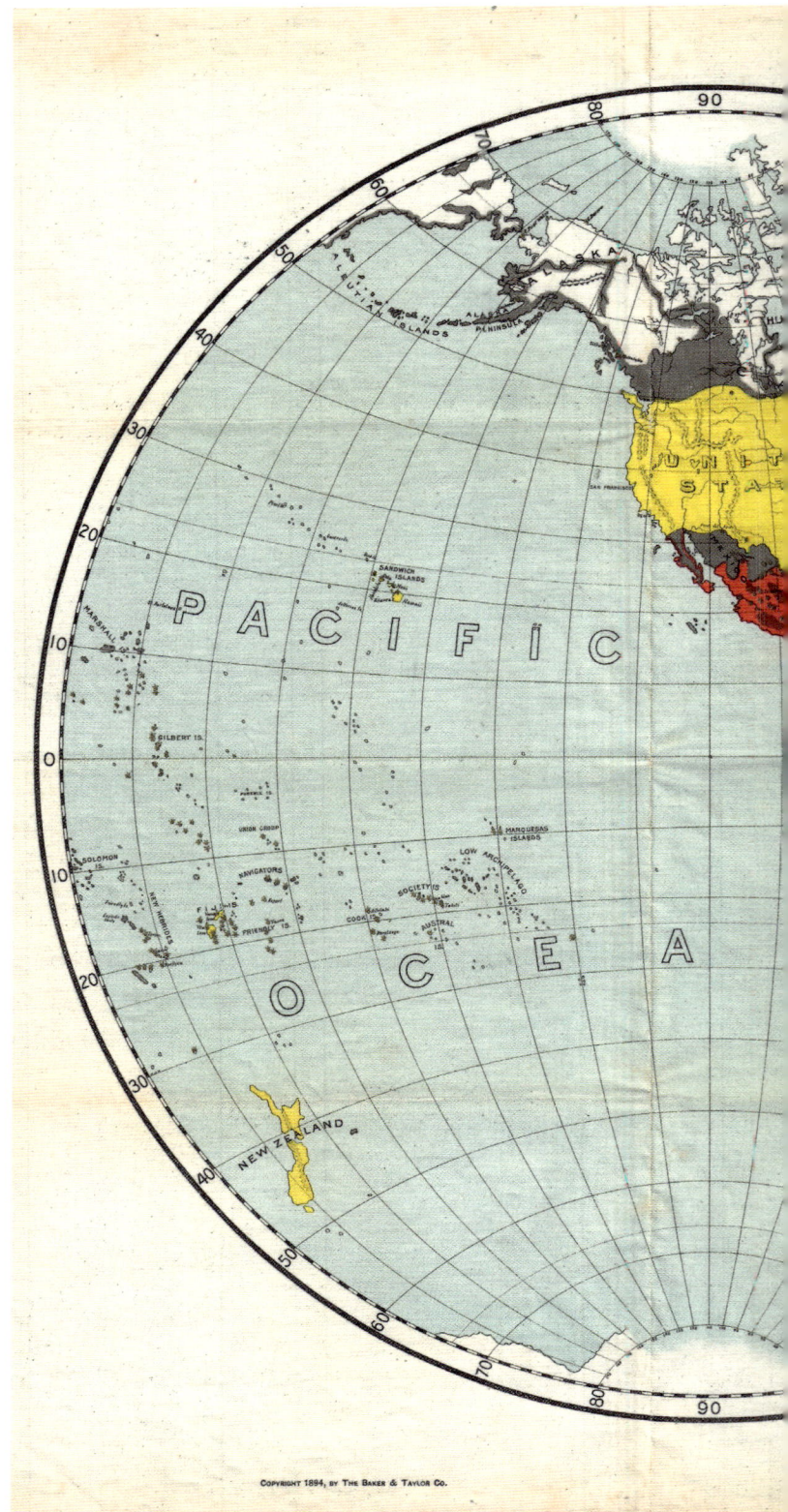

COPYRIGHT 1894, BY THE BAKER & TAYLOR CO.

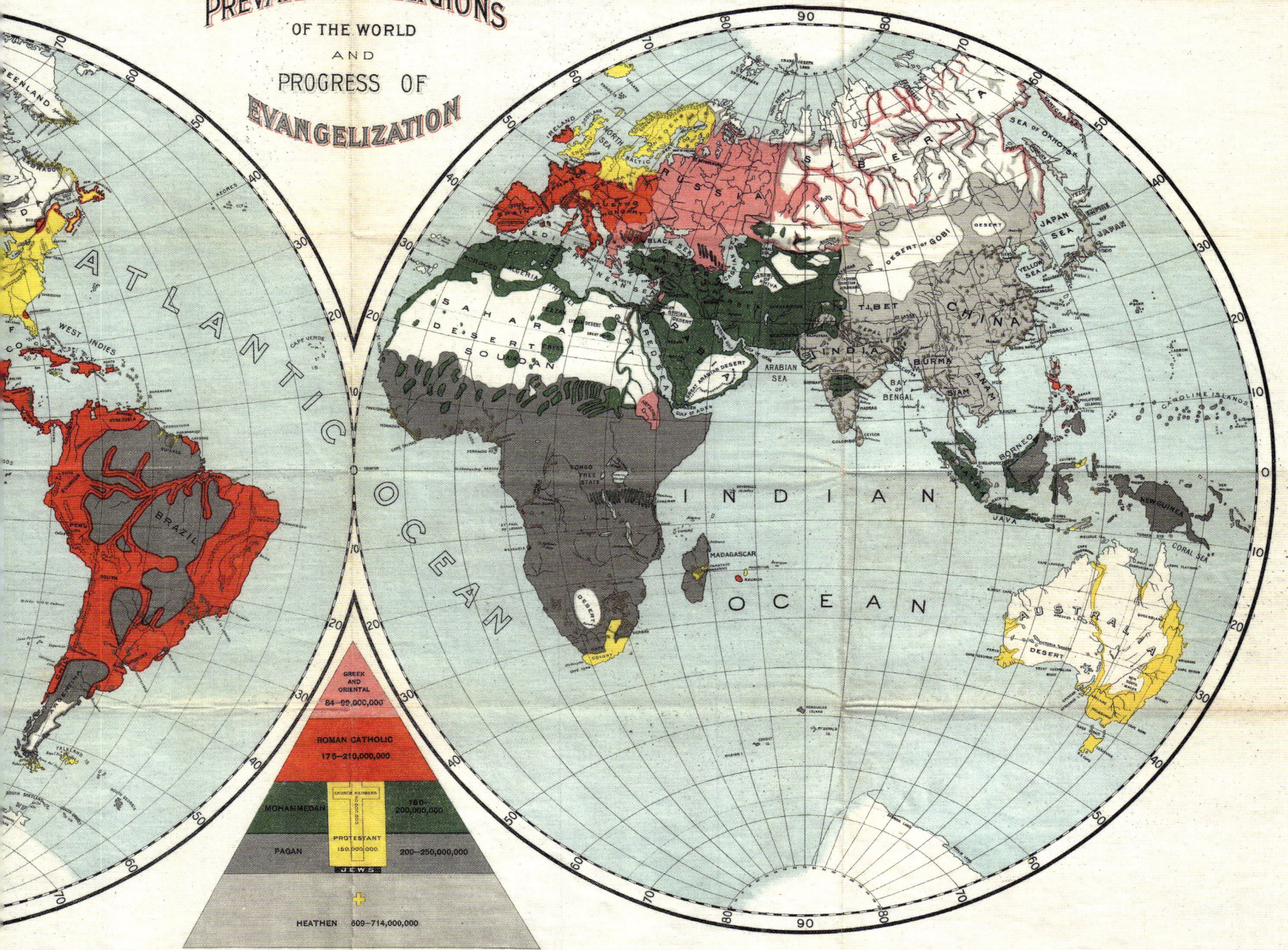

PREVAILING RELIGIONS
OF THE WORLD
AND
PROGRESS OF
EVANGELIZATION

GREEK
AND
ORIENTAL
84–99,000,000

ROMAN CATHOLIC
175–210,000,000

MOHAMMEDAN

CHURCH MEMBERS

160–200,000,000

PROTESTANT
150,000,000

PAGAN
200–250,000,000

JEWS

HEATHEN   609–714,000,000

THIS TRIANGLE REPRESENTS 1500,000,000—TOTAL POPULATION—AND THE RESPECTIVE COLORS CORRESPONDING WITH THOSE ON THE MAP REPRESENT THE
VARIOUS RELIGIONS, WITH THEIR APPROXIMATE COMPARATIVE NUMBER OF ADHERENTS. PARTS WITHOUT COLOR REPRESENT DESERTS OR SPARSELY INHABITED
TRACTS OF COUNTRY. THE SMALL CROSS IN THE HEATHEN SECTION STANDS FOR THE NATIVE CHRISTIAN COMMUNITY IN PAGAN AND HEATHEN LANDS. THE JEWS,
BEING DISPERSED THROUGH VARIOUS LANDS, THEIR LOCATION IS NOT INDICATED ON THE MAP. THE YELLOW SPOTS REPRESENT MISSION STATIONS AND CENTERS.

PRINTED IN U. S. A. BY KETTERLINUS, PHILA. AND N. Y.

163

The Arctic Regions Showing Exploration Towards the North Pole

This polar projection was issued in 1909 by Matthews-Northrup Works to illustrate the conflicting claims of Robert Peary and Frederick Cook, both of whom believed themselves to have been the first explorers to reach the North Pole. Red overprinting illustrated their competing exploratory routes.

In 1909, both Frederick Cook and Robert Peary proclaimed themselves as the official discoverer of the North Pole. Cook had been a surgeon on one of Peary's earlier, failed expeditions in 1891. In 1908, Cook left on his own privately funded expedition with only Inuit guides. Cook and the two guides reached what he believed to be the North Pole on April 21, 1908.

Around the same time, in July of 1908, without any knowledge of his former physician's journey, Peary began a fifth and final attempt to reach the North Pole. Traveling with a team of 23, Peary kept careful records and believed he had reached the North Pole on April 6, 1909.

The courts later determined that Peary would receive the honor of being named the discoverer of the North Pole due to Cook's more limited records and the conflicting reports of his guides. In more recent times, the English historian Wally Herbert offered convincing evidence that Peary most likely missed the pole by some 60 miles, thus relegating the right of discovery to Cook.

Cartographer

The **Matthews-Northrup Works** (fl. c. 1900-1930) were a Buffalo, New York-based writing, printing, designing, binding, and engraving firm. They rose to prominence by publishing maps for the railroad industry, but branched out into other areas, including their most lasting achievement, the 1910 design for the cover of National Geographic Magazine.

SMITH SOUND REGION

Explorers of Franz Josef Land
Payer and Weyprecht (Austrian) 1872-4
Leigh Smith (British) 1880-2
Frederic Jackson (British) 1894-7
Fridtjof Nansen (Norwegian) 1896
Walter Wellman & Evelyn B. Baldwin (American) 1898-9
Duke of Abruzzi (Italian) 1899-1900
Anthony Fiala (American) 1903-1905

FRANZ JOSEPH LAND

Coast Explored by
United States
British
Scandinavian (Norwegian, Swedish and Danish)
German and Austrian
Dutch
Italian
Russian

The Routes of the Explorers have the color of their native country.

Noted Explorers of the AMERICAN (Smith Sound) Route
Elisha Kent Kane (American) 1853-55
Isaac Israel Hayes (American) 1860-61
Charles F. Hall (American) 1870-73
Sir George Nares (English) 1875-76
General A. W. Greely (American) 1881-84
Capt. Sverdrup (Norwegian) 1898-1902
Com. R. E. Peary (American) 1891-09
Dr. F. A. Cook (American) 1907-08

ARCTIC OCEAN

SIBERIA

Kara Sea

Nordenskjold Sea

New Siberia

De Long Island

BARENTS SEA

FINLAND

Gulf of Bothnia

SWEDEN

NORWAY

North Cape

Center of Unexplored Region

North Pole
Cook arrived April 21, 1908; Peary, arrived April 8, 1909
Cook left April 23, 1908; Peary left April 7, 1909

Continual Day
March 21 to September 23

GREENLAND SEA

Jan Mayen

ALASKA

Gulf of Anadir

Bering Strait

GREENLAND

The INTERIOR is entirely covered with a Glacier of a probable thickness of 1000 to 3000 feet

ICELAND

BAFFIN BAY

Baffin Land

North Devon

DOMINION OF CANADA

Davis Strait

Arctic Circle

SPITZBERGEN
North East Land
West Spitzbergen
Edge I.

Explorers' Routes:
Parry (British)
Franklin and Richardson (British) 1821 & 1826
Franklin (British) 1845-47('48)
M'Clure's (ns.) Northwest Passage, 1850-'53
Second German North Pole Expedition, 1869-'70
Austro-Hungarian Expedition 1872-'73
Nordenskjöld Northeast Passage in "Vega" (Swede) 1878-'79
DeLong (s. "Jeanette" (United States) 1878-'81)
A.W. Greely (United States) 1881-84 (Cape Sabine to Cape Washington)
Nansen in "Fram" (Norwegian) 1893-'96
Duke of Abruzzi in "Stella Polare" (Italia) 1900
Sverdrup in "Fram" (Norwegian) 1898-1902
Peary (United States) 1898-1902
Ziegler Polar Expedition of 1903-'05 (A. Fiala)
Amundsen's Northwest Passage in "Gjöa" (Norwegian) 1903-1906
Duke of Orleans in "Belgica" 1905
Journey's by foot, sledges or boats

Telegraph Lines:
Railroads:
Steamship Routes:
Winter Harbors:
Average Limit of Icepack and solid Drift Ice
Tundra

Elevations and Depths are given in English Feet.
Soundings where bottom has not been reached are indicated thus:

THE MATTHEWS-NORTHRUP WORKS, BUFFALO, N.Y.

THE ARCTIC REGIONS
Showing Explorations towards the
NORTH POLE
COPYRIGHT, 1907, BY THE J. N. MATTHEWS CO., BUFFALO, N. Y.

Kilometers

Nautical Miles

Statute Miles

Cook's Route 1907-1909 thus: ----------

Peary's Route 1908-1909 thus: —·—·—·—

WHAT GERMANY WANT

HER CLAIMS AS SET FORTH BY LEADERS OF GERMAN T

Courtesy of Boston Rare Maps

What Germany Wants

Simple and direct, this dramatic wall map was issued by Stanford's Geographical Establishment in 1914, at the outset of World War I, to illustrate German aggression. Essentially a propaganda piece, the map highlighted what it believed to be German colonial ambitions. Annotations in the upper right included incriminating quotes by German officials and intellectuals. Deep red printing, the color of blood, suggested the violent extremes the author alleged Germany might embrace to achieve its imperial ends.

This is but one of many propaganda maps that were issued by Stanford and other publishers throughout the course of the war. Although earlier cartographers and artists produced pointedly graphic material, this style of persuasive map reached its height during the period between and including World War I and World War II.

Cartographer

Stanford's Geographical Establishment (fl. 1848-present) was founded in 1848 by Edward Stanford (1827-1904) and Trelawney Saunders (1821-1910). The firm continued to prosper through successive generations of the Stanford family and remains an active publisher to this day.

訪歐大飛行記念飛行双六

大阪市 川崎朝日印刷部

ロシア
C.C.P.

クレムリン宮殿

モスクワ   到着豫想   750
720

ニコリ
ドイツ   1100

ケーニヒスベルグ   520   ベルリン   700   ストラスブール   400

フランス   スラフ

パリ   エッフェル塔   375   ライン河

イギリス   355

ベルジュウム

ロンドン   ブラッセル

テームス河

ウラル山脈   600

クルガン   600

クラスノヤルスク

クラスノヤルスク   700   ノヴォシビライエスク   1180

初風

アルプス山脈   600

リオシ

1050   ローマ

イタリー

到着豫   アルプス山脈

【ハ】 天候と飛行時間表

			3・4	1・2	5・6
天候	ハレ	クモリ	アメ
	飛行に適す	注意を要す	無理をせず飛行中止

【ロ】

出た數	1	2	3	4	5	6
進む数	3	3	2	2	2	中止
書く力	2	2	1	1	1	

遊戯と人數

遊戯の仕方

（この『記し方』だした『方仕遊び』の外に普通の
『ごろく』のしうてしもも遊べます。）

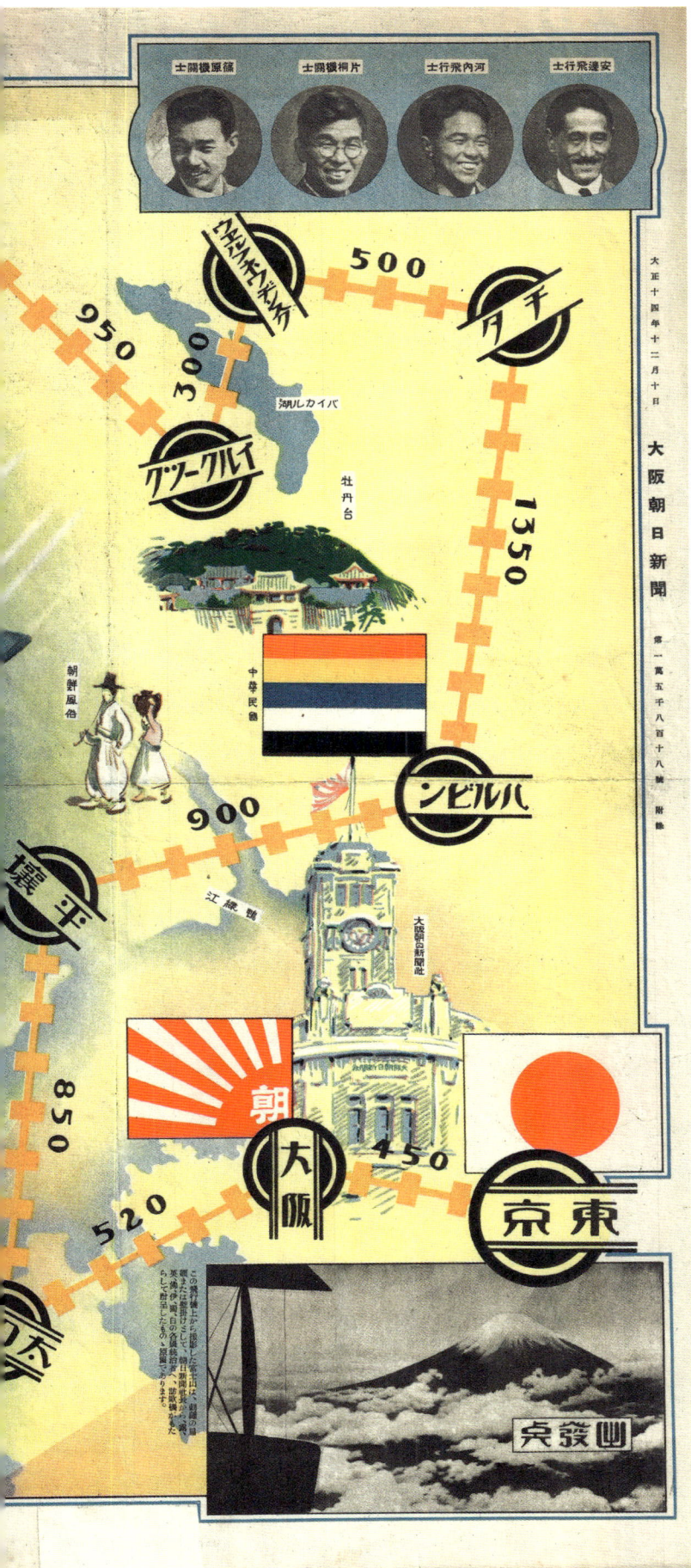

Great European Visit Memorial Flight Game

In celebration of the first, transcontinental flight from Japan to Europe, this map was printed by the *Morning Sun Newspaper* (*Asahi Shimbun*) of Japan. Although little known in the west, this famous transcontinental flight was highly significant and was comparable to Charles Lindbergh's flight across the Atlantic two years later. Photos of the two pilots, and their engineers, were included at the top right. The two Breguet 19 biplanes that made the trip were named First Wind (Hatsukaze) and East Wind (Kochikaze). The teams flew 16,565 miles and logged nearly 111 hours of flight time on this adventure.

This pictorial map, showing the Western Hemisphere, was also a *sugoroku* game board. *Sugoroku* was a snakes-and-ladders style board game popular in Japan. Beginning in Tokyo, players retraced the steps of the flight traveling from Japan to Siberia, Moscow, Berlin, Paris, and London, to finish in Rome.

As a side note, Korea and Japan have long argued over the proper name of the strait between the two countries and today it has become a matter of international intellectual contention. Japanese prefer the Tsushima Kaikyō (対馬海峡), while Korean usage is Chosŏn Haehyŏp (朝鮮海峡). Curiously, even though printed by a Japanese publication, and moreover one known to promote national pride, this map uses the Korean name.

Cartographer

*The **Morning Sun Newspaper** (1879-Present) known as the Asahi Shimbun,*
is one of the oldest newspapers in Japan. Founded in Osaka in 1879, the Tokyo branch
opened in 1888 and is still publishing today.

wie met de heele wereld wil verkeeren, moe

ARKTA OCEANO

SOVJET RU

EUROPO

ATLANTA

PACIFIKA

OCEANO

AFRIKO

FRANCA OKCIDENTA AFRIKO

NIGERIO

BELGA KONGO

SUD AFRIKO

HIN

OCEA

ANTARKTA KONTINENTO

DE GEHEELE AARDE

Esperanto, de practische en overal verbreide internationale taal, ontsluit de poorten der wereld.
Naast de moedertaal moet ieder modern ontwikkeld persoon op de eerste plaats Esperanto kennen, want Esperanto is de tweede taal voor alle menschen.
Voor een Esperantist bestaan er geen grenzen.
Esperanto is in de tegenwoordige samenleving een lichtpunt, dat de aandacht verdient van ieder weldenkende.
In de steden van alle landen zijn afdeelingen van de georganiseerde Esperantobeweging.
In het Esperanto-jaarboek komen de adressen voor van duizenden, officieel aangestelde Esperanto-Consuls, die voor Esperantisten steeds, en in alle opzichten, gratis ten dienste staan.
De Esperantist correspondeert in één taal met de geheele wereld, en leest boeken en tijdschriften op elk gebied uit alle landen.
Men bedenke, wat dit alles **groote voordeelen** zijn, persoonlijke en maatschappelijke, geestelijke en stoffelijke!

Esperanto wordt aanbevolen door alle bevoegde officieele en wetenschappelijke personen en instellingen. Esperanto wordt in de handelswereld o. m. door alle belangrijke jaarbeurzen reeds op ruime schaal gebruikt.
Esperanto is logisch samengesteld uit de bestaande talen en is daarom eenvoudig, welluidend en gemakkelijk te leeren. De studie is geen blokwerk, doch veeleer een ontspanning vooral voor hen, die weten wat talenstudie is.
Esperanto behoort thans tot de wetenschappelijke uitrusting van ieder wereldburger.
Leert Esperanto en een geheel nieuwe wereld, met groote perspectieven, zal voor U verrijzen!!

Volledige oplei

Iedere week 'n g
De lessen bevatt
kunnen ook gem

Te zamen met d
in de Nederlands
Betaling kan
Aanmelding pe

Dadelijk na g
als gratis prem

Wie met de heele wereld wil verkeeren, moet eerst Esperanto leeren!

This fascinating 1930 map was drawn to promote the study of Esperanto. The map depicts the world on a Mollweide equal-area projection with nations, and seas defined by dramatic color blocks. The text throughout the map is in Esperanto, but the title and descriptive text are in Dutch, reflecting where the map was issued.

Esperanto is a constructed language devised in the late 19th century by Ludwik Lejzer Zamenhof, a Polish-Jewish medical doctor, inventor and writer. Zamenhof believed that Esperanto would lead to better international understanding and global peace. He was inspired to create a new, neutral, and universal language after witnessing social divisions in his own city, Bialystok, now part of Russia. In an 1885 letter to the Russian Esperantist Nikolaj Afrikanoviĉ Borovko, he wrote: "In such a town, a sensitive nature feels more acutely than elsewhere the misery caused by language division and sees at every step that the diversity of languages is the first, or at least the most influential, basis for the separation of the human family into groups of enemies."

Following the horrors of World War I, Esperanto was embraced by many as a panacea for war and a gateway to universal understanding. It was even proposed as the official language of the League of Nations. Such optimism is expressed in this 1930 map which promotes the Esperanto Center at Nimegen, which offered a six-month course in Esperanto. The map's title, which is in Dutch, translates to: "Who wants to change the world, must first learn Esperanto!"

The point is further driven home by figures in the upper left and right corner, one Caucasian, the other a stylized African, who shout at one another from the far edges of the page.

Cartographer

The artist behind this map is unknown and the map itself, unattributed, but it was printed in Nijmegen by Dukkerij Gebr. Janssen.

Namen van eenige Europ. staten:

	zie hoofdstad	
SVISUJO:		Bern
AŬSTRUJO:	" "	Vieno
HUNGARUJO:	" "	Budapeŝto
BULGARUJO:	" "	Sofio
ĈEĤO-SLOVAKUJO:	" "	Praha
RUMANUJO:	" "	Bukureŝto
JUGOSLAVUJO:	" "	Belgrado
GREKUJO:	" "	Ateno
ESTONUJO:	" "	Reval
LATVUJO:	" "	Riga
LITOVUJO:	" "	Kovno
DANUJO:	" "	Kopenhagen

oor het Esperanto-diploma in 6 maanden door de bekende groote, populaire

ESPERANTO-CURSUS

les van 8 blz., die (evenals vorige jaren) óók voor de radio wordt behandeld. wat voor de studie en voor de kennis der Esperanto-beweging noodig is; en ze zonder radio geleerd worden.

Totale kosten f 4.—

peranto-cursus kan door hen, die dit noodig achten, ook een beknopte cursus al gevolgd worden. De totale prijs wordt dan voor beide talen samen f 5.—. ook in twee termijnen geschieden, n.l. op 15 October en 1 Januari. aart (of per postwissel) aan het adres:

Centrale Esperanto-Cursus te Nijmegen.

ontvangt men een 1e les, met alle inlichtingen en bovendien deze kaart

Leert Esperanto, de moderne wereldtaal!!

CARRIERS OF THE NEW BLACK PLAGUE

W. COTTON

CAUGHT here in all their peculiar beauty by the soul search-ing stylus of W. Cotton, Ken holds up for wonder the mangy motley pack of little "strong men" who are now leading the world on a backward march to the Dark Ages. Ten adult bipeds, each equipped with distended ego and outsize adrenal glands, whose ten totaled brains wouldn't counterbalance that of one Einstein in the

measurement of man's distance from the anthropoid ape. Left to right, and in the approximate order of their infamy, are Liberty's Enemy No. 1, the Hobgoblin Hitler; Man Mountain Mussolini; Generalissimo Francisco Franco, El Caudillo (literally translated means Fascism's Charlie McCarthy); the Mikado, Old Sol's Only Legitimate Child; Carol the Roumanian Cavalier, with Redheaded Heart

on Sleeve; Admiral Nicholaus (More than Royal Re Horthy of Hungary; Unhappy Schuschnigg, the Only tor Who Has Had To Take It As Well As Dish It Out (a dictator by the force of circumstance and, by comp to the rest of this gang, an angel of both peace a lightenment); Boris the Bulgar; The Unspeakable At and, off by himself, His Blood-Red Loneliness, No

Courtesy of P.J. Mode Collection of Persuasive Cartography

Comrade, Stalin. As backdrop for this Rogue's Gallery, Mr. Cotton has adapted the map devised by Dean Carl Ackerman of the Columbia University Graduate School of Journalism showing the extent of "the black plague of the 20th century," the dictatorial domination of individual and public opinion. In effect, over more than half the world, Liberty is now in Totalitarian Eclipse.

PASTEL BY W. COTTON

Carriers of the New Black Plague

This wonderfully graphic map was drawn by William Henry Cotton for the first issue of the large format *Ken Magazine* (April 7, 1938). Although the publishers David A. Smart and Arnold Gingrich, who also founded the more successful magazine *Esquire*, denied that *Ken Magazine* had any political leaning, the content of this powerful graphic, and others published in later issued, presents a definite anti-fascist prejudice.

Cotton here presents the world as a stage for large-than-life fascist dictators. The 'Black Plague' harkens to the Middle Ages and this map argues that the world is rapidly returning to those dark times. Parts of the world under cruel dictatorial control are shaded in black, while other areas dominated by censorship and intimidation appear in gray. Yellow areas, occupying only about 1/3rd of the map, represent the declining bastions of freedom.

The dictators themselves are comically rendered and assigned humorous names in mockery of the horrific truth of their deeds. Most appear in a parade at the bottom right led by 'Hobgoblin Hitler.' Following him are 'Man Mountain Mussolini,' 'Unspeakable Ataturk,' and 'Generalissimo Francisco France, El Coudillo,' among others. Stalin of Russia, identified as 'His Blood-Red Loneliness, Nobody's Comrade Stalin' is solitary in the upper right corner.

Cartographer

William Henry Cotton (1880-1958) was an American portrait artist and caricaturist active in the middle part of the 20th century. Cotton was born in Newport, Rhode Island and studied painting with Joseph DeCamp and Andreas Anderson at the Cowles Art School in Boston. He later attended the Académie Julian in Paris where he studied with Jean-Paul Laurens. While his early portrait work follows the classical mold, his later caricature work employs strong color blocks, exaggerated features, and angular lines to produce exceptionally evocative imagery.

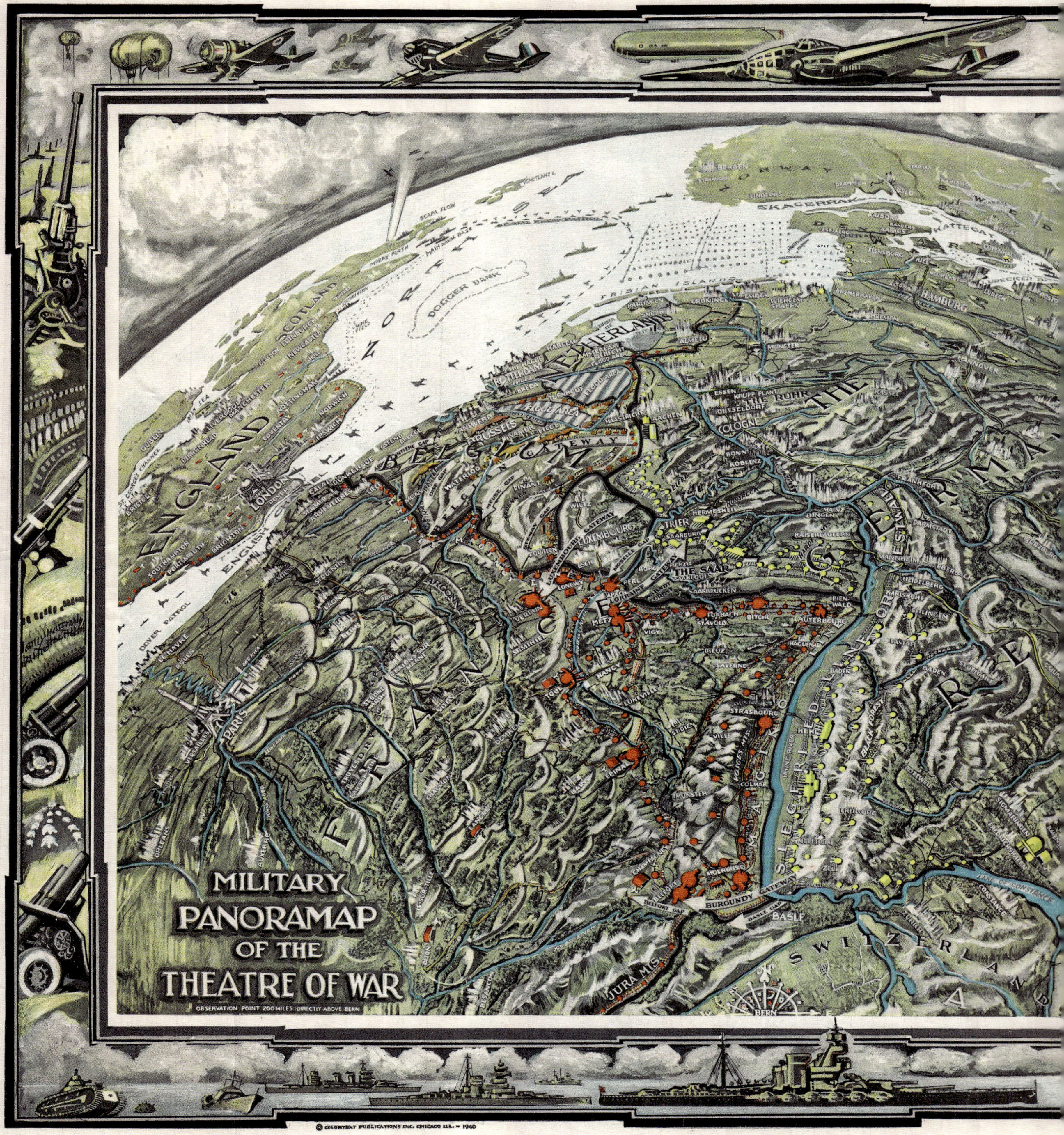
MILITARY
PANORAMAP
OF THE
THEATRE OF WAR
OBSERVATION POINT 200 MILES DIRECTLY ABOVE BERN
ENGLAND
LONDON
ENGLISH CHANNEL
DOVER PATROL
NORTH SEA
DOGGER BANK
SCAPA FLOW
SKAGERRAK
KATTEGAT
HAMBURG
NETHERLANDS
ROTTERDAM
BRUSSELS
BELGIUM
LUXEMBOURG
ESSEN
KRUPP PLANT
DUSSELDORF
THE RUHR
COLOGNE
BONN
KOBLENZ
TRIER
THE SAAR
SAARBRUCKEN
FRANKFORT
METZ
NANCY
STRASBOURG
COLMAR
PARIS
FRANCE
GERMANY
BASLE
BURGUNDY GATEWAY
JURA MTS.
SWITZERLAND
BERN
© COLORTEXT PUBLICATIONS INC. CHICAGO ILL. – 1940

Military Panoramap of the Theatre of War

This unusual 1940 map illustrates the world, but specifically northern and central Europe in the early days of World War II. Although Colortext has coined the term 'Panoramap' to describe this unusual map, which incorporates a globe-like perspective with exaggerated topography and irregular scaling, the style can be more properly attributed to Richard Edes Harrison, who pioneered it while working for *Fortune Magazine* and on propaganda *Newsmaps* for the United States War Department. This remarkably effective mapping technique has the subliminal effect of presenting regional conflicts, as in this case the war in Europe, as a global matter.

The map is centered on the Rhine River. To the west of the Rhine is the French Maginot Line, while to the east, the German Siegfried Line. Warplanes and battleships fill the North Sea and patrol the English Channel, while, to the west of Denmark, the waters are full of deadly mines. The map also has a distinctive border design, features weapons of war, battleships, tanks and bombers.

Although this map is unsigned, it does bear the mark "C:H". Given Colortext's history of employing well known pictorial mapmakers to produce the art for their maps, it is not unlikely that the "C" here refers to Colortext, and the "H" to Harrison – but we can admit no further evidence for this speculation.

Cartographer

Colortext Publications (c. 1933-1950) was an American publishing house active in Chicago in the first half of the 20th century. The firm made its debut at the 1933-1934 Chicago Century of Progress International Exposition, issuing a series of decorative maps by notable pictorial mapmakers such as Ernest Dudley Chase, Egbert G. Jacobson, Julio de Diego, A. Walker and W.E. Vogelear. The firm appears to have gone into decline following the Exposition, but briefly revived in 1938 and 1940, with it issued its most spectacular works, the Military Panoramap, as seen here, and a superb panoramic view of Chicago.

Target Berlin
Target Tokyo

These iconic images were drawn by F.E. Manning in 1943, during World War II. They were two of the most dramatic *Newsmaps* issued by the Army Orientation Course of the Special Service Division Army Service Forces, a propaganda arm of the United States War Department. *Newsmaps* were distributed to U.S. Troops fighting abroad and, on the reverse, featured optimistic reporting of Allied victories in Russia, Italy, Indonesia, and East Asia.

Target Berlin was issued just days before the first major air raids on Berlin. The series of attacks went on for nearly five months. Much of Berlin was destroyed but it did not appear to weaken the German war machine.

POLAR ICE CAP

ARCTIC OCEAN

UNITED STATES
CANADA
GREENLAND
HUDSON BAY
BAFFIN BAY
BAFFIN

NORWEGIAN SEA
BARENTS SEA
KARA SEA
LAPTEV SEA
SEA OF OKHOTSK
JAPAN
MANCHURIA
KOREA
CHINA
VLADIVOSTOK

ATLANTIC OCEAN
REYKJAVIK
ICELAND

GREAT BRITAIN
EIRE
NORWAY
SWEDEN
FINLAND
DENMARK
GERMANY
Berlin
POLAND
Warsaw
FRANCE
CZECHOSLOVAKIA
HUNGARY
ROMANIA
YUGOSLAVIA
ITALY
SPAIN
PORTUGAL
GREECE
TURKEY
SYRIA
IRAQ
IRAN
SAUDI ARABIA
EGYPT
LIBYA
ALGERIA
MOROCCO
TUNISIA
TRIPOLITANIA
CYRENAICA

UNION OF SOVIET SOCIALIST REPUBLICS
Leningrad
Moscow
Stalingrad
TIBET
INDIA

CANARY IS.
RIO DE ORO
FRENCH WEST AFRICA
SIERRA LEONE
LIBERIA
GOLD COAST
NIGERIA
FRENCH EQUATORIAL AFRICA
ANGLO-EGYPTIAN SUDAN
ETHIOPIA
BELGIAN CONGO
ANGOLA
TANGANYIKA
MADAGASCAR
RHODESIA
EQUATOR

INDIAN OCEAN

PACIFIC

TARGET Berlin

This map is a photographic view of the world with the center at Berlin. Thus, with the detachable scale, distances can be measured along any line running thru Berlin. It should be noted that an inch at the center represents less mileage than an inch closer to the edges. The detachable scale has been designed to compensate for this and should be used only with the center on Berlin.

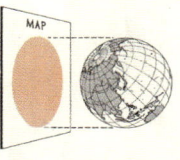

MAP

The photographic process used in making this map makes all distances measured with the tape approximate only. Distances are shown in statute miles. Lines between key cities do not represent regular air routes in all cases. They show distances between points that do not fall on a line going thru the center of the projection.

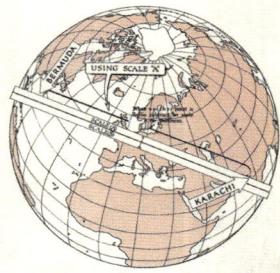

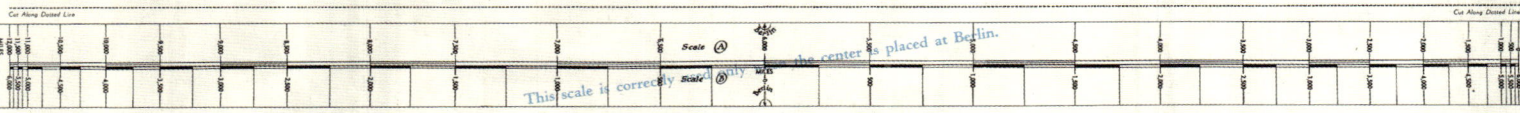

Cut Along Dotted Line

Scale Ⓐ

Scale Ⓑ

This scale is correctly only when the center is placed at Berlin.

177

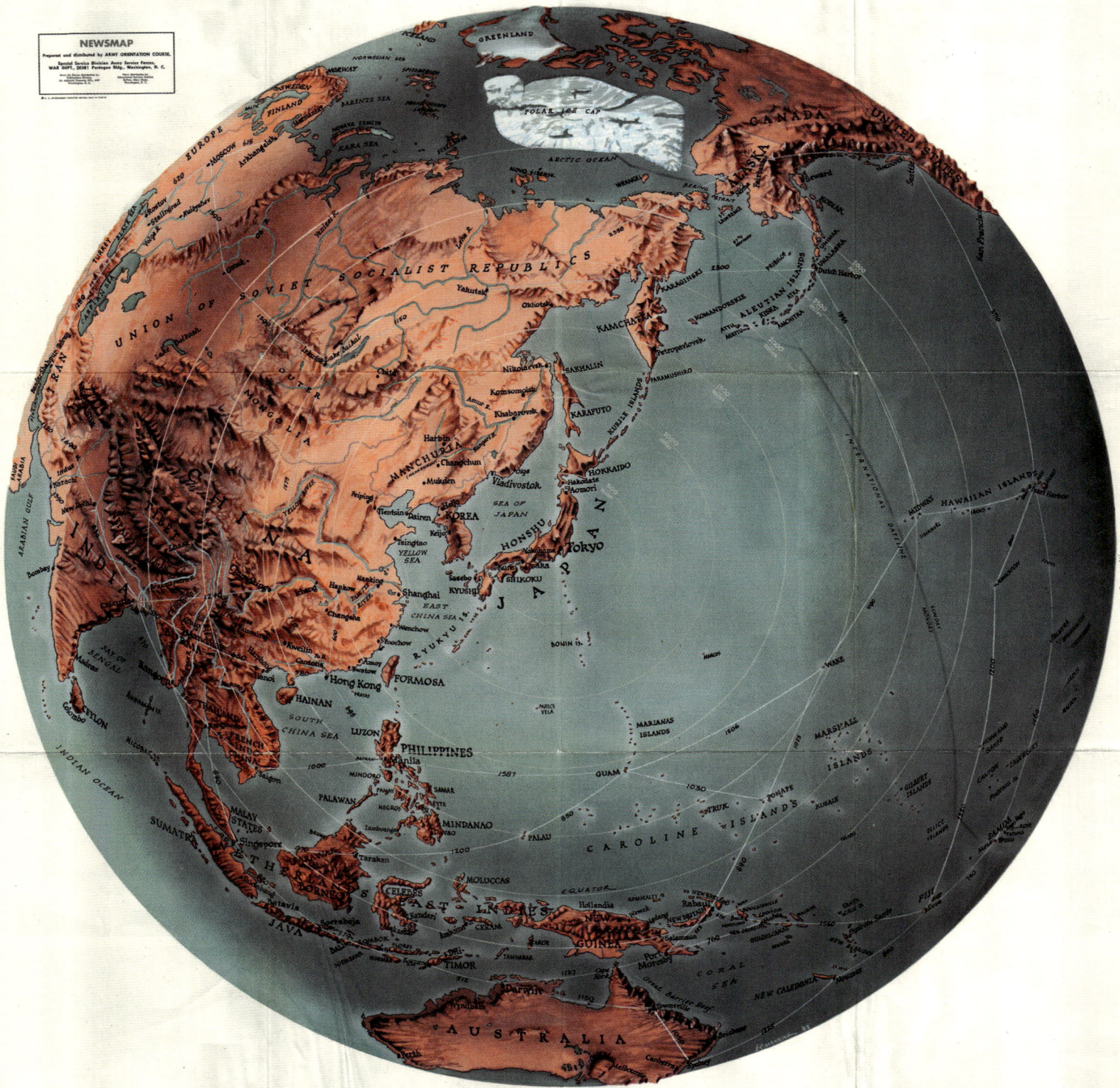

TARGET Tokyo

This map is a photographic view of the world with the center at Tokyo. Thus, with the detachable scale, distances can be measured along any line running thru Tokyo. It should be noted that an inch at the center represents less mileage than an inch closer to the edges. The detachable scale has been designed to compensate for this and should be used only with the center on Tokyo.

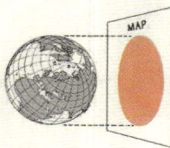

The photographic process used in making this map makes all distances measured with the tape approximate only. Distances are shown in statute miles. Lines between key cities do not represent regular air routes in all cases. They show distances between points that do not fall on a line going thru the center of the projection.

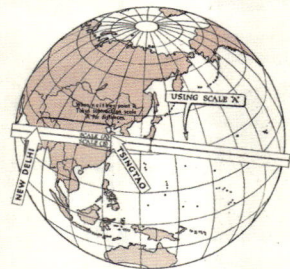

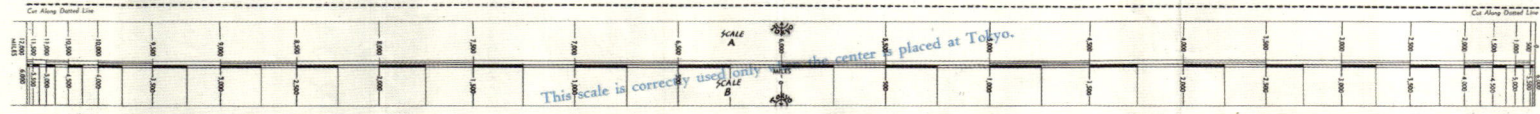

This scale is correctly used only when the center is placed at Tokyo.

Target Berlin
Target Tokyo

Target Tokyo was issued one month before significant Allied bombing began in East Asia. B-29 Super Fortresses attacked the Asia-Pacific theater for nine months until the Japan surrendered.

Manning's innovative design used a photographic shaded hemisphere with exaggerated relief. Concentric circles, narrowed, like a target, towards Berlin and Tokyo. An ingenious innovation was included below the map, a detachable scale that compensated for the distance distortion of the spherical view.

Cartographer

F.E. Manning (fl.c. 1940-1945) was a journalistic cartographer who worked at the Chicago Sun. In cartographic circles, he was admired for his introduction of the relief globular projection, a technique for adding relief to whole-Earth imagery that was used extensively to illustrate the events of World War II.

AIR
FRANCE
RÉSEAU AÉRIEN MONDIAL

208/P/6-48 - Printed in France - PERCEVAL PARIS

Air France Réseau Aérien Mondial

This 1947 Art Deco style map of the world was produced by Lucien Boucher as part of a series of maps intended to promote Air France. In this chromolithographic print by Perceval of Paris, vivid pastels, deep blacks, and browns stood in sharp contrast, while airliners filled the skies, and ships filled the waters. The bright white planes, doubtless representative of Air France, seemed even more attractive and comforting when flying over black waters. The complex network of Air France routes, demarcated in white, stood out against the backdrop of simplified, spacious, and nature-based illustrations.

Australia had ostriches and Asia, tigers. Bears populated the northern regions and the oceans were traversed with sails and steam. Showcasing the value of modern technology, the planes appeared powerful and safe compared to dangerous overland routes and ancient ships isolated in dark waters.

Boucher's work for Air France was iconic and marked a high point in the modern synthesis of cartography with graphic design and advertising. Nevertheless, he has also been criticized in recent years for some of the sexist and even racist themes evident in his material. On this map, for example, women generally appeared only partially clothed, in reclining or otherwise passive poses, while the men were clothed and engaged in a variety of more energetic pursuits. Similarly, stereotypical representations of indigenous peoples decorated several continents.

Cartographer

Lucien Boucher (1889-1971) was a French artist and writer. His cartoons appeared in Le Rire, a weekly publication known for its wit and humor. Boucher later produced a number of promotional map-themed artworks, as above, for Air France. His work was a synthesis of Art Deco and Surrealistic ethics.

The 19th Century: Gentleman Travelers and Armchair Adventurers

The dawn of the 19th century brought with it a new age of unprecedented internationalism and globalization. Over the course of the 19th century, most of the world was finally, fully mapped. Mungo Park, Speke, Stanley, and Livingstone plumbed the mysteries of the African Interior. Rubber Barons were exploiting the mysteries of the deep Amazon. Englishman Sir John Ross and John Wilkes of the U.S. were instrumental in leading explorations to map the coasts of Antarctica and the icy waters of the Arctic. The islands of Polynesia were firmly fixed on the map and British colonial cartographers sent secret expeditions to map the interior of Tibet. Both the Forty-Niners and the railroad barons forged their way westward in search of wealth and in the process transformed the American west from a barely explored frontier, to a bustling center of commerce. The once jealously guarded markets of China and Japan, under pressure from European and American powers, finally opened up to international trade. In a relatively short time, all levels of society found themselves exposed to foreign ideas, products, and cultures on a level previously unimagined. Natural curiosity about the world flourished and everyone from advertisers, to toy makers, to traditional cartographic publishers capitalized on the 19th century obsession with the exotic.

Technological advances in the 19th century also brought about two major changes in maps and mapmaking. First, the development and global implementation of steam navigation and railroads transformed travel. It was suddenly possible to cross entire oceans and continents quickly, safely, and economically. With this great change, leisure travel, once the prerogative of the nobility and the ultra-rich, became available to almost anyone with a yearning to see the world. At the same time, it also became much easier to be mobile and relocate to difference cities in search of a better life. The world was, for the first time, mobile, a state of affairs embraced by merchants, scholars, missionaries, and, quite simply, the globally curious. In Europe, this manifested itself in the rise of international tourism under the guidance of first generation travel agents like English businessman Thomas Cook. For those who were not able to travel, writers like Jules Verne, in his Around the World in 80 Days, promoted the exoticism and adventure of foreign travel.

The other major 19th century mapmaking development was the evolution of the printing process. By the third decade of the 19th century, lithography became the preferred method for map production. In the 18th century and earlier, maps were typically produced by copper plate intaglio printing techniques. These techniques involved meticulously engraving the map image onto a copper plate, then using the plate and a press to print the maps. The problem with this process was that copper was both soft and expensive. Copper printing plates wore out quickly and thus limited the number of impressions that could be produced.

Lithography, which was invented in 1796 by German Alois Senefelder, changed all of that. Instead of copper plates, lithography used lithographic limestone and depended on the fact that oil and water do not mix. Early lithography involved drawing an image on lithographic stone plates using oil or wax based paints then using acid to etch the images into those parts of the plate not covered by the protective wax. When the stone was wetted, water was retained by the etched areas of the stone. Oil-based inks would be repelled by the water but adhere to the non-etched part of the plates. The plates could then be pressed onto paper, imprinting the image. Lithography was far more cost effective than etching copper plates. Firstly, because limestone was much cheaper than copper. Secondly, lithographic limestone, unlike copper plates, did not wear out with use, so unlimited impressions were possible. Thirdly, it was much easier to paint an image than to etch it, so expensive etchers were no longer necessary in order to produce large elaborate prints.

Publishers recognized the opportunity and quickly adopted the new technique. American publishers were particularly successful with lithography. In New York, the advent of lithography gave rise to the J. H. Colton firm, one of the most prolific publishing firms in history. With railroads slowly working their way across the continent, Colton recognized the need for easily transportable maps of the rail networks. Effectively, he capitalized on economical lithographic printing to quickly produce a vast array of very specific maps geared toward the stagecoach and railway traveler.

At the same time, publishers, Colton among them, realized that they could not only use their maps to facilitate travel, but also to promote travel and thereby increase their sales. They began adding elaborate vignettes and extensive illustrative border work to their maps. These typically involved illustrations of distant cities such as Hong Kong, Calcutta, Timbuctoo, and Cape Town, as well as views of more accessible popular destinations such as San Francisco, London, Paris, and Rome. Alternatively, 19th century mapmakers also decorated their maps with images of exotic cultures that included traditional dress, activities, and backgrounds.

The addition of vignette imagery to maps was not original to the 19th century, but the ease of adding such to maps on a large scale produced a generation of highly decorative maps, perfect not only for the active traveler, but also for the armchair adventurer who wanted to familiarize themselves with far off peoples and places. Elaborately illustrated cabinet atlases by cartographers like John Tallis, Victor Levasseur, Alexander Vuillemin, became indispensable references essential for any sophisticated gentleman's library.

This chapter will examine some of those maps ranging from vignette-based game boards, to maps from cabinet atlases and grand broadsides. Each will present a unique aspect of the genre or illustrate a different perspective on a similar aspect.

JEU INSTRUCTIF DES PEUPLES
ET COSTUMES DES QUATRE PARTIES DU MONDE ET DES TERRES AU...

REGLES DU JEU. D'abord il faut convenir de ce que l'on veut jouer et payer aux rencontres et accidents. Ce jeu est

depuis 1 jusqu'à 63, et celui qui arrive le premier à ce nombre final, qui est la France, gagne la partie; mais on n'y arrive pas

Pour jouer à ce jeu il faut avoir deux dez que chaque joueur jettera une fois: autant de points qu'il sera, autant il en compte

sa marque sur le point amené. Chaque joueur aura une marque différente afin de la reconnoître. Il faut savoir que l'on ne peut s...

de l'Europe, et si le nombre amené y conduit le joueur, il redouble son nombre

Celui qui au premier coup fera 9 par 6 et par 3, ira au nombre 26 où est le Thibet.-

sera 9 par 5 et par 4, ira au nombre 53 où est l'île de Sumatra.- Celui qui du premier

de cordes, payera le prix convenu et ira se noyer dans le Fleuve des Amazones au N°12.

où est l'île hospitalière d'Otaïti, payera le prix convenu et y restera pendant que le

deux coups.- Celui qui arrivera au N°31, où est la Sibérie, lieu d'exil, payera le prix co...

ce qu'un autre joueur amenant le même point vienne l'en retirer; alors il ira à la plac...

Celui qui arrivera au nombre 42 où est le Japon, pays dont l'entrée est interdite

le prix convenu et ira au N°30 où est l'Abyssinie.- Celui qui arrivera au nombre 52

d'esclavage, payera le prix convenu et y restera jusqu'à ce qu'un autre vienne l'en retirer.

nombre 58 où est la Nouvelle Zélande, île habitée par les Anthropophages, payera le prix convenu et

Celui qui sera rencontré par un autre payera le prix convenu, et ira prendre la place de celui par qui...

V.e HENRI IV vive ce Roi vaillant

63

France.

62 Tschurtschi (Asie)

61 Baie de Nootka (Amer. mérid.)

60 Empire Mogol (Asie)

59 Italie (Europe)

58 Nouvelle Zélande

57

38 — 39 Bresil (Amer. mérid.)

37 Madagascar (Afrique)

36

35 Cafres Afrique

34 Iroquois (Amer. Sept.)

33 Nègre Afrique

32

31

52 Suisse (Europe)

30

29

28 Abyssinie (Afrique)

27 Dannemark (Europe)

26 Thibet (Asie)

25 Egipte (Asie)

24 Arabie (Asie)

23 Allemagne (Europe)

22 Amérique

Barbarie (Afrique)

Ile de Sumatra (Asie)

Portugal (Europe)

Ile de Java (Asie)

Terre de Feu (Amer. nord)

Paraguay (Amer. mérid.)

AMÉRIQUE — AFRIQUE

Peuple (Afrique)

Siam (Asie)

EUROPE

Hollande (Europe)

1	2	3	4	5	6	7	8	9
Chine (Asie)	Pérou (Amer. mérid.)	Indostan (Asie)	Laponie	Angleterre (Europe)	Mexique (Amer. mérid.) Vue d'un pont de cordes	Nouvelle Hollande (Terres Australes)	Kamtschatka (Asie)	Russie (d'Europe)

38	39	40	41	42	43
Bresil (Amer. mérid.)	Nouvelle Guinée (Mer du Sud)	Guiane (Amer. Mérid.)	Hongrie (Europe)	Japon (Asie) Navigateurs repoussés de la Côte	Nubie (Afrique)

A Paris, chez Basset M.d d'Estampes rue St. Jacques au coin de celle des Mathurins N°64.

184

Jeu Instructif des Peuples et Costumes

Geographically themed, this 1815 board game took players on a worldwide journey through 63 squares, each representing a destination. Following a spiral form, and played with two dice, the players navigated hazards and international relationships to reach the finish line in the center of the board. Printed just after Napoleon's defeat, the finish line here was France, represented by an image of Henri IV.

Invented in Italy during the late 1500s, most *jeux de l'oie* (Game of Goose) games followed a standardized structure with obstacles including a bridge, an inn, a well, a maze, a prison, and death (which required a return to square 1). In this version of the game, death was represented by being eaten in New Zealand; the maze was located in Japan, where players were refused entry due to the policy of "Closed Country"; and the well was represented by exile in Siberia where a player had to wait for an opportunity to exchange places with another player in order to escape. Instructions for the game were included in the center of the board.

Cartographer

André Basset was part of a well-known French firm (c. 1720-1865) that produced prints including maps, European city views, games, and more. His son, Andre Paul Basset took over the firm after his father's death.

39 — Nouvelle Guinée (Mer du Sud)

40 — Guiane (Amer: Mérid.)

41 — Hongrie (Europe.)

5 — Angleterre (Europe)

6 — Mexique (Amer: mérid.) Vue d'un pont de cordes.

7 — Nouvelle Hollande (Terres Australes)

186

42
Japon (Asie)
Navigateurs repoussés de la Côte.

43
Nubie (Afrique)

8
Kamtschatka (Asie)

9
Russie (d'Europe)

Most such games consist of 63 squares, a system derived from Kabalistic teachings, arranged in a spiral. Some squares involve hazards, bonuses, or penalties. In the present example the board has the standard notable squares. Number 6, traditionally a bridge, is here represented by Mexico or Central America. Number 42, traditionally a maze, is here represented by Japan where navigators are refused entry. Each game goes beyond simple cartographic representation to convey, through its rules or iconography, a deliberate 'message,' whether political, commercial or cultural. The games give insights into international relationships, perceptions and misconceptions at various times in the history of Europe. This map is no exception. European squares are generally presented as superior to non-European squares, which, as seen above, may involve being eaten or enslaved.

52

53

5

Barbarie (Afrique)
Voyageur réduit a l'Esclavage

Ile de Sumatra (Asie)

Portuga

22

23

Armenie (Asie)

Allemagne (Europe)

Arab.

55

56

(Europe)

Ile de Java (Asie.)

Terre de Feu (Amer: merid:)

4

25

26

(Asie)

Pégu (Asie.)

Thibet (Asie.)

Arrowsmith's Map of the World on a Globular Projection

An unusual 1838 world map on a globular projection by Samuel Lewis based upon the work of Aaron Arrowsmith. By the late 1810s, American map publishing was becoming well established but lacked the prestige attached to European, specifically English, maps. American map publishers, like Samuel Lewis, attempted to capitalize on this disparity by partnering with English map publishers, then revising and reissuing the maps for the American market.

Although the names of both Lewis and Arrowsmith are attached to this map, giving a clear provenance, the actual publisher was unknown, since by 1838, both Lewis and Arrowsmith had died. What was evident was that the publisher invested significantly in updates, particularly to North America, to keep this 20-year-old map contemporary. Note that Texas was an independent republic, an ephemeral period between 1836 and the Mexican-American War in 1848.

Arrowsmith's original map of 1794 was made in response to James Cook's expeditions and much remains from this edition, including a portrait of Cook, and the tracks of his three historic voyages.

Cartographers

• *Aaron Arrowsmith (1750-1823) was a meticulous and accomplished cartographer. In 1810, George III granted him the position of Hydrographer to the Prince of Wales. In 1820, shortly before his death, he was appointed Hydrographer to the King.*

• *Samuel Lewis (c.1754-1822) was an Irish geographer and engraver who emigrated to the United States in the late 18th century. Known for his work with Aaron Arrowsmith, he was the first to publish a map based on the discoveries of Lewis and Clark in the American northwest.*

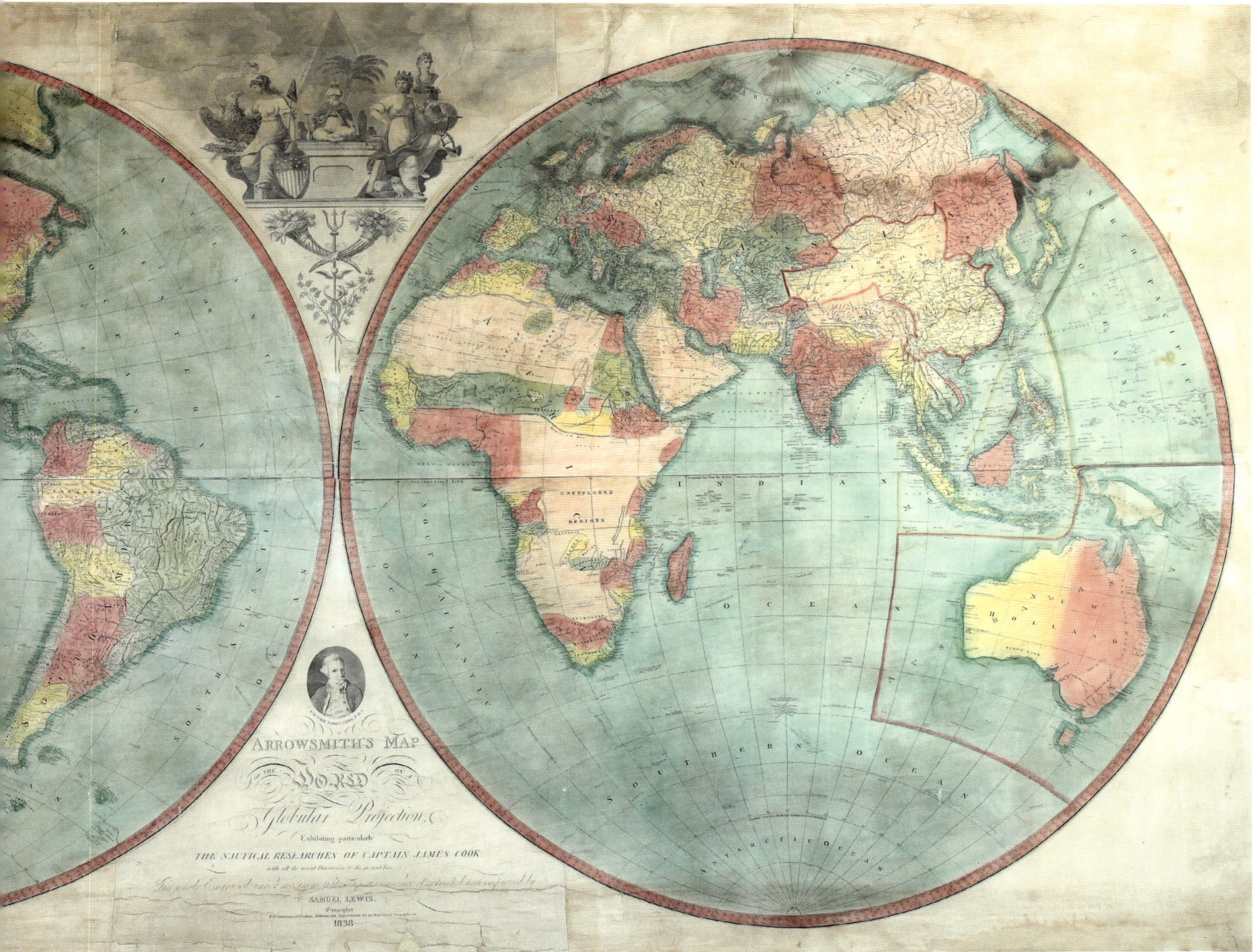

ARROWSMITH'S MAP
OF THE
WORLD
ON A
Globular Projection.
Exhibiting particularly
THE NAUTICAL RESEARCHES OF CAPTAIN JAMES COOK.
with all the recent Discoveries to the present Time.

SAMUEL LEWIS,
Geographer
1838

A New Chart of the World on Mercator's Projection

The essential library map for the educated gentleman. Published in 1844 by Henry Teesdale, this enormous map embraced the world in a sprawling Mercator Projection. It was segmented in 32 large panels which, mounted on linen, folded into a fine embossed leather binding for easy shelf placement in a gentleman's library.

The cartography was uniquely English and there were numerous annotations throughout the map testifying to that fact. For example, Texas, addressed as a fully independent republic, bore the following annotation, "Acknowledged an Independent State by England, Novr. 1840." Conversely, discoveries that were at odds with British interests or national pride, were omitted. Among these were the significant accomplishments of the American Charles Wilkes in Antarctica, which the British saw as competing with their own claims in Antarctica associated with the expeditions of James Clark Ross. Similarly, in North America, the map supported British Claims to Washington as far south as the Columbia River in opposition to American claims to the same region.

There were a number of other annotations of considerable historical interest, as in Liberia, Africa, "This district has been purchas'd from the Native Chiefs... by American(s)...for the purpose of forming Settlements for the Emancipated Slaves of the United States, and is now in a flourishing condition."

Cartographer

Henry Teesdale (1776-1856) was a British map and atlas publisher. A member of the Royal Geographical Society, he worked with several notable engravers including Christopher Greenwood, John Crane Dower, and Josiah Henshall. Later, he became a partner and founding member of the Royal Bank of Scotland, suggesting that, unlike most cartographers, his publishing business was a significant commercial success.

NORTH

HARE INDIANS

DOG RIB INDIANS

COPPER INDIANS

BEAVER INDIANS

GREAT BEAR L.

Rocky Mountains

CHESTERFIELD Inlet

HUDSON

BAY

Discovered by Capt. H. Hudson 1610 where ever mutiered and committed him & seven others to the sea in an open Boat they were never heard of after.

CUMBERLAND I.

SOUTHAMPTON LAND

STRAITS

LABRADOR

AMERICA

UNGAVA BAY

THABASCA

ENGLISH R.

SASKATCHAWAN

SWAN RIVER

SEVERN

ALBANY

JAMES BAY

LAKE SUPERIOR

NORTHWEST TERRITORY

LAKE HURON

LOWER CANADA

UPPER CANADA

CAPE BRETON I.

NOVA SCOTIA

R. Columbia or Oregon

OREGON

NEW CALIFORNIA

CALIFORNIA was discovered by Herman Cortez in 1536.

UNITED STATES

PENNSYLVANIA

KENTUCKY

VIRGINIA

NORTH CAROLINA

SOUTH CAROLINA

GEORGIA

NEW MEXICO

TEXAS

TEXAS was acknowledged to be Independent by England, Novr. 1840.

R. del Norte

ATLANTIC

Bermuda Is. (English)

GULF OF MEXICO

WEST INDIES

BAHAMA Is.

JAMAICA

CARIBBEAN SEA

St. Lucie

Barbadoes

CARTAGENA

Isthmus of Panama, the narrowest parts are thirty miles, and the Country nearly level. It is in contemplation by the American and English to cut a Ship Canal to unite the Atlantic & the Pacific Oceans.

SOUTHERN

EQUATOR or EQUINOCTIAL LINE

Galapagos

Commodore Anson in 1743

Capt. Cook in 1774

A New Chart
of the
WORLD
on
Mercator's Projection
WITH THE TRACKS OF THE MOST CELEBRATED & RECENT NAVIGATORS.
Engraved by JOHN DOWER, Pentonville.

Published
By Henry Teasdale & Co. 2 Brunswick Row, Queens Square,
LONDON 1844

ARCTIC EXPEDITIONS.

NORTH AMERICA

NORTH AMERICA

RUSSIAN AMERICA

GREENLAND

ICY OCEAN

POLAR SEA

ARCTIC HIGHLAND

BAFFIN'S BAY

SEA OF KAMTSCHATKA

NORTHERN

PACIFIC

OCEAN

NORTH ATLANTIC OCEAN

POLYNESIA

GULF OF MEXICO

WEST INDIES

CARIBBEAN SEA

SOUTHERN

SOUTH AMERICA

ETHIOPI OR SOUTHERN OC

PACIFIC OCEAN

ANTARCTIC OR SOU

194

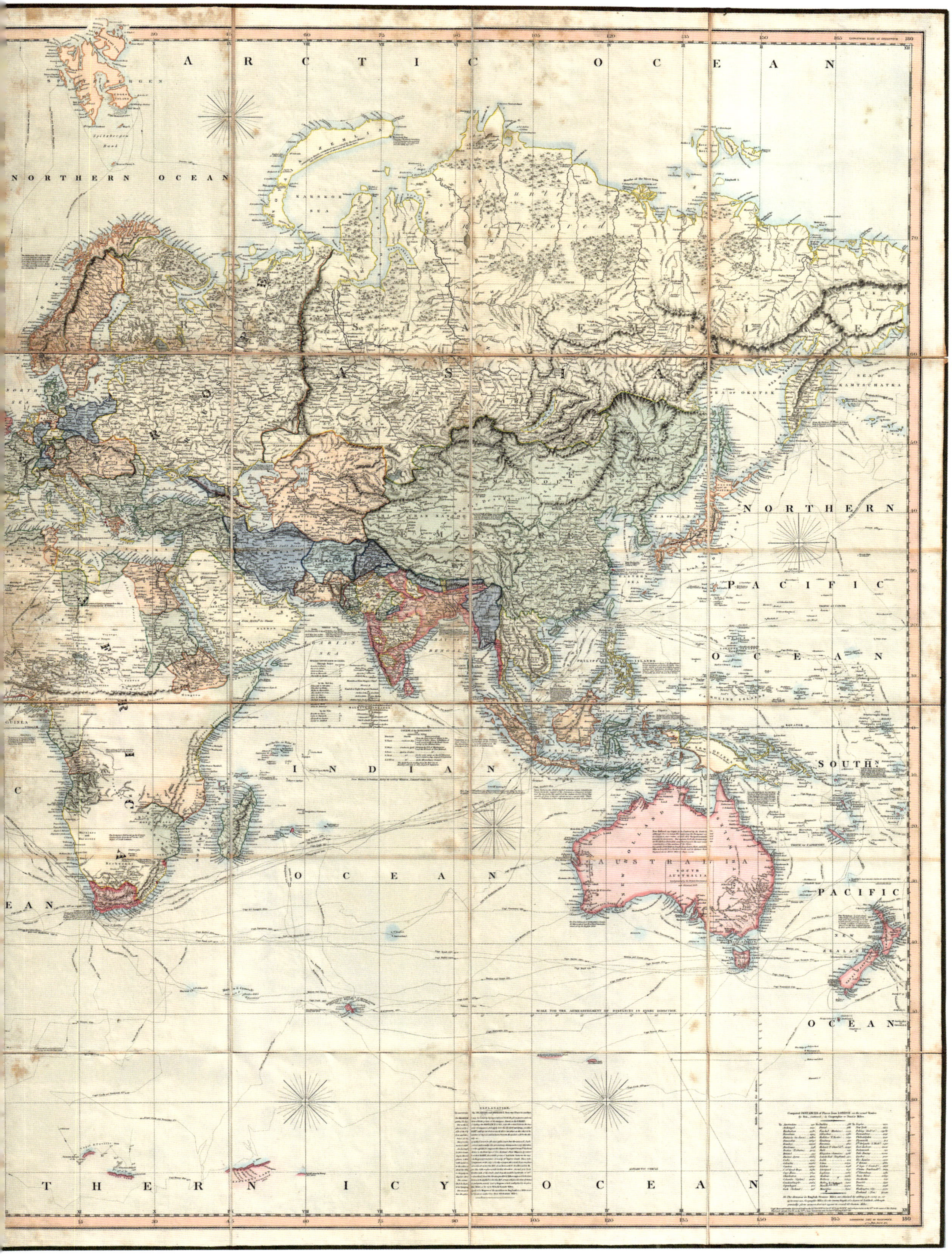

ARCTIC OCEAN

NORTHERN OCEAN

R U S S I A

A S I A

SEA OF OKOTSK

SEA OF KAMTSCHATKA

NORTHERN

PACIFIC

OCEAN

SOUTH

PACIFIC

OCEAN

INDIAN

OCEAN

AUSTRALIA

SOUTH AUSTRALIA

NEW ZEALAND

THE SOUTHERN ICY OCEAN

Western Hemisphere

This stunning 1850 map was one of the most attractive atlas maps to appear in the middle part of the 19th century. It was included in the 1850 edition of John Tallis' *Illustrated Atlas of the World*, an impressive production weak on cartography but rich in decorative appeal. The present map was exceptionally lavish, with extensive border work including vignettes depicting the peoples, plants, and animals of the Western Hemisphere. Such maps were intended for the armchair adventurer who, comfortable before a roaring fire in his gentlemanly estate, could discover the world.

Despite being primarily decorative, this map was not without cartographic interest. Color coding for example, defined the limits of the United States and, being published just after the Treaty of Guadeloupe-Hidalgo, included Texas. Nevertheless, closer examination revealed an uncolored but distinct Texas border. This, consistent with the British acknowledgement of the Texan Republic, appeared to indicate that Texas was both a part of, and separate from, the United States. This interesting choice may either be a legacy from an earlier edition of the map in which Texas was illustrated as separate, or suggestive of political uncertainty in the region.

The mythical Aurora Islands were shown to the south east of South America. Initially sighted by the Spanish ship Aurora in the mid-18th century, they appeared on numerous maps well into the 19th century. It was not until the late 19th century that the notion was abandoned and they were relegated to myth.

Cartographer

John Tallis (1817-1876) was a British entrepreneur and map publisher active in the middle part of the 19th century. Tallis produced one of the great decorative atlases of the 19th century, the Illustrated Atlas of the World. *It was an enormous success and Tallis became a wealthy man, with over 200 people in his employ and agencies representing his publications all over the world. Nevertheless, as with so many map publishers, bad business decisions late in life led to a collapse of his financial empire and, after mortgaging his furniture, he died in debt.*

The Illustrations by H. Warren & Engraved by J. Rogers.

WESTERN HEMISPHERE.

NORTH POLE

ARCTIC OCEAN

ASIA

AMERICA

NORTH AMERICA

UNITED STATES

CALIFORNIA

GULF OF MEXICO

CARIBBEAN SEA

WEST INDIES

NORTH ATLANTIC OCEAN

NORTH PACIFIC OCEAN

Tropic of Cancer

Equator or Equinoctial Line

Sandwich I.

Marquesas I.

Low Archipelago

Society I.

SOUTH AMERICA

BRAZIL

PATAGONIA

Tropic of Capricorn

SOUTH PACIFIC OCEAN

SOUTH ATLANTIC OCEAN

Falkland Is.

Antarctic Circle

South Shetland I.

ANTARCTIC OCEAN

SOUTH VICTORIA

South Pole

OCÉAN GLACIAL ARC

GROENLAND

SPITZBERG

AMÉRIQUE

Mer de Behring

Tropique du Cancer

Équateur

OCÉAN

Tropique du Capricorne

OCÉAN ATLANTIQUE

MER DES INDES

OCÉAN PACIF

OCÉAN GLACIAL ANTARCTIQ

RUSSIE D'EUROPE

SIBÉR

EMPIRE CHINOIS

SAHARA ou Gd Desert

Équateur

Hottentots   Tropique du Capricorne

NOTICE SUR LE PLANISPHÈRE.

Cette carte représente le globe terrestre sur une surface platte, d'après la projection de Mercator, les cinq parties du monde y sont indiquées de manière, a faire voir d'un coup d'œil l'ensemble de nos Colonies et notre plus facilement leur situation et leur position respective.

L'EUROPE, la plus petite mais la plus peuplée, est située entre le 35° et 71° degré de latitude nord et entre le 9° de longitude Ouest et le 65° de longitude Est.

Elle est bornée au Nord par l'Océan glacial, à l'Est par l'Asie, au Sud par l'Asie et l'Afrique et à l'Ouest par l'Océan Atlantique.

Ses principales chaînes de montagnes sont: les Alpes, les Pyrénées, les Apennins et les Monts Karpates. Ses grands fleuves sont: le Volga, le Danube, le Rhin, le Rhône, la Loire, la Seine et la Pô. L'Europe comprend 16 contrées principales qui sont: la France, le Russie, le Danemark, les Iles Britanniques, la France, la Belgique, la Hollande, la Prusse, l'Allemagne, l'Autriche, la Turquie, la Grèce, l'Italie, l'Espagne, le Portugal et la Suisse.

Ses grandes villes capitales sont: Paris, Londres, St Petersbourg, Vienne, Madrid, Rome, Berlin, Constantinople.

L'ASIE est située entre l'Equateur et le 78° degré de latitude nord, et entre le 25° de longitude Est et la 174° de longitude Ouest; elle est bornée au Nord par l'Océan glacial, à l'Est par le grand Océan au Sud, par l'Océan et à l'Ouest par l'Afrique et l'Asie.

Ses principales chaînes de montagnes sont: les Monts Stanovoï, les Altai, et la IIe chaîne de l'Himalaya. Ses grands cours d'eau sont: le Ienissei, la Lena, le Kiang, le Hoang-Ho, le Sind et l'Euphrate.

L'Asie est divisée en 12 grandes parties qui sont: la Sibérie, la Turquie d'Asie, la Tartarie indépendante, l'Arabie, la Perse, l'Afghanistan, le Béloutchistan, le Japon, l'Empire Chinois, l'Inde, Chine et l'Indoustan. Ses plus grandes villes sont: Pékin, Tobolsk, Téhéran, Ispahan et Calcutta.

FRATERNITÉ   PERFECTIBILITÉ   UNION

HARMONIE.

Imp.ᵉ de Lemercier, Paris.

PLANISPHÈRE.

Planisphère

This aesthetically rich map of the world was published by Victor Levasseur in 1852. While the cartography followed the minimalist model popular in France during the mid-19th century, the decorative border work was strikingly sumptuous, and rich with Masonic iconography. The firmament filled the top of the map that sheltered under the Zodiac. A four-breasted goddess, presumably Pandora, held her dreaded chained box. To her right Adam and Eve walked through Eden, holding hands, with the serpent, unnoticed, following just behind. To the right and left of the map, cartouches held personifications of each of the four seasons. At the base of the map, Christ was enthroned under a banner containing a masonic credo: *Fraternité, Perfectibilité, Union, Harmonie.*

The map itself was comparatively minimalist, with few place names and simple outline color. Unlike most English maps of the period, French cartographers supported American claims to British Columbia and Oregon as far north as 54°40' and this map reflected that contention. Also of interest was the open sea in the high Arctic, proving that even as late as the mid-19th century, there was still hope that the Northwest Passage would be discovered.

This map was composed for the *Atlas National de La France Illustré*, one of the last great decorative atlases of the 19th century.

Cartographer

Victor Levasseur (1800-1870) was a French engineer who produced unusually artistic engravings and cartography. Levasseur's large, decorative atlas of France, Atlas National Illustré des 86 Départements et des Possessions de La France, *is his best-known work.*

COLTON'S
New Illustrated Map of
THE WORLD
ON MERCATOR'S PROJECTION.

Published by J. H. Colton.
No. 1 36 Cedar St. New York.
1858.

ARCTIC HIGHLANDS

NOVA ZEMLA
KARSKOE SEA
IAKOUTSK SEA
LIAKHOV I[sls] or NEW SIBERIA

SAMOIEDES

EASTERN SIBERIA

CHUCKCHEES

RUSSIAN UNEXPLORED TERRITORY

BAFFINS BAY

TOBOLSK
WESTN SIBERIA
RUSSIAN EMPIRE
TOMSK

KAMTCHATKA or BHERING SEA

OKHOTSK SEA
LIMA SEA

ALEUTAN ARCHIPELAGO

COCKBURN LAND

NORTH

BRITISH POSSESSIONS
AMERICA

CHINESE TARTARY
CHINESE EMPIRE
BOKHARA
AFGHANISTAN
HINDOSTAN
INDIA

JAPANESE EMPIRE

UNITED STATES

ATLANTIC

ARABIAN SEA
BAY OF BENGAL
CHINA
PHILIPPINE ISLANDS
LADRONE or MARIAN Is
BORNEO

NORTH PACIFIC OCEAN

TROPIC OF CANCER

SANDWICH ISLANDS

GULF OF MEXICO
CARIBBEAN SEA

CAROLINE ISLANDS

NEW GUINEA

POLYNESIA

SOUTH
BRAZIL

INDIAN

NORTHERN AUSTRALIA
WESTERN AUSTRALIA
AUSTRALIA
SOUTH AUSTRALIA
NEW SOUTH WALES
VICTORIA

TROPIC OF CAPRICORN

MALAYSIA

BOLIVIA
AMERICA

OCEAN

SOUTH

PACIFIC OCEAN

SOUTH SHETLAND
SOUTH ORKNEY

PACIFIC OCEAN

ANTARCTIC OCEAN

ANTARCTIC CONTINENT

Longitude East from Greenwich   Longitude West from Greenwich

Colton's New Illustrated Map of the World

This grand, richly illustrated, wall-sized 1853 map of the world on a Mercator Projection was published in case-format by the great American cartographer Joseph H. Colton. Vivid pastels outlined nations and states. The whole was surrounded by an exceptionally lavish border work by W. S. Barnard. The border boasted large engraved views of Havana, Alexandria, Constantinople, Bordeaux, Seville, Egypt (Karnak), Ningbo, Rio de Janeiro, Hong Kong, Venice, Afghanistan (Ghuznee or Ghazni), and Nanking.

This map was issued in a case format intended for easy transport and better preservation. Maps like this were first printed in large sheets then dissected into panels, in this case 32 individual panels. The panels were then mounted onto linen sheets or sailcloth. The idea behind this was that the cloth would absorb the stress of folding and unfolding the map, thus preserving the map's integrity. Such maps were known as either pocket maps or case maps, because they were easily transported and were often accompanied by leather or cardboard cases. Typically, cartographers like Colton would offer their larger separate edition maps, like this one, to clients in multiple formats, including folding, case or pocket, and mounted on rollers.

Cartographer

Joseph Hutchins Colton (1800-1893) was one of the most significant and prolific American commercial cartographers of the 19th century. Colton began publishing maps around 1833. Initially, his work focused on the lucrative emigrant guide market. In 1858, he was commissioned by the government of Bolivia to produce a large map of Bolivia. While in production, the government that ordered the map was overthrown and the anticipated payment never arrived, forcing Colton into bankruptcy. Although savvy business deals with A. J. Johnson and others allowed his business to survive, it never fully recovered.

Planisphère Illustré

This 1857 map by Alexandre Vuillemin was drawn for the homebound scholar to unfold and explore the peoples and places of the world. Great discoveries, famous navigators, prolific annotations, and decorative elements all added to the map's educational agenda. Throughout, there was a wealth of detail, including extensive annotations on history, culture, climate, colonies, major cities, nautical routes, and even the duration of various journeys.

The map was perhaps most striking for its numerous vignette illustrations, such as horsemen in the Sahara, Eskimos in the Arctic, American Indian tribes, and whaling ships. Two large illustrations at the bottom of the map showed the dress and physiology of various ethnic groups, among them the "Espagnols," the "Mongols," the "Arabes de la Mecque," the "Grecs," the "Chinois," the "Russes," the "Italiens," and the "Francais."

Cartographer

Alexandre Vuillemin (1812-1880) was a prolific French editor and cartographer whose best-known work was an atlas illustrating industrial and commercial interests, Atlas Illustré de Géographie Commerciale et Industrielle. *He trained as an engraver and publisher under Auguste Henri Dufour (1795-1865). Despite a large body of surviving work, Vuillemin's life remains shrouded in mystery.*

OCÉAN GLACIAL ARCTIQUE

GROENLAND

SPITZBERG

NOUVELLE ZEMBLE

NOUVELLE SIBÉRIE

MER DE KARA

ISLANDE

SIBÉRIE

ASIE

MER D'OKHOTSK

MER DE BEHRING

OCÉAN ATLANTIQUE

TARTARIE INDÉPENDANTE

MONGOLIE

MANDCHOURIE

PERSE

TURQUIE

CHINE

EGYPTE

ARABIE

SAHARA OU GRAND DÉSERT

AFRIQUE

OCÉAN PACIFIQUE

ILES PHILIPPINES

ILES MARIANES

ILES KAROLINES

POLYNÉSIE

ÉQUATEUR ou LIGNE ÉQUINOXIALE

MALAISIE

MER DES INDES

OCÉANIE

AUSTRALIE ou NOUVELLE HOLLANDE

MADAGASCAR

TERRE DE VAN DIEMEN

NOUVELLE ZÉLANDE

GRAND OCÉAN

TERRES AUSTRALES

GLACIAL ANTARCTIQUE

TERRE VICTORIA

PRINCIPALES MONTAGNES DU MONDE.

TABLEAU EXPLICATIF

LONGUEURS, SOURCES ET EMBOUCHURES DES PRINCIPAUX FLEUVES DU MONDE.

COSTUMES DES DIFFÉRENTES RACES QUI PEUPLENT LA TERRE.

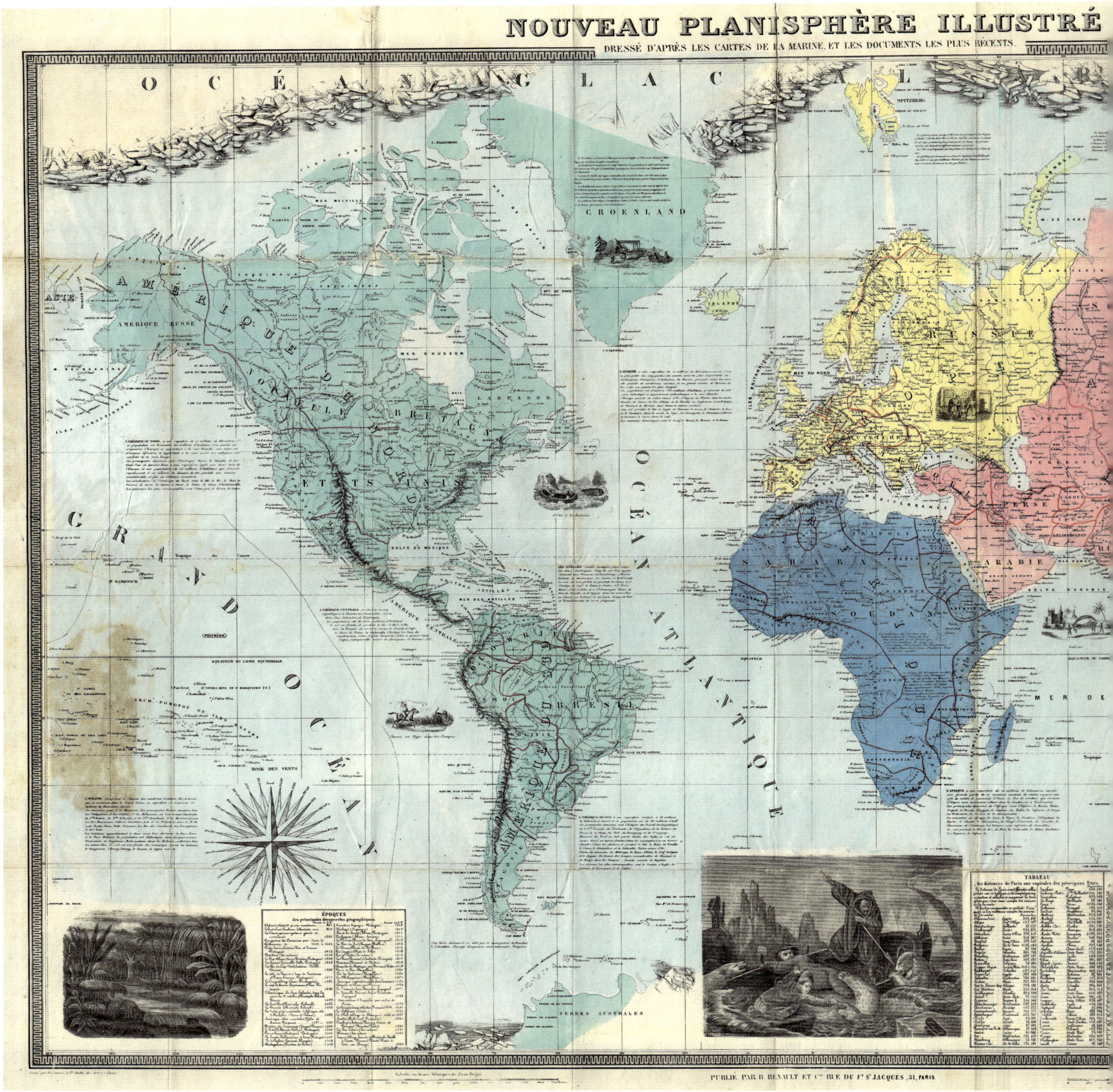

NOUVEAU PLANISPHÈRE ILLUSTRÉ

DRESSÉ D'APRÈS LES CARTES DE LA MARINE, ET LES DOCUMENTS LES PLUS RÉCENTS.

OCÉAN GLACIAL ARCTIQUE

GROENLAND

ASIE

AMÉRIQUE RUSSE

AMÉRIQUE DU NORD

NOUVELLE BRETAGNE

MER D'HUDSON

LABRADOR

ÉTATS UNIS

GOLFE DU MEXIQUE

AMÉRIQUE CENTRALE

MER DES ANTILLES

ÉQUATEUR OU LIGNE ÉQUINOXIALE

AMÉRIQUE DU SUD

GRAND OCÉAN

OCÉAN ATLANTIQUE

ROSE DES VENTS

TERRA AUSTRALES

RUSSIE

EUROPE

SAHARA

SOUDAN

ARABIE

PERSE

MER DE

ÉPOQUES
des principales découvertes géographiques

TABLEAU
des distances de Paris aux capitales des principaux États.

PUBLIÉ PAR B. RENAULT ET C.ie RUE DU F.g S.t JACQUES, 31, PARIS.

Nouveau Planisphère Illustré

A dramatic and richly illustrated 1862 map of the world by Felix Delamarche. At the bottom of the map three terrified men, in a tiny boat, attempted to fight off aggressive polar bears in the most dramatic of numerous vignettes on this monumental map. Other exciting and delightful illustrations included a man on horseback appearing to try to rope a tiger near South America; two girls in a horse-drawn sleigh in Russia; a man and a woman with cups of tea in China; and a wealthy man reclining while being carried near "Arabie." Delamarche, being more of a businessman than a cartographer, included over 15 illustrated vignettes, no doubt intended to appeal to the growing market of armchair adventurers.

In the early 19th century, illustrations were largely removed from maps in favor of a more minimalist cartographic style. By the middle of the 19th century innovative new printing technologies, which allowed highly detailed maps to be produced on a mass scale, changed the economics of cartography, making what was once only for the elite, affordable to the masses. Pictorial illustrations, popular with the public, began to appear again, notably in the work of John Tallis, Felix Delamarche, and Victor Levasseur.

Cartographer

*Félix Delamarche (fl. c. 1830-1880) was a French cartographer and
the heir to the Charles François Delamarche (1740-1817) publishing empire.
He ran the company with cartographer Charles Dien (1809-1870).*

Crofutt's New Map of the Trans-Continental, American, and Trans-Continental, European, Route Around the World

Crofutt's 1871 map of the world expressed the remarkable enthusiasm that technological innovations such as steamships and the locomotive generated. Crofutt realized that what was once nearly impossible for the common traveler, a trip around the world, was now within reach and he composed this map to prove it.

The map offered several round-the-world routes and even provided timetables and estimated costs. The best route, argued Crofutt, started from New York and crossed the United States on the newly completed Union-Pacific Railroad. From San Francisco, the traveler could embark on a steamship for Shanghai, then another to India, which could be crossed by rail or rounded by sea. From Bombay, the adventurer took to sea again to pass through the Suez Canal and into the Mediterranean. From Greece, several routes were possible, but the quickest was a train to Paris, then a boat trip across the English Channel. From London, a steamship could be easily booked to New York.

Jules Verne may have been inspired by Crofutt's guide when he sat down to write *Around the World in 80 Days*, which was published two years after this map in 1873. By Crofutt's calculations, Phileas Fogg would have taken 87 days and 13 hours to complete the fastest round-the-world route. Fogg beat Crofutt's estimate by some 7 days, but by Crofutt's calculation, also overpaid by more than 75%!

Cartographer

George Andrew Crofutt (1826-1907) was an American artist and publisher best known for his tourist guides to the American West. Much of his work focused on the growing North American railroad network and westward expansion. He was credited with inspiring the increased settlement of the American West.

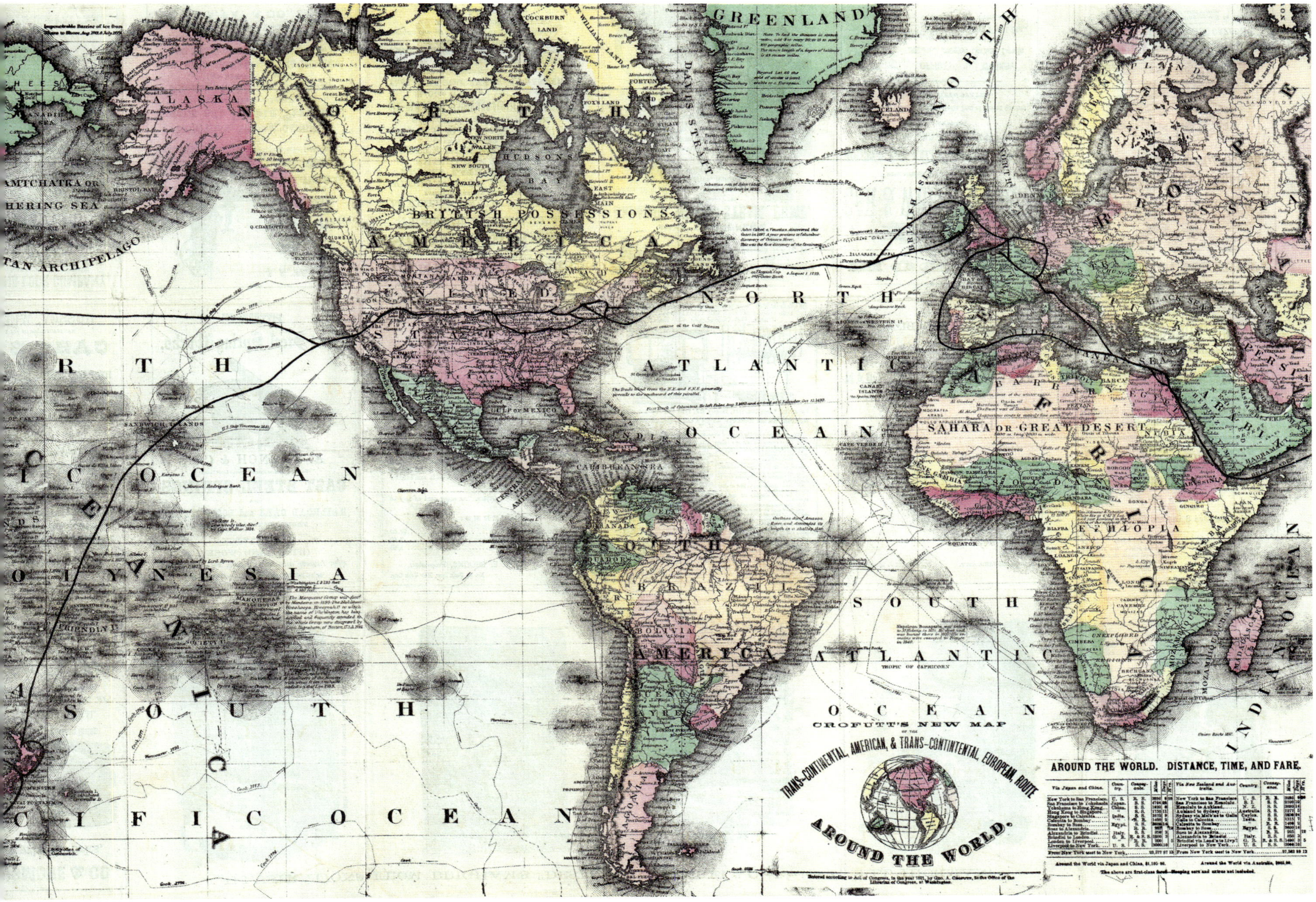

GREENLAND

NORTH AMERICA

BRITISH POSSESSIONS AMERICA

ALASKA

AMTCHATKA OR HERING SEA

TAN ARCHIPELAGO

NORTH

ATLANTIC

OCEAN

EUROPE

RUSSIA

PERSIA

AFRICA

SAHARA OR GREAT DESERT

ETHIOPIA

POLYNESIA

SOUTH AMERICA

BRAZIL

BOLIVIA

SOUTH ATLANTIC

OCEAN

INDIAN OCEAN

PACIFIC OCEAN

SOUTH

CROFUTT'S NEW MAP
OF THE
TRANS-CONTINENTAL, AMERICAN, & TRANS-CONTINENTAL EUROPEAN ROUTE
AROUND THE WORLD.

Le Tour du Monde en un Clin d'Oeil

This magnificent pictorial map offered a 'World Tour in the Blink of an Eye.' It was issued to supplement the January 1876 issue of the popular French periodical *Le Monde Illustré*. The world was presented as if it were being viewed from space, but was surrounded by such rich illustration that it remained both distant and intimate.

A hot-air balloon flew over a starry night, a lighthouse shone into dark and thrashing waters, a volcano erupted under a falling star, and meanwhile the village market carried on. Throughout the map, over 75 individuals, in "traditional costumes," were presented in meticulous detail. Vivid regional highlights incorporated both into the border work and into the map itself present a continuously interesting visual panorama.

In North America, the flag of the United States flew near the seemingly small cities of Washington, "Philidelphie," and New York. The Union Pacific railroad ran just below an industrialized view of Chicago. In far off Asia, just south of Beijing there was a "Boudhiste" temple near an opium field. Prominent explorers were noted in the Arctic and in Africa. In the seas, a wide variety of ships navigated bustling shipping lanes. At the top of the map, just below the golden cross a note read, "Mer Libre?" suggesting lingering hopes for a Northwest Passage.

Cartographers

• **Daniel Vierge** (1851-1904) *was a Spanish illustrator and watercolorist. Vierge was educated at the Madrid School of Fine Arts before moving to Paris to participate in that city's lively publishing industry. In 1870, he was invited by Charles Yriarte to work for* Le Monde illustré, *a popular French periodical. He also produced numerous book illustrations, among them, the illustrations for Victor Hugo's* L'Annee Terrible.

• **Fortuné Louis Méaulle** (1844-1901) *was a French woodcut engraver whose work appeared in* Le Monde illustré *and other French graphic periodicals.*

E TOUR DU MONDE EN UN CLIN D'ŒIL

a numéro du MONDE ILLUSTRÉ du 1er Janvier 1876 — Dessin de MM. SCOTT et VIERGE, gravure de M. MÉAULLE

Bureaux : 13, quai Voltaire, 13, à Paris.

TYPES ET COSTUMES

PAVILLONS MARITIMES

PARIS. — IMPRIMERIE TYPOGRAPHIQUE DE A. BOURDILLIAT, 13, QUAI VOLTAIRE. — 2192

209

COURANT EQUATORIAL

Sénégal

Cayenne
Poivre

Flora, fauna, historic events, cultural artifacts, and indigenous people are represented pictorially in this map. The dramatic imagery in these pages includes sketches of some 75 individuals in traditional costumes, all listed in the lower section of the map.

Noubert

ABEG Mourzouk

TOUÂREGS

O.E. Vogel

Nachtigal 1872

Kartoûm

Café Moka

Mungo Park

Barth

REGIONS INCONNUES

Osaii

Condar

Russegger 1839

Schweinfurth 1871

Mr Kozanga

Schweinfurth 1870

Miāni

Baker 1864

COMAI

Richard Lander

DuChaillu

Tucker Badian

Gorille

Kingston Tuckey

Tschébúgos 1871 Livingstone

ANGOLA

1850 MAGYARD

Golb ango

Pombeiros 1866
GRAÇA 1846

STANLEY

LIVINGSTONE

47 48 49 50 51 52 53 54 55 56 58

MER DES INDES

Iles Maldives
Ceylan

Poudichery

INCINÉRATION HINDOUE

ILE DE PAQUES

PANADE

F. MÉAULLE. SC

Worlds that Were, and Were Not

From the earliest days of cartography, mapmakers found the impulse to map alternate realities almost impossible to resist. For as long as there was a real physical world, there was an alternate metaphorical world. In the early days of human history, this world was the land of gods and monsters, great allegorical beings that manifested both our best and worse human qualities, including our greatest aspirations and greatest fears. Mapping that alternate reality was a way to bring it within the spectrum of human understanding, and by doing so, exert some control over the world and one's relationship to it.

Some of the earliest such maps are associated with astrology and the mapping of the firmament. The constellations in the night sky were seen as reflections of a divine world. In western cultures, Hercules, Pegasus, Orion and Draco cavort through the night with Andromeda and Cassiopeia. In non-European cultures, a different but thematically similar celestial pantheon reigned. The earliest known star chart, the Dunhuang Chart, was discovered on the ancient Silk Road, in the Mogao Caves, and dates to about 700 AD. The pantheon on the Dunhuang Chart derived from the Chinese system, but the essential concept is the same; out there, in space, is another world on which we can imprint our dreams.

Another kind of early map of an imaginary land is the religiously themed allegorical map. These we covered somewhat in earlier chapters, including such examples as the Hereford Map in chapter 1. Briefly revisiting the Hereford map, we can now review it in a different light. Yes, it is map of the known world, and with some imagination, the geography is recognizable, but, as discussed in that map's description, it also illustrates an allegorical path from sin towards redemption through an overlapping religio-magical pseudo-world.

Such maps, while no doubt beautiful, were also practical tools for promoting the agenda and propaganda of the government and church, which often marched hand-in-hand. In today's more literal world, allegorical messages are easily missed, but from the Middle Ages through the 19th century, they were quickly grasped. Until the early 20th century, the average educated person would have been deeply indoctrinated in Greco-Roman mythology and Biblical tradition. He or she would have instantly understood the multiple meanings associated with various gods and goddesses, or underlying scenes from the Bible. Louis XIV, France's Sun King, for example, regularly commissioned paintings associating himself with Apollo through that deity's iconography, i.e. his laurel wreath, the sun, a golden chariot, etc. By doing so, his people understood that his reign would also encourage Apollonic virtues such as music, philosophy, and learning.

Thus, it was not uncommon for maps of the 18th century or earlier to have rich allegorical content, typically embedded into their cartouche work. Allegorical cartouches could be read as easily as the map itself, giving the viewer insight into the message and intention of the cartographer, both with regard to the map, and to society at large. It was but a small step for early cartographers to segue into purely allegorical charts and maps. In this chapter we offer two such maps for study, the first being the 1743 Carte de l'Isle de la Félicité and the second, J. B. Homann's Accurata Utopiae Tabula.

Neither map is particularly religious in subject matter or content, but both arise from the Biblical tradition of allegorical imagery. The earlier of the two was Homann's Accurata Utopiae Tabula. Far from our understanding of Utopia today, this was a land of debauchery and vice, the German Schlaraffenland, quite literally "Fool's Paradise." Here every manner of excess was embraced while the true spiritual paradise, inaccessible to the fools beyond a daunting mountain range, remained Terra Incognita (Land Unknown).

The Carte de l'Isle de la Félicité has another message. It is the product of a secret quasi-Masonic society, L'Ordre de la Félicité, which, by all appearances, seems to have been dedicated to having a good time. The map speaks of the society's agenda, by which one must navigate through various ports such as wealth, beauty, virtue, etc. before arriving at the well-fortified castle of perfect happiness. The map was intended to illustrate, for initiates to the Order, the path by which its values might be exemplified.

Variations on this type of map remained prevalent well into the 19th century, when they were adapted to promote and propagandize social and political movements, ranging from the encouragement of marital felicity, to suffrage and temperance. Such maps, as in our example, an 1838 map of the Land of Temperance, typically involved a passage through various daunting realms and oceans. If one could navigate through starvation, anguish, poverty, murder, and other horrors, one may have arrived at the wonderful sounding land of "Self-Denial" where such delightful countries as "Industry," "Prosperity," and "Enjoyment," among others, could be found.

The general theme, common in many such maps, analogized life to a great journey with the destination being some sort of paradise, either in the physical word, the spiritual, or the afterlife. Along the road of life, the traveler had to conquer many dangers and avoid temptations that might have led them astray. In almost all examples there was a strong moral, even righteous, component and the perspective was, to our mind, rather narrow and limited, based upon the underpinning assumption that a singular definition of "good" and "right" must apply to all.

By the early 20th century, a different and more nuanced view of "good" emerged. World War I devastated not only the countryside of Europe but also broke down social, moral, and political barriers. The distinction between right and wrong, good and evil, was no longer completely clear. In the wake of this change, a new type of map emerged, the fantasy map. Probably the earliest example of this is Bernard Sleigh's 1918 Anciente Mappe of Fairy Land. Sleigh pulls from German and English fairy tales, Greco-Roman mythology, Norse Mythology, and more, to compile a fantastical map. Sleigh promotes no moral lesson and the map is without judgement, giving equal measure to the light and dark as two sides of the same coin. Sleigh's new map style inspired subsequent fantasy work in cartography, art, and literature, including, possibly, the pictorial maps of the 20th century.

Les marins monstres & terrestres, lesquelz on trouue en beaucoup de lieu

SS₃ 4   A . Sere

Les Marins Monstres & Terrestres

Often euphemistically referred to as "Münster's Monsters," this is Sebastian Münster's bestiary of sea serpents and other terrifying monsters, some fictional, some real, that was included in the 1545 "Cosmographia." Most of the beasts here are derived from a 1539 map of Scandinavia drawn by Olaus Magnus. Although Münster's Monsters may initially seem fabulous and scary, many are based upon or outright depictions the factual creatures that Scandinavian sailors and whalemen actually encountered.

Among the more recognizable beasts are various forms of whales with obvious blowholes, at least two enormous lobsters, a sea serpent (probably an oarfish), the whale fish (white fish at center, an Orca), and something that might very well be a walrus. Of course, there are fictional sea monsters too, including a pig faced sea beast, apparently seen by sailors in 1537, and the Sea Buffalo, something that looks like a cross between a bull and a fish.

Although much is made of Münster's sea creatures, it should be noted that his map also illustrates land based fauna, most of which is far more realistic. These include reindeer, beavers, sables, bears, a wolverine, snakes, and what might be some sort of large cat. In the lower left, there is a tree populated by "duckbirds," a curious kind of avian that Münster claims "grows on trees" but which, in his lifetime, had not been seen for some 400 years.

Although not properly a map, Münster included this catalog of beasts in his "Cosmographia" to illustrate the natural world. Today we might look at a book like the "Cosmographia" and consider it an atlas for its many maps, but the work itself is more accurately an attempt to describe, as the name suggests, the entire cosmos. It included descriptions of flora, fauna, geological and astronomical observations, historical notes, and cultural (some might even say anthropological) commentary.

Cartographer

Sebastian Münster (1488-1552) was a professor of Hebrew at the University of Basil, Switzerland. Münster had issued a call throughout Germany's academic communities for cartographic information, in preparation for putting together the "Cosmographia", and the book's accuracy and scope were unprecedented. It sold well and went through 24 editions. The intricate woodcuts, by a variety of artists, were one of the reasons for its vast influence. It was produced for nearly 100 years. Most of Münster's work was published by his sons. He died in Switzerland in 1552.

Mundus Alter et Idem

Published in Hanover in 1607, the title of this map roughly translates as 'Another World, and Yet the Same.' It was drawn to illustrate Hall's dystopian novel *Mundus alter et idem sive Terra Australis antehac semper incognita*. In the *Mundus alter et idem*, a naive young Englishman, Mercurius Britannicus, lusting for adventure, embarks on a voyage of discovery to an unknown continent far to the south, beyond the limits of the known world. Traveling on the ship *Fantasia*, Britannicus makes landfall on Terra Australis, the mythic southern continent, only to find himself lost and stranded among that far country's morally bankrupt populace.

Hall uses the speculative but undiscovered southern continent of Terra Australis as the theater for his moralistic and religious criticism. Terra Australis, situated at the periphery of most contemporary world maps, here takes center stage, occupying nearly half the page. Hall's Terra Australis features mighty rivers, dense forests, and fearsome mountains. It is populated by terrible nations, including Lavernia (the land of thieves), Pamphagonia (the land of gluttony), Ivronia (the home of drunkards), and Viraginia (the country of nagging wives).

Mundus alter et idem is a historically significant work. Predating *Gulliver's Travels* by more than 100 years, it considered the first moralistic parable to append a fictional geo-satirical land to a known factual geography. The work, while suppressed by Puritans in England, became popular in continental Europe, going through several editions until about 1664. Hall was doubtless aware that this work would arouse the ire of those he criticized, so he published under a pseudonym, that of the story's hero, Mercurius Britannicus. It was not until 1674 that Thomas Hyde, an English orientalist scholar, definitively attributed the work to Hall.

Cartographer

Joseph Hall (1574-1656) was a satirist, moralist, devotionalist, and high ranking clergyman active in England during the late 16th and first half of the 17th century. He is frequently referred to as the 'English Seneca' for his adherence to stoic principals. Hall was born in Bristow Park, England. He studied to become a clergyman at Emmanuel College in Cambridge. In 1627, Hall was appointed the Bishop of Exeter, and later the Bishop of Norwich.

Gallia
Rochel
Geneua
Baiona
Compostella
Lisboa
HISPANIA
Scuilla
Italia
Roma
Sardina
Napels
Sicilia
Constantinopolis
Turchesta
Mare Maior
Corint
Candia

A S I A
Tenduc
Cathaia
Indostan

A F R I C A
Anzica
Abassia
Mare Rubri
Mare Mediterra
Narsinga
Smagar
Sian
Maliupar
C. Comōri
Malaca

Saribano
Peru
Brasilia
Mono motapa
Insula
Hermæphroditica

AMERICA
MERIDIONALIS
PATAGO
NES
C: de la
Victoria
C: de Vegenia
C: de N: de
Iesu
Insula
Familia
Promontor: Bonæ spei
Promontorium
Nigrum
Aphrodyssia
Nova Gynia

Acaleo
Trugillo

de la Crus
Magellan

V E R
A
L arcinia

Tryphon flu
Doxia
Le Sion
Byous flu
Pla Moronia
Credulia

Ozsuum flu
PAMPHAGO
NIA
Mejonium flui
Vealgonius
I V R O
NIA
Varenia pars
LOCANIA
Vel
Euginia
Amazonia
VSRAGINIA

MORONIA
FELIX
Lisonica gens
Plorauia
Lingua dotia

MORON FATVA
Baueria
Tuberony
Colles

Scieceia
Aspera Moronia
Orgilia
Lyperia

VARIANA
Vel Morion
Mobilis

FRVGIONA
Adhuc Incognita

Planisphaerium Coeleste

A rich and fanciful 1680 double hemisphere celestial chart by Frederik de Wit. Dark clouds pushed up against the title banner and six additional astronomical diagrams surrounded the main map. The additional spheres illustrated the phases of the moon in relation to the sun, the rotation of the moon orbiting the earth, and the Copernican and Ptolemaic systems.

In the main map, each hemisphere was rendered on a polar stereographic projection and centered on the elliptical pole. Pictorial forms were drawn around the starts to more clearly illustrate the constellations, with an emphasis on Zodiacal forms. Some of the secondary constellations presented here were uncommon and may have been derived from Joan Blaeu's celestials of 1658.

This map was not officially included in any of the standard atlases of the time, but it was sometimes bound with Sanson's *Atlas Nouveau* and Allard's *Atlas Major*.

Cartographer

Frederik de Wit (1629-1706) was an engraver and cartographer in Amsterdam during the Dutch Golden Age of Cartography. In 1689, he was granted his privilege, a type of early copyright. After his death, de Wit's widow sold his maps and printing plates at auction. The plates were bought by Pieter Mortier and subsequently laid the foundation for the firm Covens and Mortier, which became one of the largest Dutch publishing houses of the 18th century.

Peg asus

Caßiopea

Cygnus

Cepheus

Perseus

Polus Eclipticæ Boreus

Lira

Capella

Auriga
Erichtonius

Circulus Arcticus

Stella Polaris

Urfa
minor

...urus

Solftitiorum

Polus Arct...

EMINI

Urfa maior
Califto

Draco

Coro
Bor.

Caftor

Dubhe

...lux

Colurus Æquinoctio...

Coma Berenices

CAN CER

Arctu...

As is the case with many celestial maps of the same period, this one by Frederick de Wit utilizes classical symbology to represent the constellations. This is particularly true of the Boötes, Hercules and Ophiuchus constellations in the Northern Hemisphere.

Accurata Utopiae Tabula

This 1694 map of Utopia was the most significant 17th century literary map to be issued in German. The map was commissioned from Johann Baptist Homann by the art dealer and publisher Daniel Funck. This vision Utopia was based upon a 16th century satirical musical work by the Nuremburg *Meistersinger* Hans Sachs. The vision was unusual but was similar to the English Land of Cockaigne.

The Holy Land, or Terra Sancta, appeared at the top of the map and was marked "Incognita." At the bottom of the map, the more familiar land "Das Hollische Reich," or "The Hellish Kingdom," with place names like "Beelzebub," "Satan" and "Lucifer," was easy to access. The greater map of Utopia was defined by every vice and vulgarity known to man, ranging from avarice and drunkenness, to murder and indolence. In all, there were some 1700 place names, most of which denoted sins and human vices. This "Utopia" was known alternatively as *Schlaraffenland*, a High German term that loosely translated into "Lazy Ape Land."

Cartographer

Johann Baptist Homann (1664-1724) was a prolific German map publisher based in Nuremberg. Homann built a prosperous map publishing empire by undercutting more expensive maps by French and Dutch publishing houses, becoming, in the process, one of the most prolific map publishers in history. After his death, the firm continued to publish as Homann Heirs (Heirs of Homann).

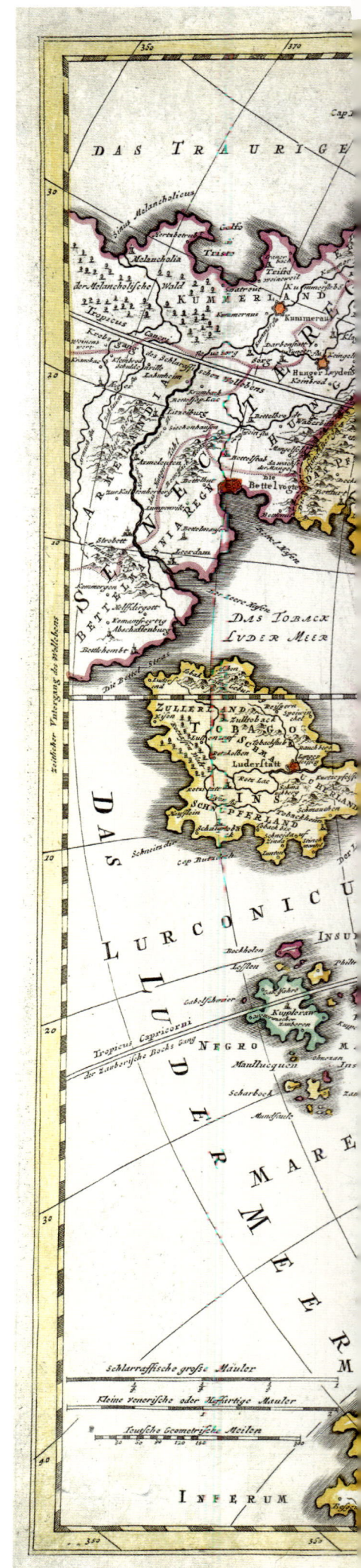

Accurata UTOPIÆ TABULA

Das ist Der Neu entdeckten SCHALCK WELT, oder In so offtbenanten und doch nie erkanten SCHLARRAFFENLANDES

TERRA SANCTA INCOGNITA

UNBEKANTE LAND DER FROMMEN

MAMMONIA

SUPERBIA REG.

CAENI IMPERIUM

RESPUBLICA

BABONIA REGN.

DAS MARE FRESSIGE MEER

DOLE EBRIUM

UND VOLLE MEER

DAS VERSOFFENE MEER

MARE

STOLIDUM

LUSORIA REG.

TARTARI REG.

DAS NARRISCHE MEER

SCHLARRAFFENBURG

ÆQUINOCTIALIS

DAS SUESSE GOLFO DI FEIN NARRISCHE VENEREA MEER

225

SISTÈME DE LA CRÉATION DU MONDE SUIVANT MOÏSE.

EUROPE

ASIE

AFRIQUE

l'Élement aride, ou la Terre sans Eaux. *Génes. I. v. 9.*

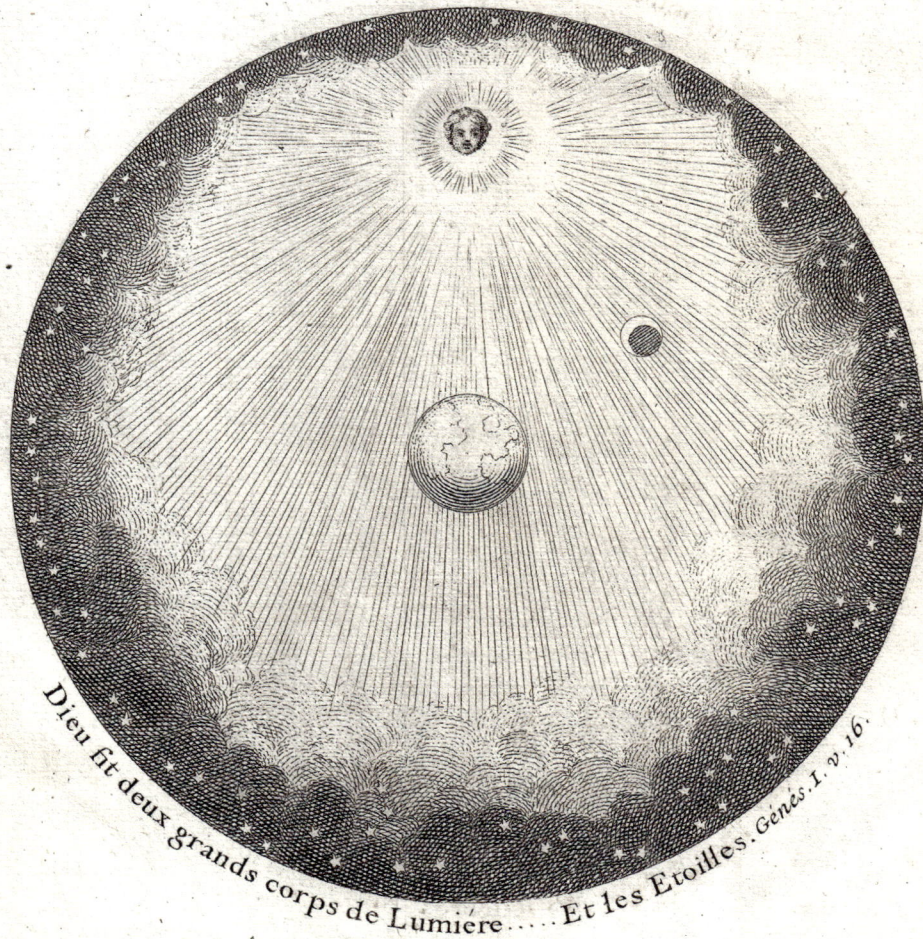

Dieu fit deux grands corps de Lumiére..... Et les Etoilles. *Génes. I. v. 16.*

Sisteme de la Création du Monde

This 1728 two-part map by Antoine Calmet was rendered from an arcane religio-scientific perspective. It was issued to illustrate Calmet's influential *Dictionnaire Historique Critique, Chronologique, Geographique et Littéral de la Bible*.

Focused on the Eastern Hemisphere, the top sphere expounded a geophysical idea promoted by Francis Bacon, ironically known as the father of the scientific method. This hypothesis suggested that the globe was a great sphere of water upon which God, during creation, caused the continents to float. The weight of the continents, it was thought, was so great that it displaced the water of the Northern Hemisphere to the Southern Hemisphere, thus submerging all but the most mountainous lands south of the Equator.

The lower sphere offered a pre-Copernican view of the cosmos. The Earth was shown at the center of the universe, with the stars and the moon rotating around it. The sun was a god-like figure warming the Earth in its divine light. After Copernicus, it became widely accepted that the Earth rotated around the sun and not the other way around.

Cartographer

Antoine Augustin Calmet (1672-1757) was a French Benedictine monk and Biblical scholar. His academic approach to Biblical research influenced a new era of Biblical exegesis that focused on a critical search for meaning. Pope Benedict XIII offered to confer Episcopal Dignity upon him, but in his piety and humility, he refused the honor.

Carte de l'Isle de la Félicité

In this unusual allegorical map of 1743, the 'Island of Happiness' was bordered by a calm sea to the south and a savage sea to the north. Painted in rich watercolor with extensive gold leaf embellishment, this masterpiece was designed for a secret quasi-masonic organization, L'Ordre de la Félicité. The Order was unique in that it encouraged female initiates. Although the existence of the order was shrouded in mystery, this gorgeous allegorical map provided some insight into its character and raison d'etre.

The map focused on the path to the "Castle of Perfect Happiness," entry to which meant successfully overcoming a number of challenges. First, your ship must not be dashed on the Rocks of Caprice or Prudery. Also, you must not become trapped on the Banks of Temptation. You must find safe harbor, the available ports being Beauty, Virtue, "Complaisance," Félicité (Happiness), and Wealth. Finally, you must navigate the dangers on land which included the Path of Coquetry and the dismal Swamp of Pleasures.

Secret shared dinners and coded nautical terminology were the cornerstones of the order's social life. Sexual innuendos seem to have been integral and it is unclear whether libertine debauchery was the true order of the day. A dictionary of the group's code words was created by journalist and member Jean-Pierre Moët. The dictionary included a variety of coded terms that can only be interpreted as risqué: breasts (promontory), thighs (capstan), stomach (dry dock), and even for lifting a woman's skirts (reefing the sails). What we do know is that an initiation ceremony was required that involved "sailing to the Island of Félicité" and eventually joining the group, after overcoming a number of "difficulties."

Cartographer

Johann Martin Weis (1711-1751) was a prominent artist,

draughtsman, and engraver based in Strasbourg.

CARTE DE L'ISLE DE LA FELICITÉ

MER SAUVAGE

MER FAVORABLE

Rocher de Prudence

Rocher de Bonheur

Philosophie

Harmonie

BONHEUR PARFAIT

Cavallerie

Montagne des honneurs

OCEAN OF ANIMAL APPETITE

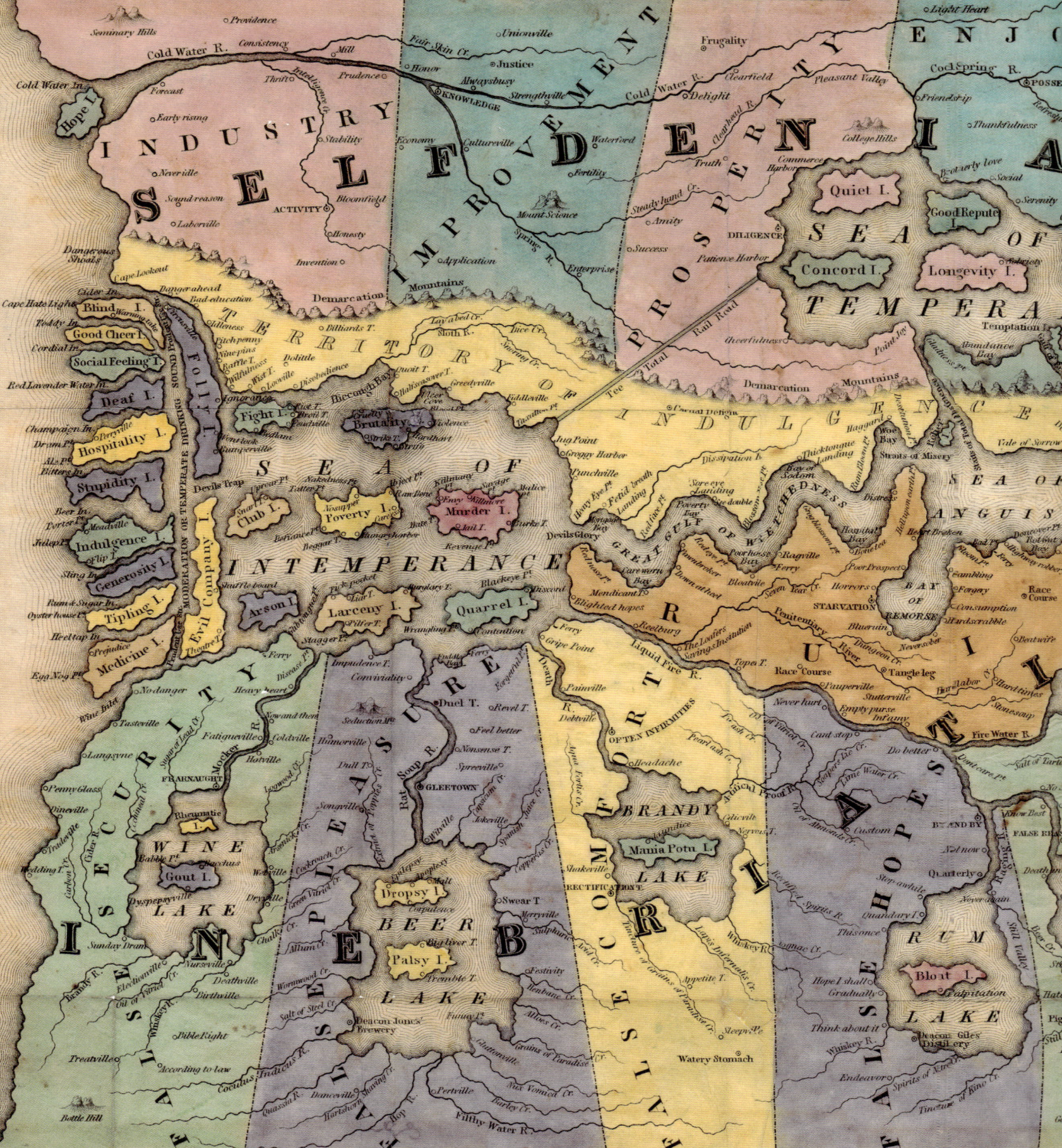

INDUSTRY

SELF IMPROVEMENT

PROSPERITY

ENJO

SEA OF TEMPERA

SEA OF INTEMPERANCE

TERRITORY OF INDULGENCE

GREAT GULF OF WRETCHEDNESS

SEA OF ANGUIS

DOMINION OF TEMPERATE DRINKING — MODERATION

WINE LAKE

FALSE SECURITY

FALSE PLEASURE

BEER LAKE

BRANDY LAKE

FALSE COMFORT

FALSE HOPES

RUM LAKE

RUIN

Quiet I.   Concord I.   Longevity I.   Good Repute I.

Murder I.   Poverty I.   Club I.   Fight I.   Brutality

Larceny I.   Arson I.   Quarrel I.

Tipling I.   Generosity I.   Indulgence I.   Hospitality I.   Stupidity I.   Deaf I.   Social Feeling I.   Good Cheer I.   Blind I.

Gout I.   Dropsy I.   Palsy I.   Mania Potu I.   Bloat I.

Evil Company I.

Hope I.

BAY OF REMORSE   STARVATION

KNOWLEDGE   ACTIVITY   DILIGENCE

Cold Water R.   Cold Water In.

Demarcation Mountains

Tee Total Rail Road

Deacon Giles Distillery   Deacon Jones Brewery

Temperance Map

A brilliant 1838 allegorical diagrammatic map by Reverend John Christian Wiltberger illustrating the challenges and rewards of abstinence from alcohol (temperance). This map revealed a dangerous world full of temptations and pitfalls, but rich with reward. At the bottom of the map was the country of "Inebriation," where the lands "False Hope," "False Pleasure," and "Total Indifference," among others, gravitated around evil bodies of water, among them "Wine Lake," "Beer Lake," etc. To the north, across the "Sea of Temperance" or the "Great Gulf of Wretchedness," lay the "Paradise of Self Denial" where one could find "Longevity I.," "Good Repute I.," "Prosperity," and "Enjoyment."

This broadside map, and others like it, were designed as didactic visual aids with the intention to both amuse and educate. Typically, they would be passed out on the street or furtively posted in bars, saloons, and other drinking establishments in the hope of luring the wayward towards the tea-totaling path of temperance.

Cartographer

John Christian Wiltberger Jr. (1766-1851) was an American minister, missionary, and temperance activist based in Philadelphia.

An Anciente Mappe
of Fairy Land Newly
Discovered and Set Forth

A NANCIENTE MAPPE of FAIRYLAND newly discovered and set forth.

This 1918 map by Bernard Sleigh offered up a world divided into darkness and light where green fields and sunny beaches were just a stone's throw away from ancient tombs and stormy waters. Offering a rich mix of characters from Greek mythology, European folk tales, and literature, this map presented a panoramic view of an "Ancient Fairyland." Set sail on the Sea of Dreams, or follow the rainbow to its end, fantastical delights were abundant there.

A Tolkienian paradise, Lancelot, Cinderella, Peter Pan, Puss in Boots, Peter Piper, Hansel and Gretel, elves and dragons could be found among these mountains and valleys. A visitor could swim in the Peace Pool, visit the tomb of King Arthur, or see Andromeda rescued by Perseus. Follow the red line to journey from the "world as it is" to the place "that never was and always will be." From the "Harbour of Dreamland" to the mermaids warming themselves on the shore, there were many places to rest your mind and remember the wonder you felt as a youth.

This map was developed in 1918, just as the "Great War" in Europe came to an end. All of Europe had suffered war's terrible losses. Perhaps this map helped soothe some of the inevitable, yearning ache for the halcyon comforts of childhood.

Cartographer

Bernard Sleigh (1872-1954) was a British illustrator and muralist. He studied at the Birmingham School of Art and was influenced by the Arts and Crafts Movement. Although he published several other maps of various regions of England this was his best-known work.

This extraordinary six foot long image let one admire fantastic details of a unique map of Fairy Land, where classic European tales mixed with Greek mythology. One can see the Garden of Proserpine, Demeter, Circe's Isle, Perseus saving Andromeda, the Argonauts and the Snow Queen, just to list few in the detail image on the left. Also, the legend is unique; one can find symbols for a wishing well, dwarf treasure, an elfin temple, a fairie shine and a village inn.

The image on the right illustrates Peter Pan's house, the King Arthur saga – from Excalibur to Lancelot and Percival – to the Harbour of Dreamland.

Silverbell Light

Here is Avalon

EXCALIBOR

King Arthur's Tomb

Amfortas

Ogier the Dane

Here du Kilwc

Floramie

Galahad lyeth here

The House of Echoe

Parsifal Titurel

Here are manie Blue Birds

Here is the Castle of Joyous Gard

Here is the Imp Tree

The H...

Lancelot

Guenevere lyeth here

Here lyeth Morgan le Fay

Percival

The Pool of Hippocrene

This is CARBONEK

Here is Kundry

Merlin

Here is Narcisus

Here is the Magic Forest of Lyonesse

Here is Sir Iwodos

Red Riding Hoode House

Courtenay Mary's House

Palace of King Cole

Knave of Hearts Cottage

...th her Prince

The River of White Nymphs

Pool of the Nereids

FAIRY WORLD / REAL WORLD

This is Actæon

These are Satyrs

Here is Rhodope

Lake

Here is the Sibyl

...are Quicksands

THE HARBOUR of DREAMLAND

The Gold Caverns

This is the Shippe of Tristram of Lyonesse

The Enchanted Sea

Oberons Shield

Scale of Thoughts
100 200 300 400

The Northe
Beacon

Here are the manie Valleys of Sleep

The Bay of Dreams

Here are
...Wolves

...ave Point
...doe swarm here

...d is
...d

West
Beacon

A Watch
Tower

Ogres Tongue
Cape

Here do they
Kennel
Nightmares

The Bridge of
Rocs' Eggs

The Bay of
Moaning

The Valley of Fire

The
Witch Wood

Landing Place
for the
Region of
Blacke
Magick

Mouth of Dream River
Castle of Seven Towers

Here is the Greate
Whirlpoole

Crowned Fish

The Three Wise
Men of Gotham

These bee Tritons

Allalonestone Rock

América primum detecta à Christophoro Colombo aº 1492 at ab Americo Vesputio latius retecta aº 1499 deqз suo nomine eam dixit hinc aº 1520 à Ferdinando Magellano, Fretum quod de nomine suo Magellanicum dictum, Traietum est: Idem prestiterunt Franciscus Draco aº 1579. Thomas Candisch aº 1587. Olivierus à Nort aº 1600. Schaldus de Weert aº 1600 Gorgius Spilberg aº 1615. Commodius vero et titius fretum deprehensum aº 1616 a Iacobo le Maire, quod et ab ipsius nomine dictum fretum le Maire.

atervatim hic homines per cam
os, societate inita in tentorus,
irtarorum more, agrestem vitam
egunt

invisit: Sed commeatus per

GROE

MARE CONGELATUM

Circulus Arcticus

Anian Regnum

Escondido

Quivira Regnum

El Streto

d'Anian

Ne Ultra

Hope advanced
C. Phillipp
Hubberts Hope
Buttons Bay
Porte Nelson

Magni huyus Oceani primus obtector Ille fuit Mr. Hudson

Fretum Davis

TERRA DE LABRADOR

AMERICA SEPTENTRIONALIS

Chichuco

NOVA FRANCIA

Norumbega

Canada

Terra dos Cortereal

Terra Nova

Sierra Nevada

Totonteac

Cevola

Rio S Laurens

Avacal
Calicuas

Capachi

LA FLORIDA

Virginia

MAR DEL

Tropicus Cancri

De Sierra

Ilhas de Ladrones

MAR DEL

Sinus Mexicanus

Nova

R d Palmas

Cuba

Spagnola

NORT

Mechoacan

Galapagos

Circulus Æquinoctialis

Caribana

OCEANUS

Amazones

BRASILIARS

AMERICA

MERIDIONA

ZUR

PERUVI

Moxos

Ouram

Tropicus Capricorni

MARE

NUS

S. Philippe
I. de Pescadores

Insul. Jean Fernando

S. Maria

ChILIS

Rio de la Plata

PACIFICUM

Chiloe

Patagonum regn

AMERICA SEPTENTRIONALIS

Circulus Archcus

Quivira reg.

Anian reg.

Nova zembla

TARTARIA

RUSSIA

Moscovia

EUROPA

SEPTENTRI

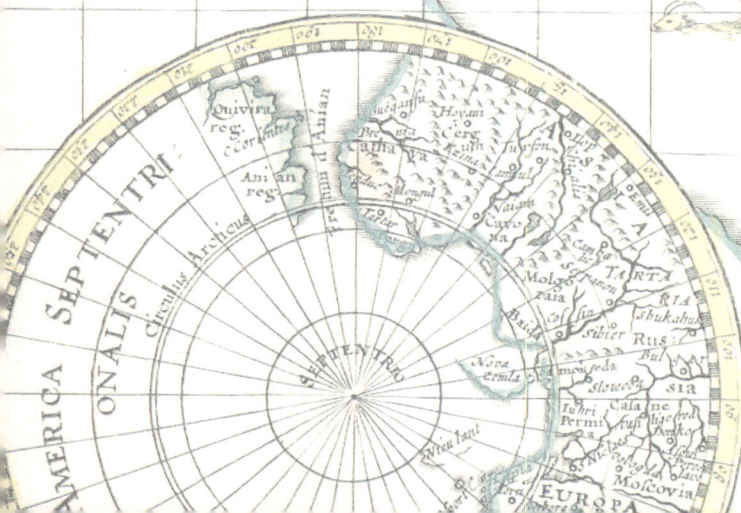

Hæ regiones cuidam Hispano apparuerunt cum disiectus à classe in hac Australi vagaretur Oceano.

Fretum Magalanicum

Terra del Fuego

Fretum le Maire

J. Barnevelt

Text

Kevin J. Brown

Project editors

Valeria Manferto De Fabianis

Laura Accomazzo

Graphic design

Paola Piacco

WS WHITE STAR PUBLISHERS

WS White Star Publishers® is a registered trademark
property of White Star s.r.l.

© 2017, 2018 White Star s.r.l.
Piazzale Luigi Cadorna, 6
20123 Milan, Italy - www.whitestar.it

New extended edition

Editing: Norman Gilligan

ISBN 978-88-544-1320-7
1 2 3 4 5 6   22 21 20 19 18

Printed in Italy by Rotolito - Seggiano di Pioltello (MI)

Acknowledgements

I would like to extend my thanks and acknowledge the support of those who helped make this book a reality. First and foremost, Laura Accomazzo, the book's editor, whose vision guided this project from day one and who was endlessly patient while I compiled the texts and images. I would also like to thank my fellow Bennington graduate Kim Hottenstein, who copy edited my text and talked through many of the ideas with me via email. Similarly, I would like to extend my appreciation to my associate Spencer Hunt, with whom I batted around ideas in the final stages of the project.

This work would have been impossible if not for the support of my friends in the rare map trade, Michael Buehler of Boston Rare Maps, Barry Ruderman of Barry Ruderman Rare Maps, and Sebastian Hidalgo Sola of H.S. Rare Books, all of whom graciously allowed to the use of map images from their collections.

We would also like to thank P. J. Mode, a visionary map collector, whose wonderful collection of Persuasive Maps is an inspiration and who also generously helped this project by allowing us to use several of his digitized map images. P. J. has donated his wonderful collection to Cornell, who have digitized many of his maps.

Last but in no way least, I would like to extend thanks to my kind and generous parents, Willard and Carol Brown.

Also, to my brilliant partner in life, Yuan Ji, whose bright plumage never fails to lighten my mood.

And finally, to my best bud, Shumi the dog, who keeps it real.

Photo credits

The Author

KEVIN J. BROWN, is the owner of Geographicus Rare Antique Maps (http://www. geographicus.com), a generalist dealer in rare maps from all periods and at all value points. Kevin attended Bennington College, in Vermont, where he majored in "Pilgrimage." Bennington fosters a "learn by doing" approach to academics, and Kevin has translated this philosophy to the map trade.

He approaches his study of early cartography from a hands-on perspective, supplementing historical knowledge and the study of primary source material with visceral experience. To better understand the experience of early travelers and mapmakers in the Amazon, for example, he spent a month with indigenous guides bushwhacking through the primary rainforests of the Guyana Shield, learning in the process traditional jungle survival techniques. Or, to better understand the experience of early merchants in Europe, he trekked the ancient Roman road system through France and Spain, eschewing all modern comforts and transport, for several months. He has also studied early engraving, printing, and drafting techniques. While Kevin understands that these adventures and studies will not turn him into a jungle survivalist, a medieval merchant, or master etcher, he believes that a better understanding the challenges that early surveyors, mapmakers, and travelers would have faced, on a multifaceted personal level, contributes to his ability to appreciate and relate to the early maps he deals in. In his spare time, Kevin enjoys walking his dog, playing with his bird, and studying Ninjutsu. He also imports artisanal mezcal from Mexico in partnership with his Nok, and enjoys the detail oriented work of restoring his historical townhouse in Bedford-Stuyvesant, Brooklyn.

Simiere Mountain

Koboldes' Caves

Cliffs of the Giants

Here are Boliaun Caves

The Witch Tarn

The Sapphire Lake

Zen Fairies Marsh

anshees' Bog

Donkey Cabbages grown here

These are Clurichaun

The Shee an Gannan House

The Oreads — They singe here at Nightfall

Here doe grow Witch Herbs

The Lake of Alhallows

Here is a Wishing Well

The Lake of Weeping

Here doe they make Wishing Caps and Cloaks of Darkness

Elfinmere

Here are horned Children

The Laidley Worm

Workshop for Seven League Boots

The Faerie Flocks

Japonel

The Peries Village

Here is the Palace of La Belle Dormonde

The Weird Wood

Beauty and her Beast

Blackadder Lake here Afanc broodeth

Bogles Corner

Here live the Seven Little Dwarfs

The Kelpies Hamlet

Valley of Dragons

Here doe Rocs' build their Nests

An Elfin Monastery

Rapunzel, her Tower

Here are the Dwarfs' Caves

Here is Will o' the Wisp

Hansel & Gretel

Here they doe Magick

To Goblin Land

Here do they blow the Horns of Elfland

Undine

No landing here

Here doe dwelle horned Monsters

These Cliffes are of Diamonde

Dangerous Shoals and Rocks are here

Sentinel Rock

Mermen

This is Ulysses, his Shippe

100 Fathoms